Vagabond Li

Gabriel Ferry

Alpha Editions

This edition published in 2024

ISBN : 9789362096494

Design and Setting By
Alpha Editions
www.alphaedis.com
Email - info@alphaedis.com

Contents

PERICO, THE MEXICAN VAGABOND.

CHAPTER I.

The Jamaïca and Mount Parnassus.

Mexico is the most beautiful city ever built by the Spaniards in the New World; and even in Europe it would take a high place for splendor and magnificence. If you wish to behold the magnificent and varied panorama which Mexico presents, you have only to mount at sunset one of the towers of the Cathedral. On whatever side you turn your eye, you see before you the serrated peaks of the Cordilleras, forming a gigantic azure belt of about sixty leagues in circumference. To the south, the two volcanoes which overtop the other peaks of the sierra raise their majestic summits, covered with eternal snow, which, in the evening sun, put on a pale purple hue flecked with delicate ruby. The one, Popocatapetl (smoking mountain), is a perfect cone, dazzling in the blue vault of heaven; the other, Iztaczihuatl (the white woman), has the appearance of a nymph reclining, who lifts her icy shoulders to receive the last beams of the dying sun. At the foot of the two volcanoes gleam two lakes, like mirrors, which reflect the clouds in their waters, and where the wild swan plays its merry gambols. To the west rises an immense pile of building, the palace of Chapultepec, once the abode of the old viceroys of New Spain. Round the mountain on which it is built stretches, in a long, waving belt of verdure, a forest of cedars more than a thousand years old. A fountain bubbles forth at the top of the mountain; its brawling waters leap down into the valley, where they are received into an aqueduct, and thus conducted into a large and populous city, to supply the wants of its inhabitants. Villages, steeples, and cupolas rise on all sides from the bottom of the valley. Dusty roads cross and recross one another like gold stripes on a green ground, or like runnels of water interbranching through the country. A tree, peculiar to Peru, the weeping willow of the sandy plains, bends its long, interlaced branches, loaded with odoriferous leaves and red berries, in the evening breeze, and a solitary palm-tree rises here and there above clumps of olives with their pale-green foliage.

But these are only the grand outlines of the picture. Turn your eye upon the city, or, rather, look at your feet. In the midst of the chess-board formed by the terraces of houses, and from among the flowers with which these are adorned, you will see rising, as from an immense bouquet, spires, churches with domes of yellow and blue tiling, houses with walls stained with various colors, and balconies hung with a kind of striped cotton, which give them a trim and jaunty appearance. On one of the four sides of the Plaza Mayor (great square) the Cathedral towers majestically aloft. This magnificent edifice overtops the turrets of the president's palace, a building devoid of all pretensions to architectural beauty, and now falling to decay. It is an immense pile, inclosing within its four walls the public offices of the government, a prison, two barracks, a botanic garden, and the legislative chambers. This palace occupies a whole side of the square. The *Ayuntamiento* (Municipality) and the *Postal de las flores*, an immense market, form the third side. The *Parian*, a market similar to the preceding, completes the fourth. Thus the legislative and executive power, the board of works, commerce—all the departments of the Mexican government, in short, are in one building, and seem as if grouped together under the shadow of the church. The people are there also; for the streets of St. Domingo, of St. Francisco, of Tacuba, of Monnaie, of Monterilla, all arteries of the great city, pour into the Plaza Mayor a flood of human beings, which is always changing, and ever in motion, and you have only to mix in this crowd for a few moments to get acquainted with Mexican life in all its diversified phases of vice and virtue, of splendor and misery.

When the hour of the Angelus approaches especially, horsemen, foot-passengers, and carriages are packed together in disorderly confusion, and gold, silk, and rags, mingled here and there, give to the crowd a grotesque and startling appearance. The Indians are returning to their villages, the populace to the suburbs. The *ranchero* makes his horse prance and curvet in the midst of the passengers, who are in no hurry to get out of his way; the *aquador* (water-carrier), whose day's work is over, crosses the square, bending under the weight of his *chochocol* of porous earthenware; the officer is bending his steps to the coffee-houses or gambling-tables, where he intends to spend the evening; the non-commissioned officer clears the way for himself with a vine-tree-staff, which he carries in his hand as a badge of his rank. The red petticoat of the townswoman is in glaring contrast with the saya and black mantilla of the fashionable lady, who holds her fan over her face to shade it from the departing rays of the sun. Monks of all colors flit through the crowd in every direction. Here the *padre*, with his huge hat *à la Basile*, elbows the Franciscan in his blue gown, silken cord, girdle, and large white felt hat; there goes the Dominican in his lugubrious costume of black and white, reminding one of Torquemada, the founder of the Inquisition; farther on, the brown drugget of the Capuchin contrasts with the white flowing robes of the Brother of Mercy. Incidents of different kinds occur continually in this motley crowd, and serve to keep one's attention alive. Sometimes, as the drum in the barracks are beating a salute, the folding doors of a *sagrario*[1] suddenly fly open, and there issues forth a carriage splendidly gilt, the slow toll of the bell is heard along with the harsh rattle of the drum, and the whole crowd uncover, and kneel with bent head to the holy sacrament which they are carrying to a dying man. Woe betide the foreigner, though bold and resolute, who, ignorant of the profound respect which the Mexican pays to his religious rites, fails to bow the knee to the host as it passes! Sometimes a military detachment of six officers, escorted by three soldiers and preceded by a dozen musicians, is seen marching into the square in all the majesty of military pomp; it is to proclaim a *bando* (law or edict) of the highest authority, for which all this display of military music and brocaded uniforms is deemed necessary. Such at this time of the evening is the general appearance of the Plaza Mayor, that square where the people of Mexico, the sovereign people (as their flatterers call them), flutter in rags, ceaselessly engaged in quest of a new master who can put down the master of the night before, quite indifferent as to political principles, mistaking disorder for liberty, and never suspecting that the continual assaults of anarchy may bring down one day the worm-eaten structure of their rotten republic, although it has not been in existence more than twenty-five years.

Every evening, however, at the first peals of the Angelus, all noise ceases, as if by enchantment, in the Plaza Mayor. The crowd becomes hushed and silent. When the last toll of the bell dies away, the din recommences. The crowd disperses in every direction, carriages rattle off, horsemen gallop away, foot-passengers hurry hither and thither, but not always nimbly enough to escape the sword or *lasso* of the bold thieves who murder or rob their hapless victims, and whose audacity is such that, even in open day, and with crowds looking on, they have been known to commit their crimes.[2] At nightfall the square is deserted; a few promenaders scurry along in the moonlight; others remain seated, or swing lazily upon the iron chains, which, separated by granite pillars, run round the sagrario. The day is past, the scenes of the night begin, and the *léperos* become for a few hours masters of the city.

The *lépero* is a type, and that the strangest, of Mexican society. The attentive observer, who has seen Mexico stirring with the joyous excitement that precedes the Oracion, and then abandoned to the ill-omening silence which the night brings on, can alone tell what is singular and formidable in the character of this Mexican *lazzarone*. At once brave and cowardly, calm and violent, fanatic and incredulous, with just such a belief in God as to have a wholesome terror for the devil, a continual gambler, quarrelsome by nature, with a sobriety only equaled by the intemperance to which he sometimes delivers himself, the lépero can accommodate himself to every turn of fortune, as his humor or idleness inclines him. Porter, stone-mason, teamster, street-pavior, hawker, the lépero is every thing at different times. A thief sometimes by inclination, he practices his favorite calling every where, in the churches, at processions, and in theatres; his life is only one struggle with justice, which is not herself safe from his larcenies. Lavish when he finds himself master of a little money, he is not the less resigned or courageous when he has none. Has he gained in the morning a sufficiency for the expenses of the day? he drops work immediately. Often his precarious resources fail him entirely. Tranquil then, and submissive, and careless about thieves, he wraps himself in his torn cloak, and lies down at the corner of the pavement or in a door-way. There, rattling his *jarana* (a little mandolin), and looking with stoical serenity at the *pulqueria* (public-house), where he has no credit, he listens distractedly to the hissing of some savory stew which they are preparing for some more favored being, tightens the belt round his stomach, and, after breakfasting off a sunbeam, he sups off a cigar, and sleeps quietly without thinking of the morrow.

I will confess my weakness: among this motley crowd, idle and brawling as it was, my attention was more engaged with the miserable tatterdemalions than with the well-dressed foot-passengers, as the former seemed to afford a truer index of Mexican society than the latter. I never met, for instance, a lépero, in all the picturesqueness of his tattered costume, without having a strong desire to become better acquainted with this Bohemian-like class, who reminded me frequently of the more uncommon heroes of Picaresque romance. It appeared to me a curious study to compare this filthy and ragged denizen of the great towns with the savage adventurers I had met in the woods and savannas. When I first came to live in Mexico, I sought, and succeeded in getting acquainted, through the kindness of a Franciscan monk, a friend of mine, with a thorough-bred lépero, called Perico the Zaragate.[3] Unhappily, our acquaintance had hardly commenced, when, for very good reasons, I was resolved to break it, for I only got the scantiest information from him about his class, and the number of piastres I was forced to pay him was so considerable as to induce me to reflect strongly upon the absurdity of taking such expensive lessons. I was resolved, then, to bring my studies with him to a conclusion, when, one morning, Fray Serapio, the worthy monk who had made me acquainted with Perico, entered my apartment.

"I came to ask you," said the Franciscan, "to go with me to a bull-fight at the Necatitlan Square; there will also be a *Jamaïca* and a *Monte Parnaso*, which will be an additional inducement."

"What is a *Jamaïca* and a *Monte Parnaso?*"

"You will know that immediately. Let us set out; it is nearly eleven, and we shall be scarcely there in time to get a good place."

I could never resist the attraction of a bull-fight, and I found an advantage in having the company of Fray Serapio while traversing in security those suburbs which surround Mexico in a formidable belt. The neighborhood of the Necatitlan Square is more dreaded than any, and it is almost always dangerous to appear there in a European garb; indeed, I never passed through it alone without uneasiness. The cowl of the monk would be a safeguard to me in my European dress. I accepted his offer with pleasure, and we set out. For the first time, I viewed with a tranquil mind the narrow, dirty, and unpaved streets, the blackened houses full of cracks running over the walls in all directions, lurking-places of the thieves and robbers who ply their calling on the streets, and who sometimes even break into houses in the city. Swarms of one-eyed léperos, their faces cut and scarred with the knife, were drinking, whistling, and shouting in the taverns, clad in dirty cotton clothes, or enveloped in their *frazadas*.[4] Their wives, dressed in tatters, stood in the doorways, watching their naked children, who were sporting in the mud, and laughing and shouting merrily. In passing through these haunts of cut-throats, the terror of the police, the judge mutters a prayer, the alcalde crosses himself, the *corchete* (bailiff) and the regidor shuffle humbly along with downcast eye but watchful look, and the honest man shudders, but the monk stalks along with lofty brow and serene face, and the creak of his sandals is more respected there than the clink of the *celador's* sabre; sometimes, even, like tame tigers who recognize their master, the bandits emerge from their lurking-places, and come and kiss his hand.

The Necatitlan Square presented an appearance at once strange and novel. On one side, where the sun darted his unpitying rays upon the *palcos de sol*,[5] stood the people, with cloaks and rebozos hung over their heads as a shade, clustered in noisy, animated groups on the steps of the circus, and keeping up a lively concert of whistling and groaning. On the shady side, the nodding plumes of the officers' hats, and the variegated silk shawls of the ladies, presented to the eye an appearance which contrasted strongly with the wretchedness and misery of the rabble in the palcos de sol. I had witnessed bull-fights a hundred times. I had seen this dirty mass of people, wearied and exhausted in body, but with as keen a relish for slaughter as ever, their tongues sticking to the roofs of their mouths, and their throats dry and parched as the sand, when the setting sun darted his long rays through the ill-joined boards of the amphitheatre, and when the scent of the blood lured the hungry vultures who were sailing in the air above, but I never saw the arena so transformed as it was at that time. Numerous wooden erections filled the space ordinarily devoted to the bull-fights; these, covered with grass, flowers, and sweet-smelling branches of trees, made the whole place assume the appearance of a vast hall, growing, as it were, out of the ground, and forming a series of shady groves, with paths winding through them. Little booths were dispersed here and there through the groves, some intended for the preparation of delicate articles of Mexican cookery, others for the sale of cool, refreshing drinks. In the cookery booths you could indulge in the luxury of nameless ragouts of pork, seasoned with pimenta. In the puestos[6] glittered immense glasses filled with beverages of all the colors in the rainbow, red, green, blue, and yellow. The mob in the palcos de sol snuffed up greedily the nauseous smell of the fat pork, while others, more lucky, seated in this improvised elysium, under the shade of the trees, discussed patés of the wild duck of the lakes.

"Look!" said the Franciscan, pointing with his finger to the throng seated at the tables in the ring; "that's what we call a *Jamaïca*."

"And that?" said I, showing him a tree five or six yards high, fixed in the ground, with all its leaves, in the middle of the arena, quite covered with handkerchiefs of every hue, which fluttered from the branches.

"That is a *Monte Parnaso*," said the Franciscan.

"Probably poets are to ascend it?"

"No; but léperos, and such like uneducated persons—which will be a great deal more diverting."

The monk had hardly given me this answer, which but half enlightened me, when cries of *toro, toro,* from the rabble in the palcos de sol became louder and more overpowering; the pastry cooks' booths and the puestos were suddenly deserted; the revelers were suddenly interrupted by the sudden rush of a band of léperos from the highest boxes round the inclosure, who, sliding down by means of their cloaks, made a terrific onslaught on the green booths inside. Among the crowd who were yelling and kicking down the booths, and strewing the whole ring with their remains, I recognized my old friend Perico. Indeed, without him the fête would have been incomplete. The *Monte Parnaso*, with its cotton handkerchiefs, stood alone in the midst of the wreck, and soon became the only object to which the looks and aims of the rabble were directed. All tried to be the first to ascend the tree, and get possession of such handkerchiefs as took their fancy; but the struggles of the one impeded the efforts of the other; the tree still remained standing, and not a single claimant had yet succeeded in even touching its trunk. At the same moment the bugle sounded in the box of the alcalde, the door of the *toril* was thrown open, and a magnificent bull, the best that the neighboring haciendas could furnish, came thundering into the arena. The spectators, who expected a more formidable animal, were somewhat disappointed when they saw an *embolado*.[7] The aspiring laureates of *Monte Parnaso* were nevertheless somewhat scared and frightened. The bull, after standing with some hesitation, bounded with a gallop toward the tree, which was still standing. Some of the léperos ran away, and the others took refuge, one after another, in the branches of *Monte Parnaso*. The bull, having come to the foot of the tree, butted at it with repeated blows of his horns; it tottered; and at the very moment Perico was busily engaged in reaping an abundant harvest of pocket-handkerchiefs, it fell, dragging with it the men who were entangled in the branches. Roars of laughter and enthusiastic cheering arose from the ten thousand spectators in the galleries and boxes at sight of the unfortunate wretches, who, bruised and lamed, were seeking to escape from each other's grasp, and from the branches in which they were entangled. To add to the confusion, the bull, seeking no doubt to separate the black mass struggling on the ground, butted several of the unfortunate léperos with his horns, and, to my great sorrow, I saw Perico, launched ten feet into the air, fall to the ground in such a state of insensibility as to deprive me of all hope of completing my studies of Mexican life under so skillful a master.

Perico had been scarcely carried out of the arena when cries of "a priest! a priest!" were raised by a hundred voices. Fray Serapio crouched in a corner of his box, but he could not avoid the duty which the people expected from him. He rose, gravely cloaking his disappointment as much as he could from the eyes of the people, and said to me, in a low tone,

"Follow me; you will pass for a surgeon."

"Are you joking?" said I.

"Not at all; if the fellow is not quite dead, he will have a surgeon and a priest of equal merit."

I followed the monk with a gravity at least equal to his own, and while descending the stairs of the amphitheatre, the laughter and loud hurrahs of the populace proved that the people in the *shade*, as well as the rabble in the *sun*, viewed the accident as an every-day occurrence. We were conducted into a little dark room on the ground floor of a house, from which issued several lobbies leading to different apartments. In a corner of this room Perico was laid, having been previously deprived of all his handkerchiefs; then, partly through respect for the Church and the faculty, so worthily represented by both of us, partly lest they should lose the spectacle of the fight, the attendants withdrew and left us alone. The lépero, his head leaning against the wall, and giving no sign of life, was seated rather than reclining; his motionless arms, and his pale, corpse-like face, showed that, if life had not quite fled, there was but a slender spark remaining. We looked at each other, the Franciscan and I, quite at a loss what to do in the circumstances.

"I think," said I to the monk, "that it would perhaps be best to give him absolution."

"*Absolvo te*," said Fray Serapio, touching roughly the lépero's foot. He appeared sensible to this mark of interest, and muttered, half opening his eyes,

"I believe in God the Father, the Son, and the Holy—Ah! the rascals have taken all my handkerchiefs—*Señor Padre*, I am a dead man.

"Not yet, my son," said the monk; "but perhaps there only remains for you sufficient time to confess your sins; and it would be best for you to profit by it, that I may open to you the folding doors of heaven. I warn you that I am in a hurry."

"Is the bull-fight not over, then?" said poor Perico, naïvely. "I think," said he, passing his hands over his body, "that I am not so ill as you imagine."

Then, seeing me, Perico shut his eyes, as if he were going to faint, and added, in a very low voice,

"Indeed I am ill, very ill; and if you please to listen to my confession, I will soon finish it."

"Go on, then, my son."

The monk then kneeled down close to the sick man, who, to speak the truth, bore no trace on his body of a single wound. Taking off his large gray hat, Perico brought his lips near the ear of the monk, and I, not to interrupt the lépero, stepped aside. He began thus:

"I accuse myself first, father, of the blackest ingratitude to this cavalier, in that I took from him so much money—and would have taken more if I could—and I hope he will bear no ill feeling toward me on that account, for at heart I sincerely loved him."

I bowed in token of forgiveness.

"I accuse myself also, father, of having stolen the gold watch of Sayosa, the judge in the criminal court, the last time I appeared before him."

"How was that, my son?"

"The Lord Sayosa was imprudent enough to put his hand into his pocket for his watch, and to express his regret and surprise that he had left both it and his gold chain at home. I said to myself then, if I am not executed for this, that will be a good stroke of business for me. Ignorant that any thing like this accident would befall me, I gave a hint to a friend of mine who was at that moment set at liberty. I ought to tell you that my lord judge has a weakness for turkeys."

"I don't understand you, my son."

"All in good time, father. My confederate bought a splendid turkey, and hastened to present it to the wife of my Lord Sayosa, saying that her husband had ordered him to give it her; my lord judge entreated her at the same time, added my friend, to deliver to the bearer his gold watch and chain that he had forgotten at home. It was thus the watch—"

"That's serious, my son."

"I did worse than that, father; the day after, I stole from the judge's lady while her husband was at court."

"What, my son?"

"The turkey, father. You see one does not like to lose any thing," muttered Perico, in a doleful tone. The monk could scarcely restrain himself from laughing outright at the confession of the lépero.

"And why," said Fray Serapio, in a shaking tone of voice, "were you at the bar before my Lord Judge Sayosa?"

"A trifle, father. A citizen in the town (his name needn't be mentioned) had engaged me to take vengeance on a person who had offended him. The man was pointed out to me whom I was to strike. He was a young, handsome cavalier, easily recognizable by a long narrow scar above his right eyebrow. I placed myself in ambuscade at the door of a house which he was accustomed to enter every night before orisons. I saw him, in fact, enter the house pointed out to me. Night came on. I waited. Two hours passed. There was not a single person in the street, which was silent as the grave. The person I was waiting for had not yet appeared. I was curious to see what kept him so long. The apartment in which I thought he was was on the ground floor. I crept slowly up to it, and looked through the bars of a window that had been left open probably on account of the heat."

Perico, in continuing his confession, either from weakness or some other motive, seemed to do it unwillingly, as if he could not brook the ascendency which Fray Serapio had over him. The lépero unveiled his thoughts like one in a state of mesmeric sleep, who is obliged to act according to the will of the manipulator. I asked the monk by a look whether I should stay or retire. His glance urged me to stay.

"Beneath a picture of all the saints," continued Perico, "slept an old woman wrapped up to the eyes in her *rebozo*. The handsome cavalier, whom I recognized, was seated on a sofa. Kneeling before him, her head on his knees, was a young and beautiful woman, her eyes fixed upon his, beaming with the most ardent devotion. The young man was stripping the leaves off a full-blown rose that he had taken from the tortoise-shell comb in the hair of the fair dame, whose head was on his knees. I saw clearly now why the time had seemed to him so short. Perhaps the feeling of compassion which rose in my bosom will be placed to my credit aloft, for I felt quite sorry at being forced to bring this sweet romance to a rough conclusion."

"Did you kill him, then, you wretch?" cried the monk.

"I sat down in the shade on the pavement, with my face to the door. I pitied the poor fellow, was quite discouraged, and slept at my post. The creaking of a door awoke me from my slumbers; a man came out. I said to myself then that my word of honor had been given, and my feelings of compassion must be crushed. I arose. A second after, I was on the traces of the unknown. The sound of a piano came stealing from the window, which was now closed. 'Poor girl!' said I, 'your lover has seen his last hour, and you are playing!' I struck—the man fell!"

Perico stopped and sighed.

"Had grief dimmed my sight?" said he, after a short silence. "The rays of the moon fell full upon the face of the poor fellow. It was not my man. I had done my duty, however; I had been paid to kill a man. I had killed him. And my conscience quieted on this score, I set about cutting off a lock of hair from the head of the unknown, in order to convince my employer that I had fulfilled my mission. 'All men's hair is of the same color,' said I to myself. I was again deceived; the man I had killed was an Englishman, and had hair red as a ripe pimenta. The handsome cavalier still lived. Chagrined at my disappointment, I blasphemed the holy name of God, and that is what I accuse myself of, holy father."

Perico beat his breast, while the Franciscan showed him the blackness of the latter crime of which he was guilty, passing very slightly over the former, for the life of a man, an English heretic above all, is of very little importance in the eyes of the least enlightened class of the Mexican people, of which the monk and the lépero were two very distinct types. Fray Serapio finished his exhortation by administering hastily to Perico an absolution in Latin, worthy of Molière's comedies. He then said, in good Spanish,

"All you have got to do now is to ask pardon of this cavalier for having fleeced him so often, which he will willingly grant, seeing that it is very improbable that you will lay him again under contribution, at least for a long time."

The lépero turned to me, and, in as languishing a tone as he could assume,

"I am a double-dyed rascal," said he, "and shall only consider myself completely absolved if you will pardon me for the unworthy tricks that I have played upon you. I am going to die, Señor Cavalier, and I have not the wherewithal to bury me. My wife must be told of my situation, and it will be a great comfort to her if she find something in my pocket to pay for my shroud. God will reward you for it, Señor Cavalier."

"In truth," said the monk, "you can hardly refuse the poor devil this favor, as they are the last piastres he will cost you."

"God grant it!" said I, not thinking about the cruelty of the wish, and I emptied my purse into Perico's outstretched hand. He shut his eyes, let his head fall upon his breast, and said no more.

"*Requiescat in pace!*" said Fray Serapio; "the sports must be far advanced by this time. I can be of no farther use here."

We went out. After all, said I to myself in leaving the circus, this recital has been the most curious revelation I have yet got from the Zaragate. Such a confession as this is ample amends for the drafts upon my purse which this singular personage has made. Besides, this would be the last lesson the lépero would ever give me; and, with this thought in my mind, I could not help pitying the poor wretch. I was wrong, however, as will be seen in the sequel, in thinking that I would have no more dealings with my master Perico.

FOOTNOTES:

[1] Sagrario, the part in a church where the host is kept.

[2] A journal, "Siglio XIX." of the 11th November, 1845, contains in its columns a petition addressed to the Ayuntamiento upon the subject of certain thieves, who, not content with the evening, had chosen midday for the exercise of their calling. The petition and answer of the municipal council are alike curious.

[3] Zaragate, a rogue of the most dangerous kind.

[4] A blanket of common wool, differing in that respect only from the *serape*.

[5] Those parts of the circus exposed to the sun.

[6] Portable shops.

[7] A bull with a ball on each horn.

CHAPTER II.

The Alameda.[8]—The Paseo of Bucareli.

There are few towns in Mexico which can not boast of having an Alameda; and, as generally happens in the capital city, that of Mexico is decidedly the finest. There is no promenade of this sort in Paris. Hyde Park in London most nearly resembles it. The Alameda of Mexico forms a long square, surrounded by a wall breast high, at the bottom of which runs a deep ditch, whose muddy waters and offensive exhalation mar the appearance of this almost earthly paradise. An iron gate at each of its corners affords admission to carriages, horsemen, and pedestrians. Poplars, ash-trees, and willows bend their branches over the principal drive, and afford a leafy shade to the occupants of the carriages and equestrians for whom this beautifully level road is appropriated. Alleys, converging into large common centres, ornamented with fountains and *jets d'eau*, interpose their clumps of myrtles, roses, and jasmines between the carriages and the pedestrians, whose eyes can follow, through the openings in those odoriferous bushes, the luxurious equipages and prancing steeds caracoling round the Alameda. The noise of the wheels, muffled by the sand on the drive, scarcely reaches the ear, mingled as it is with the murmur of the water, the sighing of the wind through the evergreen leafage, and the buzzing of bees and humming-birds. The gilded carriage of the country and the plain European chariot are continually passing each other, and the gaudy trappings of the Mexican horses contrast strongly with the unaffected plainness of the English saddle, which wears a shabby appearance in the midst of this Oriental luxury. The ladies of fashion have laid aside for the promenade the *saya* and *mantilla*, to wear dresses which are only six months behind the last Parisian mode. Stretched in dreamy languor on their silk cushions, they allow their feet, the pride and admiration of Europeans, to remain in shoes, alas! ill fitted for them. The sorry appearance of their feet is hidden when in the carriages, through the open window of which you can only see their diadems of black hair, decorated with natural flowers, their seductive smile, and their gestures, in which vivacity and listlessness are so pleasingly blended. The fan is kept in a perpetual flutter at the carriage window, and speaking its own mysterious language. Swarms of pedestrians present a spectacle not less piquant; and the sad-colored garments of the Europeans are seen less frequently here than the variegated costumes of America.

After taking a few turns, the carriages quit the Alameda, the horsemen accompany them, and the whole crowd saunters carelessly past a strongly-grated window, which hangs over the path you must traverse before reaching a promenade called the *Paseo* of Bucareli.[9] One can hardly tell what hideous scenes are daily exhibited there behind this rusty iron grating, not two paces from the most fashionable promenade in Mexico: this is the window of the Mexican Morgue, where the dead bodies are exposed. Justice only displays her anxiety at the moment when the dead bodies of men and women are thrown together in one promiscuous heap on its floor, some half naked, others still bleeding. Every day there is a new succession of victims. As for the Paseo, which is close to this melancholy exhibition, its only attractions are a double row of trees, a few stone seats for the use of pedestrians, and three fountains overloaded with detestable allegorical statues. At this spot you catch a glimpse of a part of the country seen from the towers of the Cathedral; the two snow-covered peaks of the volcanoes with their canopy of clouds; the sierra shaded with its beautiful violet tints: lower down, the whitened fronts of several haciendas; and through the arches of a gigantic aqueduct you descry fields of maize, church domes and convents, almost always half hidden at the promenade hour in the mist which generally ascends at nightfall.

On the evening of the day on which I had witnessed the bull-fight, I found myself in a crowd of idlers who ordinarily cover the space between the Paseo and the Alameda. It was twilight; the lamps were about to be lighted, and pedestrians and carriages were severally wending their way homeward. It was Sunday. Noisily repeated by the numerous bells of the churches and convents, the toll of the Angelus rose high above the murmur of the crowd, of which one portion respectfully paused, while the other made its way like a torrent that nothing could resist. The last gleams of departing day glimmered through the grate of the Morgue, and lighted up feebly the victims who were lying promiscuously on the slabbed pavement, stained here and there with large patches of blood. Women, uttering the most piercing cries of sorrow, returned to the rusty grated window, though again and again pushed back by the soldiers. Their cries attracted the passers-by; some pitied them; others contented themselves with peering curiously in their faces. Kneeling before the grated window, his head uncovered, and the bridle of his richly-caparisoned horse in his hand, stood a man praying devoutly. From his costume you could easily see that he belonged to that opulent class of inhabitants of the *Tierra Afuera*, who disdain both the fashions and ideas of Europeans. His picturesque costume harmonized well with his manly and noble features. Above the right eyebrow of the stranger extended a long narrow scar. It was doubtless the handsome young cavalier whom Perico had that very morning described to me. Was he thanking God for preserving him from danger, or for loving and being loved? The question remained doubtful; besides, the emotions which gave rise to these conjectures were suddenly interrupted. Startled by the noise of the carriages, a refractory horse struck violently against a ladder, on the top of which a *sereno* (watchman) was lighting a lamp suspended from the walls of the barrack of La Acordada. The sereno fell from a height of fifteen feet, and lay motionless on the pavement.

It would be easy to describe the feelings of the unfortunate horseman when he saw the poor fellow lying unconscious, and perhaps dangerously injured; for the cavalier, I must own, was myself; but I prefer telling what followed.

Every one is well aware of the benevolent feelings of the populace of great towns toward those who have the misfortune to be guilty of such sad accidents. It is impossible, however, to have an exact idea of the spirit of such a populace, in Mexico especially, toward a foreigner, which is there synonymous with a national enemy. Hemmed in, in spite of his mettle, amid a dense crowd of léperos, who were deliberating only what sort of punishment to inflict on the unhappy author of such a calamity, my horse was of no use to me. I could not help envying for an instant the fate of the sereno, insensible at least to the rude hustling of the crowd, who mercilessly trod him under foot. Fortunately, chance sent me two auxiliaries, on one of whom, at least, I was far from reckoning. The first was an alcalde, who, escorted by four soldiers, made his way through the crowd, and told me that in his eyes I was guilty of having caused the death of a Mexican citizen. I bowed, and said not a word. In compliance with the magistrate's orders, the still inanimate body of the sereno was placed on a *tapestle* (a kind of litter), always kept at the barracks for similar accidents; then politely inviting me to dismount, the alcalde ordered me to follow the litter on foot to the palace, which was not more than two paces from the prison. It may be supposed that I took good care not to comply at once with this invitation, and attempted to demonstrate to the alcalde that the exceptional case in which I stood nowise warranted such a procession. Unhappily, the alcalde was, like all his class, gifted with strong obstinacy, and replied to all my arguments only by insisting on the respect due to custom. I then thought of seeking among the spectators some one who might be security for me, and, very naturally, my eyes sought the place where I had seen the cavalier, who had, at first sight, inspired me with such interest; but he had disappeared. Was I then to be compelled to submit to the odious formality required by the alcalde? Chance at this moment sent me the second auxiliary of which I have spoken. This new personage, who interposed between me and the alcalde, was very jauntily dressed in a cloak of olive-colored Queretaro cloth, the skirt of which, thrown back, almost entirely hid his face. Through the numerous rents in his cloak appeared a jacket as dilapidated as his upper garment. Having, with great exertion, got through the crowd as far as the alcalde, this personage passed his hands through one of the holes in his cloak, and was thus able to touch the remains of a hat which covered his head without disarranging the folds of his cape. He courteously uncovered, while a few cigarettes, a lottery ticket, and an image of the miraculous Virgin of Guadaloupe remained sticking in his long black hair. I was not a little surprised in recognizing in this respectable townsman my friend Perico, whom I believed dead, and on the eve of being buried.

"Señor Alcalde," said Perico, "this cavalier is right. He committed the murder involuntarily, and he should not be confounded with ordinary malefactors; besides, I am here to become security for him, for I have the honor of his intimate acquaintance."

"And who will be security for *you*?" asked the alcalde.

"My antecedents," modestly replied the Zaragate, "and this cavalier," added he, pointing to me.

"But if you become security for him?"

"Well, I become security for this cavalier—he is security for me; you have, therefore, two securities for one, and your lordship could not be better suited."

I confess that, placed between the justice of the alcalde and the offensive protection of Perico, I hesitated an instant. On his side, the alcalde seemed scarcely convinced by the syllogism which Perico had enunciated with such barefaced assurance. I thought it best, then, to finish the debate by whispering to the alcalde my address.

"Well," he replied, on retiring, "I accept the security of your friend in the olive cloak, and will go immediately to your house, where I hope to find you."

The alcalde and his soldiers walked away; the mob remained as compact and threatening as before, but a shrill whistle and two or three gambols played by Perico soon caused him to be acknowledged by the people of his caste, who eagerly made way for him. The lépero then took my horse by the bridle, and I quitted this scowling rabble very uneasy about the termination of my adventure, and much depressed at the unfortunate event of which I had been the innocent cause.

"How comes it that I find you in such good health?" said I to my guide, when I had recovered a little my presence of mind. "I confess I thought your affairs in this world were forever wound up."

"God wrought a miracle specially for his servant," returned Perico, and he devoutly raised his eyes to heaven; "but it appears, señor, that my resurrection displeases you. You can conceive that, in spite of my strong desire to be agreeable to you—"

"Not at all, Perico; by no means; I am delighted to see you alive; but how was this miracle brought about?"

"I don't know," gravely replied the lépero; "only I was resuscitated so quickly as not only to resume my place among the spectators of the fight, but even to attempt another ascension. I had just been confessed and received absolution, and it was a capital opportunity for risking my life without endangering my soul. I wished to profit by it, and it brought me good fortune; for this time, although the bull gave me another pitch in the air with his horns, I fell on my feet, to the great delight of the public, who showered reals and half reals upon me. Then finding myself, thanks to you especially, with a tolerably well-lined purse, I thought it my duty to satisfy my love for dress; I went to a *baratillo*, and purchased this garb, which gives me quite a respectable appearance. You saw with what consideration the alcalde treated me. There is nothing like being well dressed, señor."

I saw clearly that the fellow had *done* me once more, and that his pretended agony, like his confession, had been only simulated for the purpose of getting more money out of me. I must confess, however, that my anger was disarmed at this moment by the comic dignity with which the lépero strutted about in his torn cloak all the time he was holding forth in this strange way. I determined to rid myself of company that was becoming troublesome to me, and said to Perico, with a smile,

"If I reckon accurately, your children's illness, your wife's confinement, and your own shroud have cost me little less than a hundred piastres; to release you of the whole debt will, I would fain hope, be a sufficient reward for the service you have rendered me. I will therefore return home immediately; and I again thank you for your kindness."

"Home, señor! What are you thinking about?" cried Perico; "why, by this time your house will be in the hands of the soldiers; they are seeking you among all your friends. You do not know the alcalde you have to do with."

"Do you know him, then?"

"I know all the alcaldes, señor; and what proves how little I deserve the surname bestowed upon me is, that all the alcaldes do not know me; but of all his fellows, the one in pursuit of you is the most cunning, the most rapacious, and the most diabolical."

Although I felt that this portrait was exaggerated, I was for a moment shaken in my resolution. Perico then represented to me, in very moving terms, the happiness his wife and children would receive by seeing their benefactor indebted to them for a night's lodging. Having a choice between two protectors equally disinterested, I allowed myself to be convinced by the one whose rapacity seemed most easily satisfied; I decided upon once more following the lépero.

Meanwhile, night came on; we traversed suspicious lanes, deserted places, streets unknown to me, and shrouded in darkness. The serenos (policemen) became more and more scarce. I felt myself hurried away into the heart of those dreadful suburbs where justice dares not penetrate; I was unarmed, and at the mercy of a man whose frightful confession I had just heard. Hitherto the Zaragate, I must confess, in spite of his crimes so unblushingly avowed, did not seem to me to stand out in glaring relief among a people demoralized by ignorance, want, and civil wars; but at that hour, amid a labyrinth of dark lanes, and in the silence of the night, my imagination gave fantastic and colossal dimensions to his picaresque figure. My position was a difficult one. To leave such a guide suddenly in this cut-throat quarter was dangerous, to follow him not less so.

"Where the devil do you live?" said I. The lépero scratched his head in answer. I asked him again.

"To say the truth," replied he at last, "having no fixed abode, I live a little every where."

"And your wife and children, and the night's shelter you offered me?"

"I forgot," replied the Zaragate, imperturbably; "I sent away my wife and children yesterday to—to Queretaro; but as for a lodging—"

"Is that at Queretaro also?" I asked Perico, discovering, when too late, that the wife and children of this honorable personage were as imaginary as his abode.

"As for shelter," added Perico, with the same impassible air, "you shall share that which I can procure for you, and which I find when my means won't admit of paying for a night's lodging, for heaven does not send us every day bull-fights and such like windfalls. Stop," said he, pointing with his finger to a glimmering light at a distance, which was reflected on the granite pavement; "that is perhaps what we are seeking for."

We advanced to the light, and soon perceived that it came from the lantern of a sereno. Wrapped in a yellow cloak almost as ragged as Perico's, the guardian of the night, squatted on the pavement, seemed to follow with his melancholy gaze the large clouds which flitted across the sky. At our approach he still kept his indolent position.

"Halloo! friend," said the Zaragate, "do you know of any *velorio* (wake) in this neighborhood?"

"Of course, a few *cuadras* from here, near the bridge of Eguizamo, you will find one; and if I did not fear some round of the Señor Regidor's, or found some good fellow to don my cloak and take care of my lantern, I would go with you to the entertainment myself."

"Much obliged," said Perico, politely; "we will profit by the information."

The sereno cast a look of astonishment at my dress, which was singularly out of keeping with Perico's.

"Gentlemen like that cavalier are little in the habit of frequenting such meetings," said the man of the police.

"This is a special case; this señor has contracted a debt which obliges him to spend the night elsewhere."

"That makes all the difference in the world," said the sereno. "There are some debts that one likes to be as long in paying as possible." And, hearing a church clock strike at a distance, the night-watch, troubling himself no more about us, cried out in a doleful tone, "Nine o'clock and stormy weather." He then resumed his former attitude, while the distant voices of the serenos answered him in succession through the silence of the night.

I resumed my melancholy march behind Perico, followed by my horse, which I led by the bridle, as, by the police regulations of Mexico, no one is allowed to ride through the streets after Angelus has rung, and I was unwilling to try another fall with the alcaldes. Shall I confess it? My curiosity was roused by the words of my guide, and I decided at this moment not to separate from him. I wanted to know what a velorio was; and this love of novelty, which finds so many opportunities of satisfying itself in Mexico, once more made me forget my troubles.

We had not walked ten minutes, till, as the sereno had told us, we came to a bridge thrown over a narrow canal. Some dilapidated houses bathed their greenish bases in the thick muddy water. A lamp which burned dimly before a picture of the souls in Purgatory threw its livid reflex on the stagnant water. On the terraces the watch-dogs bayed at the moon, which was sometimes hidden, sometimes fringed only by a movable curtain of clouds, for it was the rainy season. Except those doleful sounds, all was silent there as in the other parts of the town that we had traversed. The windows in the first story, brightly lighted up opposite the picture of the souls in Purgatory, were the only things remarkable in this double row of melancholy-looking huts. Perico knocked at the door of the house with the illuminated windows. They were rather long in coming; at last the door half opened, one of the leaves being fastened as usual by an iron chain.

"Who is there?" said a man's voice.

"Friends who come to pray for the dead and rejoice with the living," said Perico, without hesitation.

We entered. Lighted by the porter's lantern, we passed through a porch and entered an inner court. The guide pointed out to Perico an iron ring let into the wall. I tied my horse up by the bridle; we ascended some twenty steps, and I entered, preceded by Perico, a room tolerably well lighted up. I was at last going to learn what a *velorio* was.

FOOTNOTES:

[8] Alameda, a general name for a public walk; literally, a place planted with poplars, *alamos*.

[9] The name of the viceroy who presented it to the town.

CHAPTER III.

A Mexican Wake.

The company to which Perico had introduced me presented a very singular appearance. About twenty men and women of the lowest class were seated in a circle, chatting, bawling, and gesticulating. A dank, cadaverous smell pervaded the apartment, which was hardly smothered by the smoke of cigars, and the fumes of Xeres and *Chinguirito*. In a corner of the room stood a table loaded with provisions of every sort, with cups, bottles, and flasks. Some gamblers, seated at a table a little farther off, jingling copper money, and shouting out the technical terms of *monte*, were quarreling, with drunken excitement, over piles of *cuartillas*[10] and *tlacos*. Under the triple excitement of wine, women, and play, the orgie, which had only commenced when I arrived, seemed likely to mount to a formidable height; but what struck me most was precisely that which seemed to engage the attention of the assembly least. A young child, who seemed to have scarcely reached his seventh year, was lying at full length on a table. His pale brow, wreathed with flowers faded by the heat of the stifling atmosphere, his glazed eyes, and shriveled, sunken cheeks, already tinged with a violet hue, plainly showed that life had left him, and that it was some days, probably, since he had slept the eternal sleep. The mere sight of the little corpse was heartrending amid the cries, the gambling, and the noisy conversation; the men and women meanwhile laughing and singing like savages. The flowers and jewels which decorated him, far from stripping death of its gloomy solemnity, only made the appearance more hideous. A general silence followed our entrance. A man, in whom I soon recognized the master of the house and the father of the dead child, rose to receive us. His face, far from being oppressed with sadness, seemed, on the contrary, radiant with delight, and he pointed with an air of pride to the numerous guests that had assembled to celebrate the death of his son, an event considered as a favor from heaven, since God had been pleased to call the child to himself before he was old enough to displease him. He assured us that we were welcome to his house, and that to him, on such an occasion, strangers became friends. Thanks to the loquacity of Perico, I had become the focus on which all eyes were centred. I had a difficult part to play, Perico thinking it right to make it appear to all who would listen to him that no one could kill people with a better grace than I. To enable me to act my part properly, I hastened to put my gloves in my pocket, and affect the most cavalier assurance, convinced that it was prudent to follow the fashion.

"What do you think of the lodging I have found you?" asked Perico, rubbing his hands; "is not this better than what I could offer you? besides, you will now know what a velorio is; it will be a resource in the evenings when you are low-spirited, and have nothing to do. Thanks to me, you will thus acquire a title to the eternal gratitude of this worthy father, whose child, having died before its seventh year, is now an angel in heaven."

And Perico, anxious, no doubt, to have a share in this tribute of gratitude, seized, without ceremony, an enormous glass of *chinguirito*, and swallowed it at a draught. I witnessed for the first time this barbarous custom, which compels the father of a family to cloak his sorrow beneath a smiling face, and to do the honors of his house to the first vagabond who, under the guidance of a sereno, comes to gorge himself with meat and drink before the corpse of his son, and share in that profuse liberality which often brings want to the family on the morrow.

The orgie, which had been disturbed a moment by our entrance, now fell in its usual course, and I began to cast my eyes about a little. In the midst of a circle of excited females, who esteem it a duty never to neglect a night-wake, I perceived a pale face, lips attempting to smile in spite of eyes full of tears, and, in this victim of a gross superstition, I had little difficulty in detecting the mother, for whom an angel in heaven could not compensate for the angel she missed on earth. The women about her seemed vying with one another as to who should increase the sorrow of the poor woman by their ill-timed but well-meant importunities. The different stages of the disease, and the sufferings of the dead child, were described by one woman; another enumerated infallible remedies that she would have applied if she had been consulted in time, such as St. Nicholas's plasters, moxas, the vapor of purslane gathered on a Friday in Lent, decoctions of herbs strained through a bit of a Dominican's frock, and the poor credulous mother turned her head away to wipe her eyes, thoroughly convinced that these remedies, if applied in time, would have saved her child. Sherry and cigarettes were rapidly consumed during these discussions; then all the innocent games in use in Spanish America were proposed and played, while the children, weary and sleepy, lay down to rest in every corner of the room, as if envying him whose discolored face protested, beneath the withered flowers, against this odious profanation of the dead.

Seated in the deep recess of one of the windows which looked into the street, I watched all Perico's motions with some uneasiness. It appeared to me that the protection he had so suddenly bestowed was only a cloak to entrap me. My features must have betrayed my uneasiness, for the lépero approached and said, by way of consolation,

"Look you, señor, killing a man is like every thing else; the first step is the only painful one. Besides, your sereno may perhaps be like my Englishman, who is to-day as well as ever. These heretics have as many lives as a cat. Ah!

señor," said Perico, with a sigh, "I have always regretted that I was not a heretic."

"To have as many lives as a cat?"

"No, to be paid for my conversion! Unfortunately, my reputation as a Christian is too well established."

"But the cavalier you were to kill," I asked of Perico, naturally brought back to the recollection of the melancholy young man whom I had seen kneeling before the Morgue, "do you think that he is still alive?"

Perico shook his head. "To-morrow, perhaps, his mad passion may have cost him his life, and his mistress will not survive him. I have no desire to make two victims at once, and I threw up the business."

"These sentiments do you honor, Perico."

Perico wished to profit by the favorable impression his answer had produced upon me.

"Doubtless—you can not risk your soul so for a few piastres. But, speaking of piastres, señor," he continued, holding out his hand, "I feel in the vein, and perhaps there are still a few pieces left in your purse. If I break the bank at *monte*, you shall go halves with my winnings."

I thought it prudent to yield to this new demand of the Zaragate. The play, besides, would free me from his company, which was becoming irksome. I slipped, then, some piastres into Perico's hand. Almost at the same moment twelve o'clock struck. One of the company rose, and cried in a solemn tone, "It is the hour of the souls in Purgatory; let us pray!"

The gamblers arose, amusements were suspended, and all the company gravely knelt. The prayer began in a high tone of voice, interrupted by responses at regular intervals, and for the first time the object of the meeting seemed remembered. Picture to yourselves these sots, their eyes glazed with drunkenness—these women in tatters, standing round a corpse crowned with flowers; draw over all this kneeling crowd the vapors of a thick atmosphere, in which putrid miasmas were mingled with the fumes of liquor, and you will have an idea of the strange and horrible scene of which I was forced to become an unwilling eye-witness.

Prayers over, gambling commenced anew, but not with so much liveliness as before. In company, when the night is far advanced, there is always a strong inclination to go to sleep; but when this struggle is over, the spirits become more lively, and get almost delirious and frantic. That is the hour of the orgie: the time was approaching.

I had again sat down in the recess of the window, and, to drive away the drowsiness which I felt stealing upon me, occasioned by the close air in the room, had opened the window a little. Looking out into the darkness of the night, I tried to find out, by the stars, what o'clock it was, and also to trace my way mentally through the labyrinth of streets, but I could scarcely see a bit of the sky, which on that night was cloudy, above the tops of the neighboring houses. I never remembered to have seen in Mexico before this canal with its leaden waters, nor those dark, deserted lanes which ran at right angles to it. I was completely at fault. Should I remain any longer amid this hideous orgie? Ought I not to try to escape, even though it was dangerous, through the streets of this distant suburb? While I was irresolutely weighing all these things in my mind, a noise of steps and confused whispers attracted my attention. I hid myself behind one of the shutters, so as to see and hear without being seen. Half a dozen men soon issued from a lane in front of the house in which I was. Their leader was wrapped in an *esclavina*,[11] which only half concealed the scabbard of his sword. The others were armed with naked sabres. A European but newly arrived in the country would have considered them criminals from their timid deportment, but my experienced eye could not be deceived; justice alone could seem so terrified, and I easily recognized the night patrol, composed of a regidor, an auxiliary alcalde, and four *celadores*.

"*Voto a brios!*" said the man in the *esclavina*, probably one of the auxiliary magistrates, at once alcaldes and publicans, who lodge criminals during the day, and let them off to pursue them at night; "what does my Lord Prefect mean by sending us to patrol in such a quarter as this, where the officers of justice have never penetrated. I should like to see him employed about this business."

"He would take care to provide himself with fire-arms, that he refuses to us," said one of the *corchetes*, who appeared the coolest of the party, "for criminals and malefactors are not in the habit of carrying the arms we do, and the person whom we have been ordered to protect will perhaps experience it this night to his cost."

"What the devil!" said the alcalde, "when one knows that he runs the risk of getting a dagger into him at night, why does not he stay at home?"

"There are some scamps whom nothing frightens," replied one of the corchetes; "but, as the Evangelist says, 'he who seeks the danger shall perish in it.'"

"What o'clock may it be now?" asked the auxiliary.

"Four in the morning," answered one of the men; and, raising his eyes to the window behind which I was concealed, he added, "I envy those people who pass the night so merrily in that *tertulia*." Talking thus, the celadores walked along the brink of the canal. All at once the auxiliary at their head stumbled in the darkness. At that moment a man sprang up and stood before the patrol.

"Who are you?" cried the alcalde, in a voice meant to be imposing.

"What's that to you?" replied the man as haughtily. "Can't a man sleep in the streets without being questioned?"

"One sleeps at home as—as—much as possible," stammered the alcalde, evidently frightened.

The person thus caught acting so much like a vagabond gave a shrill whistle, and, pushing the alcalde aside, ran down a neighboring lane. To my great surprise, the alcalde and the celadores, like men who dread a snare, instead of following him, ran off in quite an opposite direction. Almost at the same moment a hand was laid on my shoulder. I started and turned about. Perico and my host stood before me.

"That whistle sounds wonderfully like the call of my chum Navaja, when out on an expedition," cried the former, stooping to peer through the window, while the latter, with bleared eyes, his legs tottering like a man who had too conscientiously fulfilled his duties as master of the house, offered me a glass of liquor, that his shaky hand allowed to run over. Then, with the irritability peculiar to drunkards,

"One may say, señor," said he to me, "that you despise the society of poor people like us; you don't play, you don't drink; yet, in certain cases of conscience, gambling and brandy give great relief. Look at me now! To gratify my friends, I have eaten and drunk what I have and what I haven't: well, I am happy, although I don't possess a *tlaco* in the world; and, if you like, I will play with you for my child's body! It is a stake," continued he, in a confidential tone, "which is as good as another, for I can let it out, and well too, to some lover of a velorio."

"Play for the body of your child!" I cried.

"Why not? That is done every day. Every body hasn't the good fortune to have an angel aloft, and the body of this dear little one brings luck here."

I got rid, as well as I could, of the entreaties of this tender-hearted father, and cast my eyes once more into the street, but the approaches to the canal were now silent and deserted. I was not long, however, in discovering that this quiet, this solitude, were only apparent. Some strange, vague sounds escaped now and then from one of the lanes leading to the canal. Presently I fancied I heard the crunching of unsteady steps on the gravel. With my body leaning over the balcony, and listening intently, I waited for the moment when the awful stillness would be broken by some cry of anguish. The sound of voices, loud in dispute, again drew my attention to the room on which my back was turned. The orgie was this moment at its height. The Zaragate, surrounded by a group of angry gamblers, whose suspicions had been roused by his run of good luck, was trying, but in vain, to wrap around him the shreds of his olive cloak, which had been torn into ribbons by the furious hands of his adversaries.

The most stinging epithets were launched against him from all sides.

"I am a man of substance," cried the fellow, impudently, "as much as those whose uncivil hands have torn to tatters the handsomest cloak I ever possessed."

"Barefaced swindler!" cried a gambler; "your cloak had as many rents as your conscience."

"In any other place," replied Perico, who was prudently edging toward the door, "you would have to give me satisfaction for this double insult. Señor," said he, appealing to me, "be my surety, as I have been yours; half of my winnings is yours; they were honestly come by. All this is but mere slander."

I was once more mentally cursing my intimacy with Perico, when an occurrence of a graver nature made a happy diversion to the scene in which I saw myself in danger of becoming an actor. A man rushed hurriedly out of one of the back rooms on the same floor. Close behind him another followed, knife in hand; a woman after, shrieking terribly, and her dress flying in disorder about her.

"Will you stand and see me murdered?" cried the pursued, piteously. "Will no one hand me a knife?"

"Let me bury my knife in this rascal's body, this destroyer of my honor!" gasped the outraged husband.

The women, doubtless through sympathy, shrieked in concert, and uttered the most dreadful cries, while a friend of the offender slyly slipped a long knife into his hand. The latter faced about, and rushed boldly at his adversary. The cries of the women increased; a dreadful confusion ensued. The infuriated fellows made prodigious efforts to get at one another. Blood was about to flow, when, in the struggle, the table on which the infant lay was overturned. The body fell on the floor with a dull, heavy sound, and the flowers were scattered about. A large circle formed round the profaned corpse. A piercing shriek rose over all the uproar, and the bereaved mother threw herself on her child's remains with a cry of intense agony.

I had seen too much. I rushed to the balcony to cast a second look into the street, to assure myself that escape was yet possible; but there was no egress in that way. A man had just emerged from one of the lanes which opened upon the opposite bank of the canal. Other men came behind him, brandishing their weapons. This Navaja, whom Perico acknowledged as one of the fraternity, had doubtless collected his troop, and I was about to see him terminate, without being able to help his victim, one of those nocturnal brawls, of which some of the léperos boast. The person they were pursuing soon reached the parapet, and set his back to it. I distinctly heard him exclaim,

"Back, you cowardly rascals, who fight five to one."

"At him, *Muchachos*!" cried the chief of the band; "there are a hundred piastres to be earned."

Need I tell what followed? The unequal struggle lasted only a few moments. Soon a fierce shout announced that the murderers had triumphed. The unhappy man still breathed. He was able even to drag himself to the bridge, and, waving the stump of his sword, to dare the assassins to come on. Again surrounded by these villains, he once more fell beneath their blows. By the wan light of the lamp burning for the souls in Purgatory, I saw the men lift a bleeding body and throw it into the canal, the surface of which was for a moment disturbed. A second after, the assassins dispersed, and so rapidly that I asked myself if all this was not a bad dream; but the reality was too evident for me to indulge long in this error. Another incident occurred to prove to me that I was wide awake. A man on horseback issued from the house to which a fatal chain of events had bound me, and in this man I recognized Perico, mounted on the noble animal that I had brought with so much trouble from the *hacienda de la Noria*.

"Halloo, you rascal!" I exclaimed, "this is too much; you are stealing my horse."

"Señor," replied Perico, with astonishing composure, "I am carrying away a proof which might criminate your lordship."

Such was the lépero's farewell. The spurs driven home, the horse sprang off at a gallop. Without taking leave of any body, I set off in pursuit. It was too late; I only heard in the distance his plaintive neigh and the break of his gallop. These sounds soon died away. I rushed at random down one of the lanes which led to the canal. I wandered a long time in this labyrinth before finding myself in a place I knew, and day was breaking before I discovered my whereabouts. Night had brought its counsel, and I resolved to make a declaration in a court of law about the misfortune I had caused the night before. I went, then, to the *juzgado de latras*.[12] When I entered the judge had not yet arrived, and I waited in the hall. Fatigue and want of sleep were not long in making me oblivious of all my anxieties, and I fell asleep on a bench. I was retracing in my dreams the extraordinary scenes I had witnessed. I fancied I heard a dull noise about me, then deep silence all at once. I opened my eyes; I still believed myself a prey to the nightmare. A stretcher, covered with a bloody sheet, was laid almost at my feet. A thought passed through me like a flash of lightning. I imagined that I had been recognized, and that, by a refinement of barbarous justice, they were about to confront me with him whose death I had caused. I walked to the end of the lobby; the sight of the bloody sheet became insupportable to me. I gradually reassured myself, however, and, arming myself with courage, went and raised a corner of the covering. I had no difficulty in recognizing the victim. His pale, handsome face, and forehead marked with a long, slender scar, had left too deep an impression in my memory. The marshy plants and green slime which soiled his clothes reminded me of the theatre of the crime. This was the man I had seen die so valiantly, and whose loss, I knew, would be so tenderly bewailed. I let the sheet fall over his noble face.

I hasten to terminate this too long story. Twenty days had passed. No attention seemed to have been paid to the unfortunate accident of which I had been the innocent cause, and nothing remained of my nocturnal adventures but an invincible horror of the whole tribe of léperos, when I received an order to appear before a strange alcalde. A man about forty years of age, as much a stranger to me as the alcalde, was waiting for me at the bar.

"Señor," said this man to me, "I am the lamplighter whom your lordship almost killed; and as this accident has kept me from work for a fortnight, you will not take it ill if I ask you to make it up to me."

"Certainly not," said I, delighted to know that I had not to reproach myself with the death of any body. "How much do you ask?"

"Five hundred piastres, señor."

I must confess that this exorbitant charge immediately changed my pleasure into anger, and I could not help mentally consigning the lamplighter to the devil. But these feelings cooled down almost immediately; and the alcalde advising me to compound with the man, I was glad to be let off for a fifth part of the sum demanded by the lamplighter. After all, if my studies had been too expensive, the experience I had gained had its value, and I regretted nothing that Perico had extorted from me, not even the noble horse which he had so ingeniously appropriated.

FOOTNOTES:

[10] A cuartilla is worth 1½*d*; a tlaco ¾*d*.

[11] A small frock-coat, a short cloak.

[12] Justiciary court. The *juez de latras* is the criminal judge.

FRAY SERAPIO, THE FRANCISCAN MONK.

CHAPTER I.

The Convent of St. Francis.

In the present state of society in Europe, in which the principles and traditions of the Middle Ages have been so completely broken up, one can hardly form any idea of the influence which the monk exercises in Mexico, and of the strong tie which connects him with the world. If, however, this bond had no existence, the singular picture which Mexican society presents would lose one of its greatest charms—the perpetual contrast, namely, of the customs and characteristics of the nineteenth century with those of the time of Philip II. Beside men armed to the teeth, women dressed as in the days of Cortez and Pizarro, and barelegged Indians, with feet encased in ancient sandals, the gown of the monk appears, not as an anomaly, but as a highly poetic souvenir. This figure is not out of keeping with the picture, but in perfect harmony with it. Whether in public or in private, the monk takes a share in Mexican life, not only every day, but almost every moment. Not to speak of the many religious ceremonies performed by the monks, the rules of the cloister are generally so lax as to allow them free liberty of egress at almost any hour; and thus they can mix, without difficulty, in all the gayeties of the world. You can easily understand what a picturesque element is introduced into society by this immense crowd, who issue every day from the numerous convents, each order bringing its own type upon the scene, from the black frock of the Dominican to the white robe of the *Mercedario*.

If the upper classes of Mexican society have escaped from the trammels of monkish influence, the middle classes regard them with as much superstitious reverence as they did a century ago. The fantastic eloquence of the Middle Ages still keeps its ground here. The Mexican preacher, carried away by his enthusiasm, seizes upon the most startling metaphors: sometimes he represents God *as making the sun his charger, and the moon his stirrup;*[13] sometimes it is an obscene story, to which, with the most imperturbable gravity, he attaches a religious moral. When out of pulpit or confessional, the same man who inculcated the severest asceticism, utters the raciest jokes, and sings the best songs in some *tertulia* on the ground floor. He even pushes his anxiety so far as to furnish the laity with hints about dress. He gives excellent directions about the cut of a new suit of clothes; nay, more, he charges himself sometimes with their purchase, frequenting assiduously the saloons of fashion—and there is no appeal from his criticism. Very often his complaisance is not of the most disinterested kind; too often his purchase is only a kind of tribute paid to a family whom the reverend father supports at his own expense, on condition of tasting clandestinely in its pleasures. The monk is every where except at his convent. Every thing is an attraction to him—bull-fights, cock-fights, gambling-tables, and theatres; every place gives him an opportunity of displaying his whims and oddities. Let no one fancy that his compliant manners operate against him as a priest and spiritual director. The Mexicans understand to a nicety the bond which unites devotion to worldly pleasures. When the monk, late at night, wends his way to his convent after a day spent in dissipation, the passers-by, when they see him, bow the knee with as much respect as if his pious discourses and conduct were not in startling contrast with each other.

After this account of the character and habits of the Mexican monk, no one will be astonished at the occurrence which made me acquainted with one of the jolliest members of the great monastic family, the Reverend Fray Serapio. Curiosity had led me to a popular fête in the environs of Mexico, that of San Augustin de las Crevas, a small town about twelve miles from the capital. This fête, which makes Mexico a deserted city for three days, is frequented by the élite of Mexican gamblers. Whoever does not play is looked upon with suspicion. I followed the example of the numerous card-players who had been attracted to San Augustin, and seated myself at a table. My opposite neighbor was a Franciscan of athletic mould, and I shall never forget his sunburned, swarthy countenance, his piercing look, and his shaven face fringed with clusters of long crisp hair, shaggy as a bison's mane. He was a true soldier in a monkish dress. After a run of bad luck, I left the tables just as my last stake disappeared in the pocket of the monk. I wandered for some time in the streets of the village, hearing around me every where the clink of quadruples and piastres. I then mounted my horse, and, cursing my ill luck, took the road to Mexico. I had scarcely gone more than half way when I was brought to a stand-still by a very disagreeable circumstance. A turnpike gate stood half way between Mexico and San Augustin. Just as I came within sight of it, I made the disagreeable discovery that I had not the real necessary for passing me through the gate. Wishing to give myself time for reflection, I walked my horse slowly along, but the fatal turnpike came always nearer and nearer. I was just going to turn my horse's head round and gallop back, when by chance the Franciscan who had cleaned me out came up. The lucky winner addressed me most politely, and I replied in the most courteous manner. He offered to accompany me to Mexico; and the secret hope of being able to pass the gate at the Franciscan's expense doubtless made me accept his offer with so much alacrity. I fancied that I was doing no more than an act of politeness in congratulating my companion on his run of good luck. But what was my surprise when he exclaimed, with a sigh, "Confound it! I was quite cleaned out down there; I have nothing—nothing but my debts. I must say that I counted upon you to pass me through."

I confessed that I was just about to beg the same favor of him. Upon this the Franciscan fell into such convulsions of laughter that, in spite of myself, I could not help joining him heartily. We then deliberated what course to pursue. We hit upon several ludicrous expedients, but they were rejected one after the other. After some discussion, we decided that it would be best to clear the turnpike at a gallop without paying. "We will pay double the next time we pass," said the monk. Having thus disposed of this case of conscience, he spurred his steed; I followed. We soon left the pikemen behind us; and our horses flying at full speed, a thick cloud of dust soon hid us from their sight. Once at Mexico, it may be easily understood that we did not part without agreeing to meet again. A card-table, it must be owned, is rather an extraordinary place for one to strike up a friendship with a monk.

The acquaintance thus commenced promised to be agreeable, and a few days after our first meeting I repaired to the convent of St. Francisco, the abode of my friend. After this visit I went often, at first for the Franciscan's sake, and afterward to see the convent, the most beautiful building of the kind in Mexico. To tell the truth, Fray Serapio was seldom in his cell; but his friendship insured me a constant welcome at the monastery, the library of which possessed inexhaustible treasures.

None of the religious communities scattered over Mexico is so rich or powerful as that of St. Francis. The vast extent of ground covered by the Franciscan convents in all the large towns, and the massive walls, crowned with numerous turrets, which surround them, are sufficient indications of the power and wealth of the order. The monastery to which chance had introduced me is at once worthy of the community that owns it, and of the capital of which it is one of the chief ornaments. The street of San Francisco, which leads to the cloister of this name, is a continuation of that crowded commercial street, the *Plateros*. The cloister, happily situated in the most stirring part of the town, rises at the extremity of the street Francisco, and extends as far as the entrance to the Alameda. The thick walls, flanked with massive buttresses, give to the convent the appearance of a fortress. At the same time, the spires, which shoot up into the air, and the fine cupolas, covered with burnished tiles, gave clear indications of the character of the building. You arrive at the principal chapel by a vast flagged court, which is always crowded with sight-seers, visitors, the faithful, and the poor. Opposite the first court is an inclosure reserved for the monks. The immense cloisters, ornamented with basins inlaid with white jasper, gardens, a rich library, new dormitories, three hundred cells, a refectory, in which three hundred persons can sit down to dinner, combine to form a spectacle at once imposing and magnificent, which surpasses even the expectation of the visitor who enters the convent after having admired its exterior.

All my leisure hours, on Sundays especially, I loved to bury myself in the huge dusty library, and to ransack archives of which even the monks themselves were quite ignorant. Two books, above all, captivated me completely; one was a volume of legendary stories, the other a collection of *autos de fé*, executed by the Mexican Inquisition. I forgot even the lapse of time while reading them. These atrocious recitals, which the cold-blooded chronicler always sums up with *Laus Deo*, exercised upon me, especially when the day was waning, a singular fascination. The distant droning of the organ, and the doleful chanting of the monks, sometimes deepened the impression; and, in the mysterious gloom which had already enveloped the hall, I fancied I saw rise before me the heroes of the legendary stories, or the victims of the Inquisition. When I came out of the library, and walked in the cloisters, the monks whom I met in the dark corridors seemed to me to bear no resemblance whatever to those I had seen upholding the dignity of the cowl in the streets of Mexico. There are two sorts of monks in the convent: monks still young enough to delight in a *monte* table and in a *tertulia*, and who are never in their cells; others whose age and infirmities prevent them from mixing with the world: these last form the settled population, which is not a very numerous one. Among the monks whom I met in the corridors of San Francisco, there was one, above all, who seemed to me to personify the convent life, with all its attendants of gloomy observance and secret penance. He was an old man, with a shining bald head; a kind of awe, mingled with curiosity, seized me whenever I saw him. I could have sworn that one of those sombre pictures upon the walls of the convent, from the pencil of Rodriguez, Cabrera, or Villalpando, had left its frame and come to life again.

Sometimes I mused away an idle hour in the garden; for, all the time I was in Mexico, solitude was peculiarly pleasing to me. Since my arrival in Mexico, years had been added to years, and I began to experience attacks of home-sickness. The unvarying deep blue sky, so unlike that of France, rather increased my sadness. The appearance of the convent garden, surrounded on all sides by lofty walls, was in perfect harmony with the melancholy thoughts which had taken possession of my mind. The sun had calcined the brick walls, upon which opened the windows of the tenantless cells. Weeds were growing here and there on a terrace shaded with the wide-spreading branches of the sycamore, the palma christi, and the mango. An arbor, ornamented with climbing plants, was the place to which I most frequently directed my steps. There, under a flowery arch, where the passion-flower, that favorite plant of the cloisters, the jasmine, and the clematis, with its beautiful flowers, grew in charming confusion, I passed many long hours, dreaming of my native country and absent friends. A mysterious charm drew me to this fresh and rustic retreat. A quaint device, cut on the trunk of a sycamore, which threw its branches across my bower, often attracted my attention: *In silentio et in spe erit fortitudo tua.* My soul felt strengthened and soothed in this solitude. In this wild and uncultivated garden I was charmed into a forgetfulness of the world, where the only sounds that reminded me of life were the buzzing of the humming-birds among the rose-bushes, the tinkling of bells, and the distant droning of the organ.

I scarcely ever saw any one in the garden. One monk only seemed to share with me a predilection for this peaceful inclosure, and, above all, for the arbor, from which I almost always saw him escaping at my approach. He was the same man whom I had so often watched in the cloisters with such a fearful curiosity. Sometimes I surprised him watering the garden borders, or giving his care to those flowers which grew near the grass-grown walks. My imagination soon found some romantic link between this melancholy old man and the forsaken bower. I resolved to enter into conversation with him. A conscience so troubled as his seemed to be might surely be able to make some curious revelations; but, after repeated attempts to rouse him from his habitual taciturnity, I was forced to give it up as hopeless. With hands crossed, and face turned to the ground, the monk, every time he met me, quickened his pace and vanished from my sight. I looked at him always with intense interest, as the intellectual though stern expression of his features contrasted strikingly with the vacant faces of the other monks. His face, which sometimes betrayed painful dejection, sometimes a fanatical joy, reminded me at times of the wonderful legends and dismal stories which I had been reading in the convent library. Was I right in my conjectures about this singular personage? Despairing of success in my endeavors to induce the monk to break silence, I resolved to question Fray Serapio about him; and, with the hope of meeting the jolly Franciscan, I directed my steps to one of the most charming spots in the environs of Mexico, the canal of Viga.

FOOTNOTE:

[13] Cabalgando el sol, y estribando la luna.

CHAPTER II.

The Viga Canal.

Nowhere in Mexico could there be found a spot which presents an appearance more different, according to the seasons of the year, than the Viga Canal. No place is by turns more solitary or more crowded, more noisy or more silent. This canal, about twenty-four miles long, mixes its waters with the lake on which Chalco stands, and forms a means of transport and communication between that town and Mexico. A broad open road, planted with aspens and poplars, runs along its sleeping waters. If the pedestrian did not observe, at some distance from the highway, the buildings which inclose the bull-ring, and, farther off, the towers of the Cathedral, above which shoot up the two mighty volcanoes of Mexico, he might fancy himself three hundred miles from the city. Some country houses, whose inhabitants are always invisible; the deserted paths of the *Candelaria*, a rival road to the Viga; lakelets scattered here and there in the midst of teeming vegetation, on whose surface float *chinampas*[14] looking like large baskets; a solitary *vaquero* hut here and there in the plain; then a range of hills overtopped by the sierra, form the principal features in the landscape. A placid stillness reigns over every part of the picture. Sometimes a pirogue is seen gliding noiselessly on the canal, sometimes a group of Indians kneeling in some grove before a Christ that they are decking with flowers, at whose feet they are piously depositing oranges and grenadilles, offerings which savor strongly of paganism. The flapping of the wings of an aigret hovering over the water, or that is losing itself in the blue sky, and the baying of some dogs prowling about, are the only sounds which break the stillness on this shady road. But at the approach of the Easter fêtes the road assumes quite a different appearance. Every Sunday in Lent, the entire population of Mexico assembles here, and a noisy crowd streams along the way. The day on which I went to the canal was the last Sunday in Lent. On reaching the road, I found the habitual promenaders of the *Paseo* and *Alameda* crowding every spot of the ground in the Viga; but it was not the crowd which chiefly attracted me, it was the canal itself. On that day, the reeds on the bank, ordinarily so still, waved and jostled to and fro under the continual motion of the water, produced by the passing and repassing of numberless fleets of boats. *Launches*, canoes, pirogues, were constantly coming and going; some conveying to Mexico, for the Holy Week, immense quantities of flowers, which diffused a most delightful odor around. Other boats followed, crowded with light-hearted, merry passengers, wearing wreaths of wild poppy and sweet pea, and dancing on the deck to the inspiring strains of harps, flutes, and mandolins. Light-hearted Cyprians, in gamesome mood, scattered upon the breeze the purple buds of their wreaths, and trolled out choruses of lascivious songs. The clear sky, the dazzling brilliancy of the different costumes, and the soft, sweet melody of the language, brought to my mind the national festivals of ancient Greece; while the canal, which seemed at times suddenly transformed into a carpet of flowers, generally had the appearance of a moving mass of canoes, which shot past one another in all directions; groups of people, lying lazily on the bank, bantered the boatmen as they passed. Farther off, under the green arcades formed by the aspens upon the road, which shook under the roll of carriages and gallop of horses, paraded the gay fashionables of Mexico. Parties of high-spirited, wild-looking cavaliers, dressed in the national costume, sauntered up and down amid this gay throng as if protesting by their rough manners against the whimsical appearance of the dandies habited in French style.

A striking contrast was observable to the spectator. Upon the canal one saw America in the sixteenth century, which, under the beaming sun of the tropics, had abandoned herself without constraint to pleasure. Upon the road was America in the nineteenth century, seeking to model its native appearance on the worn-out type of Europe. By way of compensation, a few Europeans, habited in the ancient Mexican costume, at times appeared on the Viga; but beneath their dress you could distinguish at a glance the Englishman, the Frenchman, or the German. I must say, however, that our compatriots of the South were distinguished above all the other foreigners for the ease and grace with which they wore the national costume.

Evening was drawing on, darkness was coming down over the surrounding country, and the moving picture before me was rapidly dissolving, when I perceived four horsemen seemingly making their way toward me. I could not at first distinguish their features, their faces being partly concealed by the wide-spreading *sombreros*, trimmed with broad ribbons, which they wore; but their appearance caused me to suspect them. These men, dressed in *mangas* and *sarapes*, seemed to be hemming me in with the intention of opposing my passage. They immediately spurred their horses and galloped up to me. "Stand!" cried a threatening voice; and, at the same moment, the four horsemen surrounded me. They were neither robbers nor alguazils, but men whose amiable character and joyous temperament I often had occasion to appreciate. In one I recognized Don Diego Mercado, student of theology in the college of St. John de Lateran; in another, the officer Don Blas; the third was the hidalgo, Don Romulo D—— F——, a political marplot, who could never be satisfied with the government of the day, but was always looking about for an opportunity to overturn it, who was admitted, notwithstanding this weakness, into the highest society in Mexico; the fourth was one whom I would have least expected to find in a company like the present, and in such a disguise: it was no other, in truth, than my worthy friend, Fray Serapio.

"Do I really see the Reverend Fray Serapio?" I exclaimed. "Do I really see my friend under this bandit costume?"

"Tut!" said the Franciscan; "I am traveling incog.; I shall tell you why some other time."

"Good," said I to the monk; "I have something to ask you which interests me as much."

"You are one of ourselves," cried the officer, "and we are going to conduct you to a place out of Mexico, where we intend to finish the Holy Week."

"Where is it?" I inquired.

"You will know when you get there," replied the hidalgo. "I know you are a lover of adventures: well, I promise you some, and of a strange enough kind."

This was taking me on my weak side, and I accepted the offer without troubling myself any farther as to its whereabouts. I was, besides, in full traveling costume; and an excursion by night was, above all, highly agreeable to me. We alighted, and threaded our way through the crowd; then leaving it, we struck along the Candelaria road, and, remounting, pursued a northerly direction. I fell behind the rest and joined Fray Serapio, and again renewed my inquiries about his disguise. On our first acquaintance the monk seemed to my taste too shy and distrustful, but I soon hit upon a sure way of stripping him of these unsocial qualities. I feigned to make the Christian virtues of my venerable friend the theme of my warm admiration; and Serapio, who had the high ambition, a singular one in a monk, of passing for a rake, replied to my eulogiums by some revelations about the old monk which did not redound greatly to his credit. At this time, too, the expedient succeeded as it ordinarily did. The Franciscan assured me, with a contrite air, that he had put on this disguise by the will of God!

"As you always do," I rejoined, gravely; "you obey him implicitly, like a humble servant."

The monk bowed and quickened his horse's pace.

"It has pleased God," replied he, "to deprive his servant of his robes for the purpose of saving the soul of a Christian who is about to quit this world."

"St. Martin gave to the poor only a half of his cloak. What was his charity in comparison with yours?"

The Franciscan shrugged his shoulders.

"Alas!" he muttered, "it is a rich man who has my gown, and I don't deserve to be compared to St. Martin."

"I am well aware that the most noble virtues are often modestly hidden from the world."

Wearied with my bantering, the monk dropped the mask entirely.

"Faith!" he replied, in a frank, open tone, "pietistic people prefer being interred in a monkish habit; and, the more threadbare the garment, the higher they value it. My gown, on this account, is of an inestimable value. I sold it a short time ago for double its original cost; and, besides the profit from the sale of it, I got a present of this costume which I am now wearing."

The sun had now set; and the moon, which was rising, diffused its beams over the solitary country. Arrived at the crest of a small eminence, I looked back upon the canals and the plains of the Viga, which, under the brilliant night of the tropics, appeared to me under quite a new aspect. The moon had lighted up the lagoons, the canal, and the road. They were all now silent. The most profound stillness had taken the place of the stir and hum of the busy crowd; the silence was broken only by the distant bellowing of the bulls in the savannas. The fire-flies sparkled in the high grass, and the watch-fires of the shepherds shone here and there in the fields.

FOOTNOTE:

[14] Floating islands.

CHAPTER III.

An Indian Village.

We had now been for some time on the road, and the night was getting darker and darker. The moon, which up to this time had lighted our way, was now becoming gradually encircled with a halo—a bad omen. At last it finally disappeared in a dense bank of clouds on the verge of the horizon. From time to time a yellowish sheet of lightning shot through the dark mass, and brought out, in strong relief, the dense blackness which enveloped the country around. The instinct of our horses alone kept us right in the thick darkness. The barking of dogs announced our approach to some solitary cabin by the wayside; sometimes we charged unwillingly among a herd of pigs which were lying wallowing in the ruts of the road, and which trotted off grunting in the darkness. In the midst of this savage scene, surrounded with the lurid light produced by the flashes, which were following each other in quick succession, we looked more like some country smugglers out on an expedition than peaceful travelers on an excursion of pleasure.

We had already passed through the village of Tacubaya, and were struggling onward in the mountain road which leads to Toluca. I knew nothing of the road they were leading me. That was of little importance, provided we reached our place of destination before the bursting of the storm, which announced its approach by distant peals of thunder. We soon arrived at a rising ground, round the foot of which ran a pine wood. There a halt was called to breathe our horses. The clouds of dust we had swallowed rendered some refreshment necessary. A skin of Valdepeñas wine, which the officer Don Blas carried at his saddle-bow, was passed round, and served for a moment to quench the burning thirst which had begun to torment us. I profited by this opportunity to renew my inquiries about our place of destination. The theological student undertook to satisfy my curiosity.

"I have been invited," said he, "to spend the Easter holidays at the hacienda of a friend of mine, about a dozen leagues from here; I thought it no bad thing to give my friend the honor of receiving a few more guests, and I am sure you will all be very welcome."

The hidalgo Don Romulo, on his part, was not unwilling to allow, during his absence, the agitation caused by a very violent pamphlet which he had written against the government of the republic to subside, while he was anxious, at the same time, to visit the ruins of a celebrated convent, the Desierto, which was on our way. The officer hoped to escape in the Desierto and the hacienda the importunities of his numerous creditors, and was disposed to make himself happy in every place but where they were. As for Fray Serapio, he confessed that, having been forced, as he might call it, to purchase a habit ill suited to a monk, he had embraced with delight the invitation of his friend, Don Diego Mercado.

"And yet I got a hundred piastres for my old habit," added the Franciscan, gloomily, taking another pull at the skin of Valdepeñas.

"That's where your soft-heartedness leads you," said I. "You have doubtless flung it away in charity."

"*Mon cher* (these were the only French words that Fray Serapio knew, and he made use of them on all occasions), know then, once for all, that I don't deserve your praises. Nature cut me out for a soldier, but conventionality made me a monk."

The Franciscan confessed, readily enough, that when he was on the point of buying a new frock, an inconceivable distraction made him spend the money on other things quite useless for a man, and, above all, for a monk; things which—(Fray Serapio whispered the remainder in my ear). The skin of Valdepeñas being now half empty, we resumed our journey. Large drops of rain began to fall; the storm was going to burst over us in all its fury. To push on was our only resource. Stimulated by a secret instinct, our horses increased their pace. Sometimes they shyed or stopped suddenly, terrified at the fantastic forms of some projecting root, or the sudden growl of the thunder; but these annoyances were only temporary, and we flew over the ground with inconceivable swiftness. We descried at last, in a plain, a little Indian village, still more than a league in advance. We covered this league in a few minutes, and entered the village, saluted by a legion of hungry dogs, who snarled and bit at our horses' heels. Our arrival set every one in motion. Copper-colored faces appeared and disappeared at the doors of the huts. We were asking ourselves, in no small consternation, if we must give up all hopes of finding a shelter in a place where every door seemed to be shut against us, when Fray Serapio, catching an Indian by his long hair, forced him to lead us to a house that did duty for an inn.

Scarcely had we stopped before the door of the pretended hostelry than a great hulking fellow, one of the half-breeds so numerous in Mexico, very easily known by his complexion, opened one of the leaves of the door, which was secured by the invariable iron chain. This was the master of the inn, who had come to parley with us.

"I have neither stables, nor maize, nor straw to offer your lordships," said the half-breed, in a gruff tone; "be so good, then, as to continue your journey."

"Go to the devil," said the officer, "with your straw, your maize, and your stables; all we want is a room fit for Christians and officers. Open, or I will smash the door to pieces."

To give full force to his threat, Captain Don Blas struck the door such a furious blow with his sabre, that the *huesped*, in a fright, dropped the chain, and, excusing himself for his obstinacy by the plea that there were a great number of suspicious characters abroad, ushered us into an apartment little better than a stable.

"I hope," cried Don Romulo, putting his pocket handkerchief to his nose, "that we sha'n't be obliged to pass the night in this cursed hole!"

"You are very squeamish, *mon cher,*" said Fray Serapio; "the room seems tolerable enough."

In spite of this assertion, we determined to push on after the storm had passed. We remained, then, standing till we could take the road again, as we wished to reach the *hacienda* as quickly as possible, where a hospitable reception had been promised us. I thought this halt presented a favorable opportunity for making some inquiries about the mysterious monk I had met in the garden of San Francisco. To my first question: "I can guess whom you are inquiring about," said Fray Serapio, shaking his head; "it is Fray Epigmenio whom you saw in the arbor in the garden of the convent, of which you and he are the only visitants. A trial, to which he was subjected by the Inquisition, turned the head of the poor soul, and for fifty years his life has been only one long penance."

"Well, I'll tell you frankly," I rejoined, "I had a suspicion that some painful mystery was wrapped up in the life of this man. I counted upon you for its solution, and it was you I was in search of when chance brought us together on the Viga."

The monk was about to reply, when an extraordinary noise arose in the court-yard of the *posada*, which was suddenly lit up by the red glow of torches. Almost at the same moment a man, whom from his copper-colored visage and strange costume we easily knew to be an Indian, entered, followed by several inhabitants of the village, some carrying torches, others brandishing knotty clubs, some even with bows, and arrows in reed quivers. The Indian who seemed to be the chief of the party advanced, and told us that, as our noisy arrival had disturbed the peace of the village, the alcalde wished to see us without delay.

"And what if we don't want to see the alcalde?" said the officer.

"You will then be taken by force," said the Indian, pointing to his armed escort. This gesture was sufficient. It was impossible for us to resist, for the ministers of Indian justice had very prudently seized our horses and arms. We looked at one another in no small dismay. The Indian *mansos*, who rule their villages according to the laws of the republic, and even choose from their brothers of the same race their municipal magistracy, behave in the most merciless manner to all the Mexicans who may have committed any crimes in the district intrusted to their care. The worst of all cruelties, the cruelty of weakness, is resorted to on such occasions. It was quite useless to struggle against those sturdy rough alguazils with the bare legs and long hair. We went quietly enough to the house of the alcalde.

"Have patience," said Fray Serapio to me, in a low voice, while going along: "instead of the history of Fray Epigmenio, which I will tell you at some other time, you will behold a sight which few foreigners have an opportunity of seeing in Mexico. If I am not mistaken, we have fallen upon this cursed village at the very time when the Indians celebrate, in their way, the fêtes of the Holy Week. The house of the alcalde is one of the ordinary resting-places of their nocturnal processions."

I had often heard of these singular ceremonies, in which the remains of Indian idolatry are mixed up with the rites of Catholicism. Just when I was going to reply to Fray Serapio, some melancholy monotonous sounds met our ears. The plaintive wail of the reed flute, called by the Indians *chirimia*, was sadly intermingled with the tapping of several drums struck at regular intervals.

"Three hundred years ago," said Don Diego Mercado to me in a whisper, "it was to the sound of these *chirimias* that the ancestors of these Indians butchered their human victims at the feet of their idols."

Round a lane, which ran at right angles to the road, came the procession whose approach was announced by this funereal music. Engaged during the day in cultivating their grounds, the Indians devote the night to certain religious solemnities. The time thus adds to the lugubrious effect of their ceremonies. At the head of the procession, borne by four men, was an image of Christ, of a hideously gigantic form, bedabbled with blood. At the two arms of the cross hung two Christs of a smaller size; behind came a disorderly throng of Indians from the village and its environs, carrying crosses of all shapes and dimensions. I remarked that the size of several of the crosses was by no means in harmony with the height of the person who carried them; their dimensions were, in fact, only regulated by the higher or lower sum paid by the person who wished to figure in these processions. The most splendid images were carried in the van by the head men of the village; the poorer inhabitants followed, and nothing could be imagined more grotesque, more sadly ludicrous than this motley crowd of tatterdemalions; some, too poor to purchase Christs, were carrying little images of the saints; others, less lucky still, were forced to hoist on long poles, for want of better, faded pieces of colored cloth and tawdry tinsel, while some had even been forced to carry hen-coops. We bent the knee respectfully as this singular procession slowly wended its way through the streets, while the odd collection of hideous and incongruous objects, and the grotesque faces of the men, lighted up by the dim, ruddy glare of the pine torches, and seen through the smoke, struck us as being more like some infernal procession revisiting this earth than a body of Christians engaged in the celebration of a religious festival.

We arrived at the alcalde's house. The sinister appearance of this Indian magistrate did not tend to soothe our apprehensions. Long gray hair, encircling a face deeply furrowed with wrinkles, flowed down behind to the middle of his back; his muscular arms were hardly covered by the sleeves of his *sayal* (a tunic with short sleeves); his shrunken, sinewy legs were only half covered by his flapping trowsers of *calzoneras* skin. On his feet were leather sandals. In such a dress this singular personage seated himself, with an air of comic grandeur, under a sort of canopy formed by the branches of *xocopan* (a kind of sweet-smelling laurel). The red-skin alguazils ranged themselves behind like a group of stage supernumeraries. We were now asked, "Who and what are you?" This question, delivered in bad Spanish, was put to Fray Serapio, whom his long beard, jaunty costume, and free manners had undoubtedly caused the alcalde to regard as the most suspicious of the party. The monk hesitated. The alcalde continued:

"When people come with arms to a village, it is to be presumed they have a right to carry arms. Can you prove your right?"

It was, then, to examine us as to our right of carrying arms that we had been arrested. The alcalde thought he had us in a trap, and would have an opportunity of inflicting upon us, without going beyond the strict letter of the law, some of those petty insults, for which opportunities are eagerly seized on, to satisfy the traditionary hatred of the Indians against the whites. We understood this perfectly, but we could not counterplot him. We were all obliged to make the same reply. We were traveling incognito, and had no right to carry arms. With the exception of the monk, who seemed ill at ease in his disguise, we were eager to tell our names and quality. As it was a point of the very highest importance to let the Indians know the powerful protectors we had in Mexico, the student fancied he was acting prudently when he said that he was the nephew of the most celebrated apothecary in the city. The clerk wrote down the answer, stopping every now and then to break in pieces little branches of *xocopan*. As for the alcalde, he seemed to triumph at having in his power five of the enemies of his race. When the student avowed his relationship to the Mexican apothecary, the wily Indian did not consider himself foiled. He seemed lost in thought; but suddenly an expression of malignant joy shot across his features as he hastily put this question to Don Diego:

"If you are the nephew of an apothecary, you must know something of botany?"

Don Diego replied in the affirmative, with an air of perfect satisfaction.

"You must, then, be acquainted with the virtues of *matlalquahuitl*?"

The alcalde had intentionally chosen a strange Mexican plant very little known, with an Indian name of the most uncouth sound. When he saw the blank look that immediately appeared on the countenance of the student, he guessed that his ruse was successful, and he rubbed his hands with an air of satisfaction. You know nothing of botany; you were trying to cheat me; you are not the nephew of an apothecary; you have all a suspicious air about you. I have a right to detain you, and I'll do it, too. Such was the reasoning which we saw written on the face of the alcalde, who looked with a cool air of disdain both on Don Diego Mercado and on us. At this moment the religious fête, in which the alcalde had to play an important part, luckily created a diversion in our favor by putting a stop to this examination. A band of Indians hurriedly entered the room. They dragged along, or rather pushed before them, a man crowned with a wreath of rushes, and draped in a tattered red cloak which had very probably been used as a *muleta*[15] in a bull-fight. His face and body were quite bespattered with mud. I looked at this man with astonishment as a living enigma, when the student, who was better acquainted with the manners of the Indians than with the virtues of the *matlalquahuitl*, said, in a low tone,

"There is nothing in this but a religious joke. They are going to get up here a dramatic representation of the Passion. We are no longer in an Indian village, but in Jerusalem. This fellow with the bespattered face personates Christ, and the alcalde, confound him! is Pilate."

In fact, we were about to have produced before us all the scenes of a genuine mystery of the Middle Ages. The alcalde, seated under his canopy of laurel, having gravely listened to the calumnious accusations of the Jews, rose and pronounced in the Indian tongue the historical sentence of condemnation. Such a storm of cries and yells greeted the sentence, that the unfortunate lépero (for it was one of that class, who, for a few reals, was personating Christ) seemed to think that the drama was becoming rather too serious. He cried out in Spanish,

"Caramba! I think it would have been better had I taken the part of the good thief. Señor Alcalde, don't forget to pay me three reals more for personating the Divine Redeemer!"

"You are a fine fellow!" said the alcalde, pushing the lépero back, who, in violation of all historical truth, took refuge in the tribunal itself. At the same time, one of the soldiers who surrounded the Christ, more faithful to his part than the bespattered lépero, struck him a smart blow on the cheek. The lépero could contain himself no longer; he rapped out a fearful oath, and struck out right and left at his astonished persecutors. There was a general melée; a fierce struggle arose between the actor, who had completely forgotten the spirit of his part, and the Indians, who attacked him with a vigor worthy of the agents of Herod. The contest was brought to an end by a heroic sacrifice on the part of the alcalde, who, to overcome the obstinacy of the lépero, promised him six reals more than he was originally entitled to. On this condition the fellow agreed to walk to Calvary in the midst of the Indians. They dragged him along to the place of execution, dealing him a more than ordinary allowance of blows.

This business finished, the alcalde returned to us. He had pronounced the sentence upon the pretended Christ with an ill-disguised anxiety. When we saw him conversing with the clerk, I looked somewhat dejectedly at the monk. To my amazement, a smile appeared on his lips which set me completely at my ease. The cause of this sudden change in Fray Serapio was soon explained. To avoid the imprisonment which he saw impending over us, he resolved to appeal to the religious feelings of the alcalde and his followers, of which they had just given such striking proofs. Fray Serapio had reasoned justly. Just when the alcalde was rising to pronounce our sentence, the monk gravely approached the tribunal, snatched off the neckerchief which encircled his head, and showed the Indian magistrate his tonsure. This was truly a theatrical stroke. The man who, scarcely a second before, was affecting to look upon us with such stubborn pride, threw himself trembling and confused at the feet of the Franciscan.

"Ah! holy father," cried the Indian, "why did you not discover yourself sooner? Taking every thing into consideration, one can be an honest man without knowing the virtues of *matlalquahuitl.*"

Fray Serapio need not have answered the terrified Indian. He condescended to confess that, under this disguise and with this escort, he was traveling to execute a mission of religious interest; and the alcalde, who crossed himself devoutly at every word of the monk, took good care not to press him with imprudent questions. An instant after, we marched majestically out of the cabin into which our entrance had been so humble and crestfallen. The Indians returned us our arms and horses. They pressed us in vain to return to the hostelry where we had been so scurvily welcomed. We were very ill pleased at the reception they had given us; and, in spite of the thunder, which had again begun to growl, we galloped out of the village without lending an ear to their entreaties.

FOOTNOTE:

[15] A red cloth shaken before the bull for the purpose of exciting him.

CHAPTER IV.

Fray Epigmenio.

Already the Indian village lay a league behind us. The route we were pursuing was through a ravine, the road through which could with difficulty be believed to have been made by the hand of man. We soon entered a pine forest which ran along a chain of precipitous hills. The darkness, which was rendered thicker by the interlaced branches of the trees overhead, was so profound that our horses could literally advance only by the gleam of the vivid flashes of lightning. Soon the storm increased; the trunks of the pines cracked and swayed to and fro in the wind, and the hollows in the mountains resounded with the multiplied echoes of terrific thunder-claps. The flashes now became less and less frequent, and at last, the intermittent gleams, which had hitherto lightened our advance, failed us entirely. A deafening thunder-clap was followed by a torrent of rain. It had now become impossible for us either to advance or to regain the road. Forced to remain immovable like equestrian statues, we were obliged to shout to one another to find out our respective positions. I then discovered that I was very near Fray Serapio. The voices of our three companions reached us like a distant echo borne along amid the whistling of the squall. We at last found ourselves separated from one another, without any probable hope of joining each other during the whole night, each of us being forced to stay where the darkness had overtaken him, exposed to all the dangers of the forest.

"Since we are condemned to remain here, as motionless as the statue of Charles IV. in Mexico," said I to the Franciscan, "don't you think this is a very good opportunity for telling me the history of your friend, Fray Epigmenio?"

"Fray Epigmenio!" cried the monk. "This is not a story suited either to the time or place. When I hear the trees groaning like spirits in Purgatory, and the torrents raging like wild beasts, I have not the courage to go over a history that is frightful enough in itself."

A long pause followed. "Where are we?" I at last asked.

"We ought to be only a mile and a half from the *Desierto*. We have kept on the right road; but I have strong fears that we have got entangled in a ravine, from which escape is almost impossible amid this darkness. In a few hours, should the rain continue, this ravine will be no longer a road, but a torrent, that will carry us along on its rushing waters like dead leaves. God succor our poor souls!" He crossed himself devoutly.

I had seen too often in America torrents suddenly swollen by thunder-showers to such a degree as to uproot trees a hundred years old, and carry down rocks, to doubt for a moment the imminent danger of which I had been apprised by Fray Serapio. To this disheartening reply I had but one answer to make—we must have a fire, at any price. Unluckily, the monk had left his flint and steel with the student. I was not discouraged, however; and, unwilling to throw away any chance of extricating ourselves from our disagreeable position, I alighted from my horse, took in one of my hands the *reata* attached to the neck of the animal, and with the other tried to guide myself while holding on to the rocks. I was not long in finding my progress stopped by a precipitous bluff. I tried the other side; always a perpendicular wall of rock. Forced at last to stop after having unrolled the *reata* to its utmost length, I came back step by step to my horse, and, gathering it up again in my hand, remounted.

"This ravine is in truth a prison," said I.

"It is not the torrent alone that I fear," replied the monk. "Even if we escape drowning, we may be burned to death if the trees are set on fire by the lightning."

"Could we not leave our horses here, and try to gain on foot a place less exposed to danger?"

"We run a risk of tumbling into some quagmire. By the way the wind hits my face, I know that this ravine is of great extent. Let us remain where we are, and trust to Divine Providence."

I had exhausted all my expedients, and could find nothing to reply to those last words of Fray Serapio's, which were uttered in a truly mournful tone. Some moments passed. The storm was still at its height, and I could not shut my ears to its wild music. In the depths of the forests, a wail as of a thousand spirits came booming on the wind; torrents raged and dashed from rock to rock, the pines creaked like the masts of a vessel caught in a hard gale, and above our heads the wind whistled strangely among the leaves. During the temporary lulls of the tempest, we heard our companions, who, whether from ignorance or a wish to drown their sense of danger, were shouting and singing with all their might.

"Don't you think," said I to the monk, "that this gayety is somewhat out of place? I have a good mind to make them sensible of the danger they are running, to cause them to change their song for the 'De Profundis.'"

"What good would that do?" said the monk, gloomily. "Would it not be better for them to remain ignorant of their danger, and let death surprise them in their joyous thoughtlessness? At this moment, when the spirits of darkness are hovering about us, the human voice seems to bring with it an undefinable charm. I have not yet told you the story of Fray Epigmenio. I'll do it now. I would rather hear the sound of my own voice than the whistling of the wind among the firs. And now, when I think of it, it was in the convent of the Desierto, in the vicinity of this forest, and exactly at this time of the year, that the most interesting occurrence in the life of Fray Epigmenio took place."

"This circumstance," said I, "must add particular interest to your recital; but, at such a moment as this, I hardly feel disposed to listen to you. However, if you like to tell the story, I—"

"Fray Epigmenio," began the Franciscan, interrupting me, "was, even in his youth, but a melancholy companion. That is to say, he was not at all like me. Far from having wished, as I did, to be a soldier before donning the monk's habit, he was, when a mere boy, admitted as a novice into the Carmelite convent of the Desierto. At the time I refer to, that is, fifty years ago, the Desierto was not abandoned as it is now. It was then a retreat inhabited by several monks, who wished, by thus withdrawing themselves from the cities, to push austerity to its utmost limits. You may guess what influence a wild solitude like that would exercise upon a weak brain. For my part, I don't think I should be long in my right mind were I to live in such a place. The superiors of the young novice were soon alarmed at the ferocious exultation that soon took the place of his former solid piety. They represented to Epigmenio that the devil, jealous of his merits, was setting a trap for him, into which he would fall. It was a wise advice; but Epigmenio paid no heed to it. Worse than all, he isolated himself almost entirely from his brethren, and shut himself up more closely than ever in his cell—a sort of dark dungeon, whose windows opened upon the wood which surrounded the convent. This was the gloomiest cell in this gloomy cloister. Fray Epigmenio had chosen it in preference to those whose windows looked out upon the garden. The sight of the flowers seemed to this rigid cenobite too much of a worldly pleasure. The heavy masses of the dark woods, constantly agitated by the wind, and surrounded by an amphitheatre of rocks in fantastic forms, was the kind of landscape which had the greatest charm for Epigmenio. I told you before that the soundest head in the world could not long resist the combined influences of solitude and prayer. The monk confessed, when too late, that strange visions passed before his eyes in those long days of contemplation and silence. Mysterious voices assailed his ears, and it was not always the concerts of angels that he heard: the murmurs of the forest were often changed into voluptuous sighs and—"

At this moment the Franciscan suddenly paused, and, turning to me, said, "Are you listening?"

"I confess," I rejoined, "that I am paying more attention to the noise of the water which is now rising about our feet."

"Fray Epigmenio," said Serapio, without attending to my remark, "fancied himself a saint, since temptations like these assailed him, and that he was struggling against the devil, like the monks in the old legends. One day, about sunset, not content to wait for the tempter in his cell, he resolved to beard him in the forest itself, which was peopled with such phantoms. He had not wandered far among the pines when he heard the sound of stifled sobbing not far from him. He stopped and listened, and then advanced in the direction from which the moaning seemed to proceed. For a long time his search was fruitless. At last, after many turnings and windings, he arrived at a glade in the wood, in the centre of which lay, on the turf, a man, who invited him by signs to approach. Fray Epigmenio hesitated a moment. At last, having crossed himself devoutly, he falteringly approached the wounded man. 'In God's name,' cried he, 'of what unfortunate accident are you the victim?' The holy name of God appeared to rouse in the stranger a painful emotion, and his voice was hardly perceptible when he told Epigmenio that, as he was traveling with his daughter, he had been set upon by robbers, stripped of all he had, and left bleeding on the ground. He added that it was not for himself that he was asking assistance, but for the feeble creature by his side; and, at the same time, parting the branches of a bush near which he lay, he showed the monk a young lady lying in a swoon upon the grass. The rays of the moon fell full upon her marble countenance and white dress. You may imagine the confusion Epigmenio was in when he saw this beautiful female, who seemed to realize to him the most beautiful visions of his dreams. After a short silence, he represented to the stranger that the convent of the Desierto was not far off; but, were it nearer, a female could not be received within its walls. The unknown was grieved that he could not continue his journey, as his horse had escaped when the robbers attacked him. Plucking up his spirits, he declared, as his wound now gave him less pain, he would like to rise and seek for his lost steed. They set out together, but soon after agreed to separate, and—"

A blinding flash of lightning interrupted the monk's story. The storm was increasing. The muddy water had now risen as far as our stirrups. Our horses, that had stood without motion a long time, now turned and presented their chests to the current, which was surging up higher and higher every minute. Around us, in the depth of the woods, the noise of the torrents was mingled with the wild harmony of the brawling winds, that seemed to blow from every point of the compass.

"The water is rising," cried Fray Serapio, "and our horses will soon be utterly powerless against its force."

Almost at the same moment the poor animals turned quickly round, and, whether guided by instinct, or carried away by the force of the current, they moved toward the bottom of the ravine. A cry of distress, wafted to us by the wind, apprised us that the torrent was also bearing away our companions in misfortune. A second flash lighted up the forest, and was followed by a clap of thunder which shook the air. A sulphurous odor filled the atmosphere, and immediately, to our inexpressible satisfaction, a pine, which had been struck by lightning a few paces from us, blazed up, and soon illuminated the surrounding objects.

"We are saved!" cried Fray Serapio: "I see near us a rock low enough for our horses to mount."

Our companions had already escaped from the torrent; they encouraged us by voice and gestures to do the same. My horse, by a desperate effort, reached the top of the bank. I had kept close by Fray Serapio, whose horse had twice attempted the ascent, and had twice fallen back; but the third time, like a true Mexican, he accomplished it. We were still not out of all danger. A shelter must be found, as it was now out of the question to push on to the hacienda.

By the pale light in the sky, which was now comparatively clear, we could discern a narrow bridle-path running along the edge of the ravine. This road doubtless led to the Desierto, the very convent in which Fray Epigmenio had first taken his vows. We hurried along this path, certain this time of not missing our way; and a few minutes after, having escaped the most imminent peril, our little troop stopped, with heartfelt satisfaction, before the ruined walls of the ancient monastery.

CHAPTER V.

The Desierto.

After fastening our horses in the outer court of the convent, we chose, near the entrance of the building, the cell which seemed to be most convenient for shelter. The first moments of our halt were devoted to an interchange of reflections, half merry, half serious, upon the danger we had run. Don Romulo confessed that he had taken part in seventeen conspiracies; that he had been banished, under circumstances of great aggravation, from three republics—from Peru, Ecuador, and Colombia, but that the danger he had just escaped was the most imminent he had ever experienced in his life. As for the monk, the student, and the officer, they owned frankly enough that, when the danger appeared most imminent, and they had seemed callous to it, they were far from feeling so in their minds. After some more talk of a like kind, our eyes roamed around the old monastery to which chance had directed us for shelter.

Situated in the midst of a tract of country which reminds one of the Grande Chartreuse of Grenoble, the convent of the Desierto is, to all outward appearance, far from being in a ruinous condition. Its cupolas and spires still shoot as high as ever above the pines which surround it; and although half a century has rolled away since the monks quitted it, ivy has not yet entirely covered the embrasures of its deserted cells. The green moss which grows upon its walls shows only the want of repair and the ravages of time. You must pass through the first quadrangle, which is still in good preservation, so as to reach the interior of the convent, before seeing the spectacle of melancholy and desolation which there meets your eye. The dilapidated cupolas admit the daylight through large chinks, the pilasters in the cloisters are crumbling away, large stones have been forced from their sockets, heaps of ruins block up the choir and the nave of the chapel, and a thick mantle of pellitories covers the rubbish. The vapors which hang in a dense curtain round the summit of the mountain, at the foot of which the convent is built, fall in fine rain on the bare stones, and cover every thing with an icy moisture. Above the high altar, through one of the numerous fissures in the dome, the condensed vapor escapes, and falls drop by drop with the regularity of a water-clock, as if to mark the flight of time, and to relieve, by the light noise it makes on the marble, the melancholy silence which reigns in this dreary solitude. Such is the convent of the Desierto, seen by the light of day and under a clear sky. Let any one fancy its appearance at the time we sought refuge within its walls, when the storm, which had lasted since twilight, was scarcely over. Imagine the beams of the moon, fitfully streaming through its deserted arches, and the wind whistling in the empty nave, in its organ loft, in its solitary cells, and he will have some idea of the shelter in which we spent the remainder of the night.

We stood shivering in our wet clothes, and our first business was to seek materials for a fire. We took each a different part of the convent. The quarter in which I was engaged happened to be the most ruinous in the whole building. The remembrance of the old monk of St. Francis often came into my mind; and, in passing along the deserted galleries, I could not help fancying I saw him flitting through the gloomy arches. Around me the pillars stretched their great shadows upon the ground, whitened by the moonbeams. A stillness, as of the grave, rested every where. The ivy curtains alone shook in the wind.

From the cloister I entered a vast corridor. Through the large chinks in the vaulted roof above the moonbeams stealthily penetrated. In the distance I thought I observed a red glow on the flagstones playing amid the surrounding whiteness, and imagined I heard the snort of a horse which did not seem to proceed from the court where we had fastened our steeds. At the same instant my companions called me; I eagerly joined them. They had collected some brushwood, as they could find nothing better. The officer, Don Blas, affirmed that he had seen, by the light of the moon, in a distant court, a horse which was not one of ours. The student pretended he had met the ghost of one of the monks who had been buried in the convent. A short silence succeeded. Don Romulo was the first to break it.

"Here is a charming variety of horrors; the horse of a bandit; the ghost of a monk; spectres and malefactors!"

We tried to induce Fray Serapio to pronounce the classical formula of exorcism in his formidable Latin, but the monk replied tartly,

"My Latin won't drive away the spectre you talk of; it will rather attract it. God grant it may not appear! Be assured this is no freak of the imagination. The phantom seen by Señor Don Blas is a reality. It is my superior, the Reverend Father Epigmenio, who comes here every year, at the return of the Holy Week, to fulfill a penitential vow imposed on him for some sins of his youth. If he recognize me, how can I justify my present disguise and foolish excursion?"

The Franciscan's reply set us completely at our ease, and we sympathized very little in his anxiety. Wishing, however, to have no meeting between the two, we resolved to light our fire in a cell in a retired part of the convent, and to stretch ourselves on our wet cloaks round it. The student, the officer, and the hidalgo were soon sound asleep; the monk and I remained awake. Fray Serapio, on the watch to catch the slightest noise, trembled all over at the thought of being surprised by his superior, while my mind was filled with the story of Fray Epigmenio, so unfortunately interrupted. Seeing the Franciscan was not inclined to sleep, I pressed him to finish it. My companion, who could not shut an eye, was overjoyed at finding this means of whiling away the time. He consented with a very good grace, and crept more closely to the fire.

"I left," said he, "Fray Epigmenio at the moment when chance had delivered to his care a female in a swoon. His first impulse was to run away; his second was to remain, and he remained. He ceased even to shout for the wounded horseman, whose return he did not now particularly desire; and when the young lady, coming out of her faint, opened her languid eyes, the reverend father lost his senses entirely. If at this moment the stranger had appeared, the monk would have strangled him, for you have doubtless guessed by this time that the stranger in black was no other than the devil!"

To this unexpected assertion my only reply was a shake of the head. Fray Serapio, believing I agreed with him, continued:

"Fray Epigmenio yielded to temptation. He fell deeply, madly in love. For a time his vows were forgotten, but the prickings of conscience at last aroused him, and he resolved to confess his fault. He was taken before the tribunal of the Inquisition.[16] Till the final judgment was pronounced, they were both kept in confinement, the monk in his cell, the female in a dungeon. Some weeks passed in miserable anticipation. One evening, the cell of Fray Epigmenio was the theatre of a scene, in which the intervention of the devil was as clearly seen as in the meeting in the forest. Kneeling before his crucifix, the monk was asking from God that peace which his soul had lost. All at once he was startled by a footfall in his cell. A man stood before him, who regarded him with a stern, watchful eye. This man was no other than the stranger who had appeared to the recluse a month before in the wood; his dress was the same, and he appeared still paler than on the night in which the monk had found him bathed in blood. Fray Epigmenio stepped back, but the stranger did not stir. The formula of exorcism, hastily stammered out, had no effect upon him. The monk then called for help, but it was too late. When they entered the cell the stranger had disappeared. Epigmenio, bleeding from a dagger thrust, lay in a swoon before his folding-stool, and you could see the impress of the villain's bloody fingers. Time has not effaced these marks; they are still there."

"I can guess the conclusion of your story," said I to Fray Serapio; "the female was condemned as a sorceress, and the monk was acquitted."

"The female," said Serapio, "confessed on the rack that she had been in league with the devil, and was condemned to expiate the crime *by a public act*; but she did not undergo that punishment. Her keepers found her one morning lying dead on the floor of her dungeon, strangled with the beautiful black tresses which had proved so fatal to Fray Epigmenio. As for the monk, his wound was slight; it soon healed. Condemned to five years menial servitude in the convent of St. Francis, he was made the convent gardener. Almost at the same period the Inquisition ceased to exist, and the convent of the Desierto was abandoned as unhealthy. The visit which Fray Epigmenio makes at the same time every year to this ruined building is the only memorial of this event."

Fray Serapio paused. I was weary for want of sleep; he seemed also ready to drop with fatigue, and I forbore troubling him with any remarks on the story I had just heard. I had already lain down by the side of my companions, who were all fast asleep. Suddenly the Franciscan shook me by the arm, and invited me precipitately to follow him. I rose and accompanied him to a window which commanded a view of the inner courts of the convent, which were still bathed in the silvery light of the moon. The monk, whose stern and forbidding countenance had awakened my attention in the garden of St. Francis, was at this moment traversing one of the courts. We remarked that his steps were more tottering, and his body more bent than usual. When he disappeared, "Follow me," said Fray Serapio, "to the cell which was his, which he has just quitted." We soon arrived at the cell, but nothing distinguished it from the others. The walls were quite bare; the wind whistled through the parasitical plants which clung to the disjointed stones. A pine torch, stuck into an interstice of the wall, was just expiring. Fray Serapio fanned the dying flame, and, with all the obstinacy of a conscientious cicerone, he pretended to point out upon the wall the traces of the five fingers of the unknown who had stabbed the monk in his prison. I did not tell Serapio that the black stains on the wall had been produced by damp, and not by the hand of Satan. I seized, however, this opportunity of informing the worthy monk that the story of his unfortunate superior could be perfectly well explained without the intervention of the devil. The superiors of Fray Epigmenio, jealous of his rigid virtue, had probably set the trap into which he had fallen. They had found an adroit monk and a female willing to work through their plans, and the brutal fanaticism of the monk had unhappily spoiled every thing. The Inquisition had got wind of the matter. The farce was then turned into a tragedy. The vengeance of the father, who repented the selling of his child, her unhappy end, and the blighted, melancholy life which Fray Epigmenio had been afterward doomed to lead, were the unhappy consequences of the shameful intrigue hatched in the very convent in which we now were. Such was my commentary on Fray Serapio's story; but he, with an obstinacy only equaled by his credulity, held fast by his own interpretation.

Next morning we arrived at the hacienda of the friend of Don Diego Mercado, where the cordial reception we experienced soon made us forget the dangers and sufferings of the previous night.

On my return to Mexico I resumed my visits to the convent of St. Francis, and I read with more interest than ever the narratives preserved in these valuable archives, for I had now a thorough conviction that the old Spanish fanaticism, of which there were many instances in these documents, had still firm root in the minds of the people of Mexico. There is a close connection between the past and present race of the inhabitants of the cloisters, which the frivolous manners of the monks, as seen by me in the streets of Mexico, had not led me to suspect. The Inquisition has passed away, but it has left in the clergy a well-defined outline, a singularly deep-rooted tradition of demoralization, superstitious ignorance, and fanaticism.

Every time I went to the convent of St. Francis I met Fray Epigmenio, sometimes in the cloisters, sometimes sunk in reverie in the arbor. One day, however, I traversed the whole convent in search of him, but in vain. Just as I was quitting it I met Fray Serapio. The presence of the Franciscan in his convent was so very rare an occurrence that I could not help inquiring why he had condescended so far as to break through his usual habits.

"It is a pity," cried Fray Serapio, "but don't ask me why. Fray Epigmenio has just breathed his last. A lingering fever hung about him a long time; he died this morning, and the duty of watching the corpse of the reverend father has been assigned to me. Could any one have played me a more scurvy trick?"

"I don't understand you," I replied. "You surely don't mean poor Fray Epigmenio?"

"Who then, if it isn't he? Do you know what this duty makes me lose? A charming assignation, *mon cher.*" And, as a commentary on these words, there darted from his eyes an expressive glance which, told more than he said. I had not the heart to reproach the monk for his heartless talk, uttered, too, in such a cavalier tone. At this moment the first strokes of the passing-bell interrupted our conversation. "Good-by!" said Fray Serapio; "the bell calls me to my post." I shook him by the hand, and, on retiring, could not help reflecting on the singular contrast which these two men presented, inhabitants of the same convent, both under the same rules, both regardless of the sanctity of their mission; the one uniting libertinism with credulity, the other pushing piety to fanaticism, till it degenerated into cruelty. This contrast, I said sadly to myself, is a faithful picture of Mexican life. Who can tell how many unhappy wretches there are, in the numerous convents in Mexico, who have commenced with the first and ended with the second?

Among the persons who have figured in this narrative, one only succeeded in securing a peaceful life after a youth of stirring adventure: this was the student Don Diego Mercado, who, belonging to a rich family in Mexico, had always looked to the future without uneasiness. As for Don Blas, he met his death in a petty encounter with some robbers on the high road. Don Romulo's lot was at once more brilliant and more varied. After having, as I said before, taken part in seventeen conspiracies, and been banished from three republics, Don Romulo, after engaging in another political intrigue, was forced to quit Mexico in the same way as he had left Peru, Colombia, and Ecuador. On returning to the last-mentioned state, in which he had been born, he was raised to the presidency; and this time, being at the head of affairs in his own country, one would think he ought to have renounced his revolutionary principles. We do not know, however, if his conversion was sincere. There are some political agitators whom the attainment of supreme power can not correct, and who still prefer the precarious advantages gained by intrigue to the pleasures of unlimited authority.

FOOTNOTE:

[16] Suppressed in Mexico in 1810. The old palace of the Inquisition, situated on the street St. Domingo, is now used as a custom-house.

DON CADEO CRISTOBAL, THE THIEVES' LAWYER OF MEXICO.

There is an old document in the National Library of Paris which has hardly ever been consulted, I dare say, since the day on which it was placed on the dusty shelves of the manuscript room. It is an essay on the idioms of the Indian tribes of the New World, written toward the end of the sixteenth century, by Fray Alonzo Urbano, a monk of the order of St. Augustin. The chain of circumstances which was the means of bringing this curious document from Mexico to Paris is perhaps known only to myself, and that for an excellent reason. It was I who carried thither the unknown work of the monk of St. Augustin. The person from whom I obtained it is very likely dead. Be that as it may, the way in which I got possession of this manuscript will never be effaced from my memory; and the essay of Fray Urbano, although I am no judge of its philological merits, has still a great interest in my eyes. It brings to mind the intercourse I once had with one of the strangest personages that I ever had the good fortune to meet in Mexico. That intercourse was very short, but the recital will enable one easily to understand the deep impression it left upon me. I do not require to add that this story, though it appear romantic, is strictly true. In Mexico, you must remember, romance is ingrained in the manners of the people, and he who would faithfully picture these exceptionable manners would be set down as a somewhat unscrupulous story-teller, *when he is, in fact, only a simple historian.*

CHAPTER I.

The Public Scribe.—Pepito Rechifla.—The China.—The Callejon del Arco.

At the commencement of the year 1835 I happened to be in Mexico, engaged in the prosecution of a troublesome piece of business. This concerned the somewhat problematical recovery of a very considerable sum of money due me by an individual of whom I could not find the slightest trace. The business demanded the most energetic measures, and I addressed myself, in consequence, to several lawyers, well known for their success in dealing with such difficult cases. They all at first promised their assistance, but when I mentioned my debtor's name (he was called Don Dionisio Peralta), one and all of them excused themselves from having any share in the business. One said he could never pardon himself if he gave the slightest cause of uneasiness to so gallant a man as Señor Peralta; a second, that he was attached to him by a *compadrazgo*[17] of long standing; a third suddenly remembered that he had been a bosom friend of his in his youth. A fourth, more communicative than the others, enlightened me as to the cause of such friendly scruples; these gentlemen had the fear of a dagger before their eyes, a mode of procedure of which Señor Peralta had availed himself more than once, to shake himself free of creditors who had been too pressing. "I don't know," he added, "a single person who will undertake your business, if the licentiate Don Tadeo Cristobal refuse: he has a heart of rock and a hand of iron; he is the man for you." I ran immediately to the *Calle de los Batanes*, where I was told he lived; but another check awaited me there. Don Tadeo had quitted that place, and no one could tell me his present abode.

Wearied and dejected in the evening, after a whole day spent in running up and down to no purpose, I was walking listlessly to and fro in the Merchants' Arcades (*Portales de los Mercadores*), which stands on the grand square of Mexico. Despairing of success, I resolved to ask for some information about Don Tadeo from some of the numerous public writers, whose stalls under the gallery are so many public intelligence offices; but, once there, I completely forgot the motive which had brought me into this kind of bazar, the daily resort of all the idlers of Mexico, and my attention was completely distracted by the animated picture which was unrolled before my eyes. The spectator will be less astonished at this if he figure to himself the almost magical appearance the Plaza Mayor presents an hour before sunset. The *Portales de los Mercadores* occupy, in fact, almost one complete side of this immense square. The Cathedral, the Ayuntamiento, and the President's palace form, as the reader already knows, the other three sides. The most beautiful streets in Mexico debouch between those buildings; there is the street Primeria Monterilla, crowded with elegant shops; another, called *los*

Plateros (the street of the goldsmiths), whose shops are almost exclusively occupied by jewelers or lapidaries, while the petty Mexican merchant seems to have chosen, for the display of European commodities, the dark arcades of the *los Mercadores*. At the time of my stay in Mexico, French innovation had not yet ventured to alter the picturesque appearance of these arcades, which, in their general aspect, bore a remarkable resemblance to the Piliers des Halles in Paris. The heavy arches are supported on one side by vast warehouses, on the other by pillars, at the foot of which are ranged shops (*alacenas*) well stocked with religious books, rosaries, daggers, and spurs. Close by these shops, as if to represent all the grades of trafficking, léperos, in rags, hawk about articles of glassware, and, sticking one of them on the tip of their finger, they search for customers with great eagerness. Every now and then the venders of wild duck ragouts, or *tamales*,[18] seated in the shade of the arches, strike in, amid the din of the crowd, with their well-known cry,[19] *Aqui hay poto grande, mi alma; senorito venga sted*, or that as popular but shorter call, *Tamales[20] queretanos*. The passers-by and purchasers are as worthy of observation as the sellers. The ever-varying color of gowns and *tapalos*,[21] the gold of the mangas, and the motley color of the serapes, form, under the dim, hazy light which prevail in the pilastera, a brilliant mixture of different colors, which reminds one strongly of the most fantastical Venetian masquerades. In the evening, when the stalls and shops are closed, the *Merchants' Arcades* become a kind of political club. Seated on the threshold of the gates, or striding along in this kind of cloister, officers and townsmen talk about revolutions that have been effected, or are to be effected, till the time when the almost deserted galleries serve only as a retreat for lovers, and their low whispers is all that is heard beneath the silent arcades.

I had now sauntered for a long time in the Merchants' Arcades, when the sight of a writer's stall reminded me of my business there. Among the working population of the *Portales*, the public writers form a considerable portion of the community. You must remember that in Mexico primary instruction is not at all general, and that the office of a public writer, among this illiterate population, has lost nothing of its primitive importance. The tractable pen of the *evangelists* (that is the name they bear) is required for a thousand commissions, more or less delicate, and often of the most equivocal character—from the venal love-letter down to the note sent by a bravo to lure his intended victim to some secret ambuscade. The evangelist whom I had remarked among the rest of his tribe was a little squat fellow, his head almost bald, scarcely encircled with a few gray hairs. What principally drew my attention to this man was an expression of sardonic joviality which shone in his otherwise insignificant face. I was just about to make some inquiries of him about Don Tadeo, when an incident made me suddenly pause, and continue to look on in silence. A young girl came to the stall of the evangelist. The long wavy hair, which escaped in plaits from her open *rebozo*, her complexion of a slight umber tint, the brown shoulders that her chemise of fine linen, fringed with lace, left almost bare, her slender figure, which had never been deformed by stays, and, above all, the three short petticoats of different colors, which fell in straight folds over her pliant haunches, all pointed out the young woman as a genuine specimen of the *China*.[22]

"Tio Luquillas," said the maiden.

"What is it?" replied the evangelist.

"I need your assistance."

"I don't doubt that, since you come to me," replied Tio; and, fancying he had divined the message she was going to send, he began complaisantly to fold a sheet of rose-tinted vellum paper, highly glazed, and embossed with cupids. But she made a gesture of impatience with her little brown hand.

"What," said she, "would a man, who is almost breathing his last, care for your rose-tinted billet-doux?"

"The devil!" said the scribe, in a passionless tone, while the girl wiped her streaming eyes with one of her long plaits: "is it a farewell epistle, then?"

A sob was the only reply; then, stooping to the scribe's ear, she forced herself to dictate a short letter, not without frequent pauses to take breath and to wipe away her tears. The contrast between the unsusceptible old man and the passionate girl appeared to me most striking. I was not the only observer; every one who passed the booth of Tio Luquillas could not help casting a glance of pity, not unmingled with curiosity, upon the young *China*. The evangelist was about to fold the letter, but had not yet written the address, when a passer-by, bolder and more curious than the rest, came unceremoniously to have some conversation with the old man. The new-comer's features were not unknown to me, and I remembered that he had, when standing next me at a bull-fight a few days before, dilated, in the most attractive manner, on a sport which I passionately loved. The time did not seem to me suitable for making any inquiry of the evangelist, and I thought it best not to approach the three. I consequently remained a few paces from the booth, waiting patiently till the visitor would take his departure. The man, with whom an hour or two's chat had made me acquainted, had inspired me with a certain degree of interest. He was about forty years of age. His features were marked with a certain kind of nobility, in spite of a sarcastic expression which he sometimes threw into them. Although I might have forgotten we had ever met, the odd costume in which he was habited stamped him on my recollection. At the bull-fight he wore a wide-flowing blue cloak, lined with red, and on his head an enormous *sombrero* of yellow vicuna cloth, trimmed with gold lace.

"For whom is the letter, my dear?" he asked of the *China*, somewhat authoritatively.

The girl pointed to the prison of the presidential palace, and muttered a name which I did not catch.

"Ah! for Pepito?" said the unknown, aloud.

"Alas! yes; and I don't know how to get it conveyed to him," replied the girl.

"Well, never despair. Here's an opportunity that Heaven sends you."

At this moment the people hastily left the galleries, and scattered themselves hastily upon the *Plaza Mayor*. What motive had they for leaving? The commission of a deed but too common in Mexico; an assassination had been perpetrated on the public street. They had seized the murderer, raised the victim, and the melancholy cortège was on its way to the nearest prison. This place of confinement happened to be precisely that in which the lover of the young girl was imprisoned, and I could easily comprehend the tenor of the words of hope which my new acquaintance had addressed to the *China*.

The procession, which was now making its way across the square, had partly a comical, partly a mournful appearance, with an originality in its arrangement truly Mexican. A *cargardor* (porter) marched in front, bearing on his shoulders, by means of a leathern belt passed round his forehead (as all Mexican porters do), a chair, upon which was strapped a man, or rather a corpse, wrapped in a bloody sheet. The assassin, guarded by four soldiers, followed closely behind. Some gaping idlers, and a few friends of the dead man, who seemed to be making a sorry attempt to appear sad, closed the procession. Of all the individuals of which that crowd was composed, the man most at his ease was the criminal himself, who, with a cigar in his mouth, marched along with perfect coolness, addressing himself every now and then to the bloody corpse, which, to his great surprise, uttered not a word in reply. "Come, now," said he, "none of your waggish tricks, Panchito; you know quite well that I can't make your wife any allowance. You are shamming death well; but I am not to be done in that style." But Panchito was quite dead, let the assassin say what he might, and I could feel a cold shudder creep over me when the hideous corpse was borne close past me. Its eyes (for the sheet did not cover the face), with a stony glitter, stared at the sun with immovable fixity. The bull-fight amateur, who was doubtless more accustomed to such sights, walked right up to the procession, stopped it, and holding the letter of the *China* out to the murderer,

"Pay attention!" said he. "Have you not some acquaintance with the illustrious Pepito Rechifla—he who is to be garroted to-morrow?"

"Of course; I am a chum of his."

"Well, as you will, in all probability, not be executed before him, you will see him just now in the prison. Give him this letter from me."

"Ah! Señor Cavalier," said the Mexican girl, suddenly, who, with face bathed in tears, and a palpitating bosom, made her way through the crowd, threw herself at the murderer's feet, and seizing the corner of his cloak, after the ancient fashion, said, "By the blood of Christ, and the merits of the Virgin in her seven sorrows, do not forget to give him this letter, which contains my last farewell! I am so unhappy at not being able to see him!"

"Yes, *Linda mia*, I will," replied the murderer, carrying his hand to his eyes, and trying to give his voice a pathetic tone. "I have as feeling a heart as you; and had not this d—d Panchito been always thwarting me, I should not have been here, I swear; but keep up your spirits, *preciosita de mi alma.*"

A piece of money which the sporting character threw to the prisoner cut short his eloquent speech; the soldiers surrounded him, and they resumed their march to the prison. The procession soon disappeared round a corner of the *Ayuntamiento*, while some women, with a delicacy peculiar to Mexican females, surrounded the young *China*, but were unable to persuade her to go home. In a short time, in spite of all their entreaties, I saw her walk to the prison, seat herself at the foot of its dark wall, and, veiling her face with her rebozo, remain there immovable. My friend of the bull-fights was lost in the crowd, and I had now a fitting opportunity for consulting the evangelist. I stepped up to the old man, and tapped him gently on the shoulder.

"Can you tell me," said I, "where the licentiate Don Tadeo Cristobal lives?"

"Don Tadeo Cristobal, do you say? He was here a minute ago."

"Was Don Tadeo here?"

"Did you not see how obligingly he caused a message to be delivered to the bandit Pepito Rechifla, that one of the prettiest *Chinas* in Mexico dictated to me?"

"What! was that man in the *sombrero* and red cloak Don Tadeo the licentiate?"

"It was."

"And where shall I find him now?"

"I do not know; for, to say the truth, he has no settled abode, but lives a little every where. If, however, you wish to consult him on urgent business, go this very evening, between the hours of nine and twelve o'clock, to the *Callejon del Arco* (blind alley of the arcade); you are sure to find him in the last house on the right as you pass the square."

I thanked the scribe, and, after giving him a few reals for his trouble, directed my steps to the Callejon del Arco. Although it was scarcely seven o'clock in the evening, I went to try to find out, before nightfall, the house which I intended to visit two hours afterward. Experience had taught me that such precautions were not useless in Mexico; besides, the Callejon del Arco had long been notorious as one of the most dangerous places in the Mexican capital.

The appearance of the alley justified but too well the reputation which it had acquired. The dense mass of houses, of which the Merchants' Arcades form a part, known by the name of the *Impedradillo*, does not form one compact *cuadra*. On the southwest side of the Cathedral, a narrow lane runs into the Impedradillo; this is the Callejon del Arco. It is like one of those caverns which the sea sometimes hollows out in the face of a cliff. When still blinded by the overpowering rays of the sun with which the square is flooded, and which beat in all their intensity on the white walls and granite pavement, the eye, at first dazzled by the glare, sees only after a few moments another street cutting this one at right angles, and forming with it a dark cross-road. There, as in the caverns by the sea-shore, you can not hear the noise without, except it be a dull, mournful hum, which resembles as much the wail of the wind-tossed waves as the tumult of a populous city. A few rope-spinners' shops, their massive doors fast closed, and here and there a few dark passages, are the only signs which remind you that you are in a city, and in the midst of inhabited houses. Water is constantly oozing out of the walls; a perpetual moisture reigns every where; and scarcely, even at midday, at the time of the summer solstice, does a sunbeam visit this dismal den. A little new life then begins to stir, till the sun has advanced into the winter solstice, when it relapses into its former gloom and silence.

It was there, then, in one of these sinister-looking houses, that I was to meet a man able to settle a piece of business for me from which all the other lawyers in Mexico had recoiled. I stopped some moments to gaze with wonder and amazement upon the situation chosen for the office of the lawyer; but had not the episode, which I had witnessed a short time before, already prepared me for the eccentricities of Don Tadeo? How could I explain the easy, familiar tone which he had employed with the wretch to whom he was consigning the message to Pepito Rechifla? How the relations which appeared to exist between the bandit and the licentiate? The strange intimacy of a lawyer with thieves and assassins seemed, at first sight, not at all to be expected. The hope, however, of obtaining a solution of this seeming enigma decided me, and I left the Callejon del Arco with the intention of visiting it again two hours afterward.

FOOTNOTES:

[17] Lit., a compaternity.

[18] A kind of meat pudding, strongly seasoned with pimenta.

[19] Here's your fine duck, my jewel; come, buy, my young master.

[20] *Tamales*, made in Queretaro, a town about forty leagues from Mexico.

[21] A shawl, which is sometimes used as a head-dress.

[22] A China is, in Mexico, what the manola is in Madrid, and the grisette in Paris.

CHAPTER II.

A Mexican Gambling-house.—Navaja, the Mexican Bravo.—John Pearce, the Yankee.

Night had come; one of those nights in May in which Mexico, seen by moonlight, assumes an appearance almost magical. The pale light of the moon sheds its soft radiance upon the stained steeples of the churches and the colored façades of the monuments. The moon here scatters her voluptuous light over the earth in a bounteous fashion, unknown in our northern regions. The crowd upon the Plaza Mayor was not so dense as before sunset; it was less noisy, and more scattered. The promenaders spoke in a low tone, as if they feared to break the silence which was brooding over all. The light noise produced by the waving of fans, the rustle of silk dresses, sometimes a peal of female laughter, melodious and clear as the tone of a crystal bell, or the striking of a church clock at a distance, alone broke the general silence. Veiled women, and men wrapped in long cloaks, glided like shadows over the sand, that hardly crunched beneath their tread. I saw more than one mysterious couple, whose appearance there would probably furnish dainty food to the scandal-loving denizens of the drawing-room. Besides young and beautiful women, there were also those who, to use an English expression, were on the shady side of thirty years. You could see also a considerable number of those *doncellas chanflonas*, those beauties of easy virtue mentioned by Perez of Guevara. I say nothing of the adventure-seekers whom you find every where in Mexico—bullies, who wear the pavement with their sabres and spurs. Such was the motley crowd which pushed and jostled one another on the Plaza Mayor at the very time I was betaking myself, not without some fear, I must say, to the Callejon del Arco.

I had hardly reached the mouth of the dark lane, when a current of cold air, as if it had issued from a cave, struck my face, and chilled me to the bone. I stood for some seconds at the entrance of the alley, trying to discover some gleam of light from the windows or grated doors, but there were no signs of life in a single house. I then advanced, groping along in search of the house which I had discovered a short time before. I had almost arrived at the cross-road of which I have already spoken, when I heard a noise of footsteps behind me, and saw a man who, coming from the square, was advancing toward me. I wished to keep on the pavement, but my legs getting entangled in the long rapier of the stranger in some way or other, I stumbled, and, to keep myself from falling, grasped his cloak. The man immediately stepped back, and, by the grazing of steel, I knew he was drawing his sword.

"*Capa de Dios!*" cried he. "Whether is it my person or my cloak you are fancying, Sir Robber?"

I thought I knew the voice, and I hastened to reply:

"I am neither a robber nor assassin, Señor Don—"

I thought the unknown was going to assist my memory, and state his name. He did nothing of the kind; but, putting his back to the door of a house, he said, roughly,

"Who are you, and what do you want?"

"I am seeking for the dwelling of Don Tadeo the licentiate," I replied; "and, if I am not greatly deceived, we are standing before it at this very moment."

"Ah! who told you he lived here?"

"Tio Lucas, the public scribe. I wish to consult Don Tadeo on a very important affair."

"Don Tadeo! It is he that is speaking to you just now."

The costume of this man I could not distinguish; his features were precisely similar to the bull-fight amateur, with whose name Tio Lucas had acquainted me. I hastened to reply to Don Tadeo, counting myself happy in having met him, and begged a few minutes' private conversation.

"With the greatest pleasure," he replied. "I am quite ready to take up your affair; but let us first enter the house; we can then speak more at our ease." At the same time, he struck the pommel of his sword against the door behind him. "My profession," added he, "obliges me to employ many precautions. You will immediately comprehend why. Do not be astonished at my queer domicile. You may think me an original, and may have reason."

Don Tadeo paused, and the door of the mysterious house opened with a great clanking of chains. The porter, with a huge lantern in his hand, bowed respectfully to the licentiate, who motioned me to follow him. We walked rapidly along the *zaguan* or lobby, and, after mounting a very steep stair, stopped before a serge curtain, surmounted by a transparent lantern, on which was inscribed, in large letters, *Sociedad Filarmonica*. Voices and confused cries escaped from the hall which bore this ambitious title. "Are those your clients who are making such a great noise, Señor Licentiate?" I inquired. Without a word, he lifted the curtain of green serge, and we found ourselves in an immense hall, indifferently lighted. A long table, covered with green baize, and surrounded with players, stood in the middle of the room. Besides the lamps which hung from the walls, the place was lighted up by four candles stuck into tin holders. Some small tables, with refreshments, placed at regular distances from each other, furnished the players with infusions of tamarinds, rose water, or Barcelona brandy. At the bottom of the hall rose a high estrade, ornamented with some size-color paintings, representing, for the purpose, no doubt, of showing the original design of the establishment, a confused group of bassoons, hunting-horns, and clarionets. My surprise may be easily conceived when I found myself in a gambling-house like this at the very time I fancied I was stepping into a lawyer's office. I contemplated my companion as if I were looking upon him for the first time. He was assuredly the very man I had met in the circus and in the Merchants' Arcades. With this strange costume, long rapier, and thick, black curly hair, his appearance partook more of the bandit than of the lawyer. He had taken only a few steps in the hall when he was accosted by two individuals—worthy habituès of such a den. The first was a tall, awkward, shambling fellow, with a ferocious air, who held out to the licentiate a hand large as a shoulder of mutton, and said, in Spanish, with strong English accent, "How is Señor Don Tadeo to-day?"

"Better than those to whom you wish well, Master John Pearce," replied he, darting upon his interlocutor a look of cold disdain, which pierced him like a sword. "You know well that your reputation here is ruined as much as it was in Texas. Above all, since—"

"Tut!" said the American, evidently not at all desirous that the licentiate should finish his sentence. "With your permission, I have come to consult you."

"Immediately," replied the man of law. "I must, however, give the preference to this gentleman, whom I met before you."

"Do me a favor; listen to me first, Señor Licentiate," cried another personage, with squinting eyes and gray hair, dressed in the national costume of Mexico. "I wish also to ask your advice."

"Ah! is it you, Navaja," replied Tadeo, eyeing the Mexican, who seemed to tremble under his stern glance. "Are you going to trouble me any more about that ugly affair?"

"Tut!" cried the Mexican in his turn. "Since it pleases you, I will take the third place."

It was quite sufficient for Don Tadeo to remind them of these two episodes, which doubtless did not redound to their credit, to shake himself free of their importunities. I admired the power that gave my companion an experience, evidently acquired at great personal risk, among the most dangerous bravos of the Mexican brotherhood.

"Ah!" said Don Tadeo, turning at last to me, "will you now enlighten me, Señor Cavalier, about the affair which has brought you hither? It must be something very delicate, since only those cases are brought to me which my brother lawyers consider insurmountable. It was doubtless one of these lawyers who advised you to address yourself to me."

I named the licentiate who had extolled the intrepid heart and good sword of Don Tadeo. He shook his head with a disdainful smile.

"The business in question is a dangerous one," replied he, "I can easily see that. The man who recommended me to you is my declared enemy, and he does not send me such jobs for nothing. Besides, perhaps I am a little too ready to draw in the public streets after nightfall. What of it? I am of Seville, and one hasn't passed several years of one's life among the fighting men in the suburb of Triana for nothing."

"Are you a Spaniard?"

"Of course; and, before being a lawyer, I was what you call a go-ahead fellow—*uracan y calavera*. You see before you a student of Salamanca—of that beautiful city:

"'En Salamanca, la tuna

Anduve marzo y abril.

Niñas he visto mas de mil

Pero como tu, ninguna.'[23]

"I once made some songs myself, and even set them to music; and it was in consequence of a serenade unhappily broken up, and followed by the death of a man, that necessity compelled me to seek my fortune in New Spain. To insure my success here, I possessed two valuable qualities, which rarely go together—I was a thorough master of law and of fence. You yourself can acknowledge that my old humor of sword-playing has not yet left me; but I think, Señor Cavalier, I owe you some amends for the unintentional insult which I lately put upon you. To tell the truth, at that time I was just about to pass my sword through your body. Allow me to offer you, as a slight compensation for my rudeness, some tincture of rose water or Catalonian *refino*."

Without giving time for reply, the licentiate drew me to a table, where we sat down. My astonishment increased as I became more acquainted with this singular personage. It was not till after we had partaken of some slight refreshment that Don Tadeo would consent to listen to my business, which I told him as clearly and briefly as I could.

"Good!" said he; "you are seeking a debtor you can't find; but won't you tell his name?"

"Ah! his name is one that touches the sympathies of your brethren very nearly, for no one dares take up my case against him."

"Let's hear this terrible name. I am curious to know if it will have the same effect upon me."

"I'll tell it you in a whisper. His name is Don Dionisio Peralta!"

The licentiate never moved a muscle of his face.

"How much does he owe you?"

"Four hundred piastres."

"No more," said Don Tadeo, after a moment's silence. "Let us go to the terrace at the top of the house, where we can converse more at our ease. But, first of all, allow me to finish the business of those two fellows who are waiting for me. The interest even which I take in your case obliges me to put a stop to our conversation for the present, for the purpose of getting some indispensable information among the frequenters of this gaming-house. All I ask of you is to manifest no surprise if you see or hear things you don't exactly understand."

I shook hands with the licentiate. We rose and crossed to a group of players, that had increased considerably since our private conversation began. A crowd of spectators, two deep, surrounded the green board upon which the piastres rolled with a most attractive clink.

The licentiate passed before his two clients, the Mexican and the American, signing them to wait upon him, and walked up to a young man, who, like the other spectators, was devouring the green board with greedy look. This fellow, of a sallow and cadaverous aspect, wore an almost brimless hat over his long, thick hair, and a well-worn *esclavina* on his shoulders. He was the beau ideal of a lawyer's clerk, sorry at being unable to stake his master's fortune on a card.

"Ortiz!" said the licentiate, "have you writing materials with you?"

"Of course," the clerk replied; and he drew from his pocket a roll containing paper, pens, and ink. The licentiate sat down by himself, wrote a few lines, folded the paper, and passed it to his clerk, who replied to his master's directions, given in a low voice, only by a bow and a hurried exit. The licentiate then begged me to have patience for a few minutes longer, till he had given his two clients their promised consultation, and I mixed with the throng round the table. It was certainly an extraordinary sight; adventurers of all kinds surrounded me, reminding me strongly of the heroes in the old picaresque romances. I was struck by a remarkably characteristic feature. The banker had on the table by him a Catalonian knife, with an edge as keen as a razor. An intimation which he gave the players let me into the secret of this strange proceeding. "I warn the gentlemen now present," said he, "that if any one affects to confound the bank with his stake, I shall nail his hand to the table with this knife." This strange threat seemed not to astonish or offend any one; and I concluded that the mishap provided against by the banker had occurred more than once.

In spite of the extraordinary scenes I was witnessing, I could not help feeling the time rather long till the licentiate drew me away from the green board to a retired corner of the hall, where his two clients, the tall Yankee and the squinting Mexican, were seated together at a table. The American was just finishing a bottle of Catalonian *refino*, while the Mexican slowly sipped some iced tamarind water.

"Well," said the licentiate, regarding me with a look full of meaning, "here are two gentlemen who will remove your conscientious scruples regarding the four hundred piastres you owe me, and who affirm that you can very easily pay me by making over a similar debt due you by Señor Peralta, who will honor his signature with the greatest grace in the world."

"I did not say that," cried the American, with a roar of laughter. "I don't know if he will pay with pleasure. All I know is that he will pay, or—"

"Softly!" interrupted Don Tadeo. "From the moment that Peralta becomes my debtor, his life is valuable to me, and I require you to respect it."

"Señor Peralta will pay with pleasure, I uphold," said the Mexican, softly, sipping his liquor by mouthfuls as if it burned him, while the American emptied his glass of *refino* at a single draught, like so much water.

"Make him pay, that's all I care about," said the licentiate. "But is not that Pepito Rechifla with my clerk over there? That's capital! Ortiz has not been long about his business."

The name of Pepito reminded me of the pretty *China* that I had seen with such a sad face in the Merchants' Arcades. I contemplated the man pointed out by the licentiate with some curiosity. He was a fellow with a sunburned complexion, shaggy, unkempt hair, and a bold, shameless face—such a one as is met with nowhere but in the tents of the wandering Bohemians or in the streets of Mexico. "Ah! Señor Licentiate," cried he, "I shall never forget that I owe my life to you. I was to be garroted the day after to-morrow, and it was you who extricated me from the claws of the *juez de letras* (criminal judge). Some reals from your purse restored me to freedom. Yes, Señor Licentiate, don't be astonished; I know you are my savior; your clerk has told me all."

"Ortiz is a fool!" replied Don Tadeo, dryly; "but I am rejoiced at your good fortune, for I wished to speak with you. I need your assistance. Here's a piastre for your supper."

"Thank you. I am never hungry but when my pocket is empty. When I have a piastre I stake it."

And the fellow hastened to the table. The Yankee and Mexican rose also, and followed him. Don Tadeo, freed from their importunities, drew me aside. "You see these three men," said he, with a smile. "Do you think there is any debtor who can resist three such bailiffs—above all, when the debt has been made over to Don Tadeo the licentiate? You understand me, of course. When I wished the debt made over to me, my name confers additional power in this dangerous war; but when the conflict is over, all the advantages will be yours, less the expenses of the campaign, which, along with the honors of victory, you will allow me to retain."

"But how will you light upon Peralta? Up to this moment I could never get a trace of him."

"That is my concern, and that of the three precious vagabonds you saw just now. Don Dionisio Peralta is a bad payer, but a good fence. However, we shall see."

I then reminded Don Tadeo that he had expressed a wish to know more about my business with him, and I offered to satisfy him in this respect. At bottom I wished to examine more thoroughly this singular character. Don Tadeo seemed to guess my real intention. "It is half past ten," he replied, looking at his watch. "I am at your service till midnight. Let us go up to the *azotea* (terrace). There is nobody there at this hour. The night is beautiful, and you can tell me your story without any risk of being overheard."

FOOTNOTE:

[23] At Salamanca I led a very dissipated life in the months of March and April. I saw more than a thousand women, but none so fair as you.

CHAPTER III.

The Convent of the Bernardines.—The young Creole Lady.

Arrived at the terrace, we stood for some time in silent contemplation. At our feet lay the ancient city of the Aztecs, with its domes and spires innumerable glittering in the pale moonlight. Not far from us, the Cathedral threw its gigantic shadow and the profile of its towers on the *Plaza Mayor.* In the distance, the Parian[24] reared its black mass in the midst of spaces whitened by the moon, like a dark rock surrounded by foaming billows. Still farther off you recognized the elegant cupola of Santa Teresa, the fine domes of the convent of St. Francisco, the steeples of St. Augustin and the Bernardines, and behind this majestic crenulated mass of buildings, cupolas, and colored spires, you saw the country bathed in a white vapor, which, rising from the lakes, encircles the city like a luminous halo.

Don Tadeo was the first to break silence by asking me some questions about the business which had been intrusted to him. I eagerly replied, hoping that he would soon make me some revelations about himself, which could not fail to be interesting; but the licentiate had fallen into a profound reverie, and I was beginning to despair of success, when the merest accident came to my relief. This was the toll of a distant bell, which suddenly rose, like a mysterious wail, from amid the mournful silence. At the sound he shook his head, then put his hands over his face, which became gradually overspread with a deadly pallor. At last he took me by the hand, and, interrupting me in the midst of my explanation, cried, "Don't you hear that bell?"

"Yes," I replied. "And, if I am not deceived, it is the sound of the passing-bell in the convent of the Bernardines."

"In the convent of the Bernardines!" he repeated, in a strangely altered tone; "in the convent of the Bernardines, do you say?"

"Assuredly. I recognize the direction of the sound; I can not be wrong."

"Let us descend immediately, for the sound drives me mad."

"Why descend? Is the light of the moon not better than those smoky lamps in the hell we have just quitted?"

The licentiate made no reply for a long time. The bell, whose strokes became more and more distinct, exercised upon him a kind of influence quite inexplicable. I can not tell whether Don Tadeo remarked my surprise, but he probably relieved his bursting heart by taking my hand, and letting escape, in the midst of stifled sobbing, these strange words:

"You must listen to me. I never hear the peal of that bell without seeing, as in a bad dream, the saddest event in my life rise before my eyes. Nothing in me will more excite your astonishment when you are acquainted with the horrible occurrence of which that bell reminds me."

I made him aware, by signs, that I was ready to listen to him. This is the story he told me, with a coolness that I could hardly have expected, from the sad introduction with which it was prefaced.

"In the year 1825, that is, ten years ago, an attempt at assassination was made in the streets of Mexico. This is, unhappily, such an every-day affair in the capital of Mexico, that the public mind would not have been called to it had it not been accompanied by some strange circumstances. These were so strange, that, instead of being briefly narrated in the last column of the journals, as is commonly the case, it figured among the events, more or less important, which have the privilege of engaging the attention of the idle inhabitants of Mexico for more than a week. A singular mystery, in fact, hung over this attempt at murder. Early in the morning, when the Paseo of Bucareli is quite solitary, a hackney-coach was seen standing in a retired part of the promenade. The coachman had descended from his box, and was standing prudently aside, as if he guessed the meaning of this early drive. Was it a man or a woman whom this coach of *providence* (you know that is the name given to the hackney-coaches in Mexico) had driven to a love appointment? The blinds, carefully drawn down, left every thing to conjecture; but it transpired afterward that a young female of dazzling beauty was in it, who, prompted by female vanity, was richly adorned with jewels for this occasion. The Creoles, you know, have a strange fancy for appearing to be as rich as they are beautiful; however, although that was the case with this young lady, she was still more beautiful than rich. A few minutes passed, when a man enveloped in a large cloak approached the vehicle. The coachman opened the door of the carriage, and the stranger sprang in precipitately. A meeting of this kind was too much in the Mexican fashion to astonish the coachman, who stretched himself upon the grass under the poplars, and fell into a deep sleep. When he awoke the carriage was still in the same place, only the shadows of the poplars, instead of leaning to the west, as at the time when he fell asleep, were stretching toward the east, as much as to say that the sun had nearly set, and the evening was succeeding the morning. This is the time when the Paseo is most thronged with promenaders. The coachman was astonished at having slept so long; he ran to the carriage, called aloud, and, not receiving any answer, opened the door. A horrible spectacle met his eyes. Upon the cushions lay the young lady in a swoon, the cause of which was sufficiently explained by the blood with which the carriage was flooded. The blood flowed from a large wound, struck by the unerring hand of a skillful practitioner; and this wound, at its first appearance, seemed mortal. Of all the diamonds which sparkled on her neck and dangled from her ears, not one remained. The unhappy female had thus found an assassin instead of a lover, and theft was followed by an attempt at murder. The cries of the coachman were not long in drawing a crowd, among which was luckily a surgeon, who maintained that the lady was still alive. He got her conveyed to the nearest convent, which happened to be that of the Bernardines. The first duty of humanity fulfilled, justice commenced its task; but while the physicians were restoring her to health, the efforts of the ministers of justice were not crowned with a like success. The coachman was first arrested; but he was soon released, having proved his perfect innocence. A young Spaniard, whose attentions to the fair Creole had been very marked for a long time, was then apprehended. He learned at one and the same time both the infidelity and death of her whom he wished to become his wife. This was a terrible stroke." Here Don Tadeo's voice evidently broke, and he seemed as if he had lost his senses. "At the end of a year," continued the licentiate, "the Spaniard was released for want of proof; but he left the prison ruined by law expenses, and with a heart dead to all his former dear illusions. He then learned that she who had deceived him, and whom he had bewailed as dead, was still alive, but that she had renounced the world, and taken the veil in that convent to which she had been carried after the unhappy incident in the Paseo. He never attempted to see her; but all his efforts, all his thoughts were directed to one sole end—vengeance! Mexican justice had been unable to discover the assassin. He set on foot inquiries himself, and succeeded, although the judges declared that success was impossible."

The licentiate here paused; the bell was still tolling, and I began to understand the emotions these melancholy sounds awoke in his bosom.

"This Spaniard, you have guessed already, I dare say, was myself. A letter had been found on the young Creole's person, inviting her to that private interview which had nearly terminated in her death. This was the only clew I had to guide me in the intricate labyrinth where Mexican justice had been at fault. Since then commenced a dark and uneasy period of my life, which death can alone put an end to. I condescended to live among thieves and murderers in the hope of unraveling, by their revelations, that secret which entirely absorbed me. Under color of exercising my profession, I mixed myself up in all those cases which would give me an opportunity of interrogating malefactors, and of penetrating into their haunts and places of amusement. Since then, not a single crime has been committed in Mexico whose perpetrator I could not hand over to justice. The most secret societies of criminals are well known to me in all their most intimate workings. You may perhaps have heard of that band of *ensebados* who for a whole year kept the Mexican capital in continual alarm. The *ensebados* were men who, after besmearing their naked bodies with grease or oil, threw themselves upon the benighted pedestrian and robbed him, and, in the event of resistance, plunged a dagger into his body. Only one of the bandits, as slippery as an eel, escaped from the soldiers who had managed to hunt down all the rest. Well, he was their chief. I know him; and even now I could put my hand on him, if I chose. This is not the only singular discovery I made. I could mention a thousand. Thanks to the perilous and watchful life I have led, I acquired an experience which soon made me of incalculable benefit to the miserable cutthroats with whose singular antecedents I had thus become acquainted. Often, for days together, has my life been in danger, and more than one wretch has tried to stab me as a spy; but the services which my knowledge of the law rendered to many of the rest proved my protection. Now, I am not a little proud of the influence which I exercise over the most redoubtable robbers in Mexico, and you see that I have under my orders an army willing to assist honest people who stand in need of my assistance."

"Mine is a case in point," I replied, "and I am glad that I fell in with you; but you have not informed me whether you were successful in finding the assassin of the Paseo of Bucareli."

"I was completely successful. I was lucky enough to fall in with the public scribe who had been employed to write those fatal lines which had enticed my mistress to the Paseo. The evangelist knew the wretch, and he set me on his track. I found him out. I had but to denounce him, and justice would have pounced upon him; but this would have defeated the object to which I had devoted my life. I did not betray him, therefore. Many years had rolled away since the attempt; and, during that time, on account of my intercourse with such characters, I had learned more to pity than hate them. Nay, I often employ them to do certain pieces of business for me, which Mexican justice gives up as impossible. The assassin is still a useful instrument for me; one, too, that I can crush at a word, but whom I prefer employing in the service of my numerous clients."

Another pause. The toll of the bell was still heard. "I never saw my beloved again, who is now in a convent," continued Don Tadeo; "but I learned from a sure quarter that she has been long in a deep consumption. You will now understand why the bell-peal of the Bernardines made me shudder."

I was trying to persuade Don Tadeo to descend, that he might no longer hear the dismal toll of the passing-bell, when the trap-door of the *azotea* creaked lightly on its hinges, and the squint-eyed Mexican, called Navaja, glided rather than walked toward us. He was pale with fright, and looked uneasily behind him.

"He is the devil in person!" cried he, leaning to take breath against the railing of the *azotea*.

"Whom do you mean?" asked the licentiate.

"The American. He is just about finishing his third bottle of *refino*, and is shouting in a loud voice what he calls his war-song. He is a ferocious Indian, with a white man's skin. He is recounting all the hair he has raised, all the murders he has committed. And, would you believe it, he claims my scalp as an addition to his treasures. I tell you again, he is a devil."

"What a saint you have become all at once!" said the licentiate, who again began to fling his sarcasms at the Mexican. "How long is it since you began to hate the smell of blood?"

The gayety of Don Tadeo was terrible to behold. This question of the licentiate's raised a hatred in his mind, fierce and implacable as the tiger's. Don Tadeo did not seem to take any notice of the impression he was producing, but, on the contrary, to delight in irritating the wretch, who foamed with anger under his cold, biting sarcasm. An allusion to the criminal attempt on the Paseo suddenly enlightened me as to this keen, bitter irony. Before me stood the man on whom the licentiate could take vengeance if he chose, at whose mercy he lived, and who had treacherously attempted the life of the unhappy female for whom the passing-bell was perhaps tolling at this very moment. "Does the peal of the Bernardines remind you of nothing?" said Don Tadeo; but this last sally deprived the Mexican of all patience, and, instead of replying, he bounded forward to snatch the licentiate's rapier, but with a vigorous thrust of the arm he was hurled violently to the ground.

"Come, now," cried the licentiate, "you forget the crime you committed. I forgive you, miscreant; but out of this, instantly."

The Mexican, stunned and stupefied, did not wait for a repetition of the order, but shuffled off precipitately. I could not help complimenting Don Tadeo on his coolness and courage. "What of that?" he said, with a melancholy smile. "You know the university in which I took my degree. I value my life only at its true worth. Let us go below. I understand your case thoroughly; and, before many days are passed, I hope to have some good news for you."

We went down, and soon reached the great square upon which the Callejon del Arco opens. There we separated, the licentiate repairing to his abode, and I to mine, by the street Monterilla. "We shall meet again soon," said Don Tadeo to me on bidding me good-night. "I hope so," I replied, although I did not partake so heartily in that belief as did the intrepid lawyer. I could not help comparing Don Tadeo in my own mind with those wild-beast tamers, who often astonish us by their deeds of courage and address, but whose least false step may transform them from masters to victims.

FOOTNOTE:

[24] An old bazar, not unlike the Temple-market in Paris.

CHAPTER IV.

Manner of taking Possession in Mexico.—Tragical End of the Assassin of the Paseo.

A month passed away without Don Tadeo giving any signs of life. At last a note, that he had sent me by his clerk Ortiz, explained the reason of his long delay. There were two causes that hindered my case from being proceeded with according to his customary activity. "One of these you may probably guess," he said. "The passing-bell that we heard tolling was for *her*! After the first burst of grief I was about to take up your case, when I received a dagger-stab from an invisible hand, the effects of which forced me to keep my bed for a considerable time. However, I am happy to be able to announce to you that your case is now progressing favorably. I succeeded in discovering, not without some trouble, the abode of Dionisio Peralta, and have set upon his traces the three knaves whom you saw the other night. Good-by; take no step without consulting me, and in a short time you will receive more satisfactory news."

Eight days had scarcely elapsed when I received another note from the licentiate. This letter contained a detailed account of the campaign which he had conducted against Dionisio Peralto, and its happy termination. Pepito Rechifla, John Pearce the Yankee, and Navaja the Mexican, went, one after the other, to the house of Dionisio Peralta, claiming, as they said, the recovery of a debt with which they had been intrusted by their friend the licentiate, Don Tadeo. Dionisio Peralta, in spite of his gentlemanly airs, was, to speak the truth, a knave of their own stamp, and received them at first with all the arrogance of a bully; but the significant threats of the three ruffians soon brought him to terms. Peralta knew but too well the character of the men with whom he had to deal, and the influence of the licentiate, who directed these bullies, rendered the odds decidedly against him. He at last ended by proposing a compromise, which the licentiate had been constrained to accept. Peralta had a small villa in the little village of Tacuba, about a league from Mexico, the value of which was almost equal to the amount of the debt. He consented, in lieu of payment, to deliver up this house to Don Tadeo, who had taken possession of it from the very first. There remained nothing now to wind up the affair but to receive the house from the hands of its new owner. Don Tadeo invited me to wait upon him the following day. We proposed to go together to the domain of my old debtor, of whose property he would install me as rightful owner.

Next day we set out together on horseback for the village of Tacuba. I was somewhat curious to see my new property, and, above all, to witness the ceremonies which, in Mexico, ordinarily accompany the act of taking possession. On the road I congratulated the licentiate on the lucky star which seemed to favor him, and that had on a recent occasion saved his life a second time. I expressed at the same time my regret that perhaps he had drawn upon himself the vengeance of Dionisio Peralto; but he replied that I was wrong in my supposition, and that, to all appearance, the man who had attempted his life was no other than the same wretch who had assaulted the Creole lady in the Paseo of Bucareli. "Be that as it may," he added, "my suspicions of Navaja have not hindered me from employing him in this business of yours, in which his zeal has been very conspicuous. Men of this class, when not in their cups or in a sullen mood, are blindly obedient to the person who has made them feel his superiority. In a letter which Peralto wrote me, announcing his acceptance of my terms, I read without regret the terrible menaces which he launched against this ruffian, whom I strongly suspect to have attempted my life, and who has shown himself the most active of the three in pursuit of your debtor. Peralta is hardly a man that will threaten in vain, and I fear his vengeance will follow quickly."

In conversation like this, we soon left the town behind us and got into the country, if the desert and arid plains that we crossed at full gallop could be so termed. The heat was stifling, and a deep silence lay around. All at once a horse's hoof broke the stillness, and we were joined by a cavalier, in whom I could hardly have recognized Pepito Rechifla. The ruffian had attired himself with some degree of elegance; he wore a blue manga lined with yellow cotton, and his horse's equipments were of a character thoroughly Mexican. He saluted us with an air at once courtly and patronizing. "You will pardon me," he said, "Señor Licentiate, if I take the liberty of traveling in your company; but, aware of your intention to take a short ride to-day, I thought you would not be the worse of having an additional companion. This road does not bear a very good character;" and, casting an expressive look at the arm which the lawyer carried in a sling, he added, "it is not always prudent to run into dangers at a distance from home. I am, however, pretty sure that we shall not need to draw upon any body to-day."

Having finished this last sentence with a drawling affectedness, Pepito whispered into the ear of the licentiate some words which I could not make out. I only remarked that he pointed out to Don Tadeo a group of hillocks on our left, over which hovered a flock of great black vultures. Without replying to Pepito, the licentiate stopped his horse a moment, and looked in a different direction. His face had a painful expression in it. He then signed to us to continue our route, spurred his horse vigorously, and a few minutes after we clattered through the streets of the village in which my new property was situated.

The house which Don Tadeo had gained (for he had at first taken possession in his own name) was situated at the extremity of the village. Crowds of villagers, who had assembled to share in the largesses which are usually distributed on an occasion of this kind, stood before the house, and assisted us in recognizing it. It was a little building of a very sorry appearance, with a small porch before the door, supported by brick pillars. Numerous cracks furrowed the walls in every direction, clearly indicating a sad state of disrepair. Behind the house was a garden choked with weeds, surrounded by a wall thickly covered with moss, and crowned with pellitories. The porter, whom the licentiate had put in charge of the house, opened the door. "You are in your own house," said Don Tadeo to me. We entered. The interior of the house was as desolate as the exterior. The ceilings were gaping with chinks, the disjointed boards in the stairs creaked sadly under foot, and the garden was nothing more than a collection of sentern, nettles, and thistles, in the midst of which rose some sickly-looking fruit-trees. This wretched house and garden, however, were almost equal to the debt, and that was sufficient; the more in the case of such a debtor as Peralta was, with whom one could not be too exacting.

After visiting the ground floor and the garden, we went up stairs. The room which we first entered seemed to have been a dining-room, and had not been entered for many years, if one could judge from the musty smell which pervaded the apartment. We hastened to let in the air and light by opening the strongly-barred window-shutters. A collection of spiders' webs, thickly matted together, covered the entire ceiling. We looked into the presses, but they were all empty; one only contained a large dusty tome, in an antique binding, which the licentiate put under his cloak after hurriedly glancing over its contents. Our inspection was over. "Let us call the witnesses," said Don Tadeo to Pepito, whom we have constituted upon this solemn occasion master of the ceremonies. The lépero, magnificently dressed in his blue manga, advanced to the casement, and made a short speech to the worthy people in rags, who were collected in groups beneath the windows. The eloquence of Pepito had the desired effect, and a few minutes afterward the court was filled with a far greater number of witnesses than the law required. I had never seen such a rich collection of gallows-birds. Preceded by Pepito, we descended into the court, and thence into the garden, followed by the crowd. "Señores," cried Pepito, in a loud voice, "you are witnesses that, in the name of the law, his lordship here present," and Pepito pointed to me, "takes regular possession of this estate. *Dios y Libertad!*" Don Tadeo then came forward. By his instructions I first plucked a handful of grass and threw it over my head, and then pitched a stone over the garden wall. These, by the terms of the Mexican law, are the ceremonies which accompany the act of taking possession. A general hurrah now burst from the throats of the respectable company assembled in the garden. All that now remained, according to national usage, was to present some gratuity to the dirty ruffians who had crawled from every corner of the village to wish me joy of my new possession. I gave them a few piastres to drink, and, headed by Pepito, they went to spend them in the neighboring cabaret.

"Well," said the licentiate to me, when we were alone, "you see you have got payment of your debt. What do you think of my plan for making stubborn debtors pay?"

"I fear, Don Tadeo, that you are playing a very dangerous game for yourself; and, if you would take my advice, you would give up business immediately as redresser of wrongs, as I think the losses exceed the profits."

"You see, however, that I am fortunate in my enterprises. Never mind. But as I may prematurely receive a dagger-thrust some day or other, I would like you to keep some remembrance of me. Here is a book which was not comprised in the inventory of the house. It is an old work, and not without its value."

"Thank you," said I to the licentiate, taking the dusty tome. "The story that you told me on the *azotea* of the house in the Callejon del Arco will ever live in my recollection. One can not easily forget such revelations; and I was very fortunate indeed in listening to such a romantic history."

The time had now come when we must return to Mexico. Without waiting for Pepito, who would probably finish the day at a wine-shop, we pushed along. The heat was as insupportable as before. The flock of vultures that Pepito had pointed out to Don Tadeo had evidently increased, and a fetid odor was wafted by the wind in our direction from the little mounds above which the birds were fluttering. The licentiate drew up suddenly.

"If you are curious to read the last page of the history of which we were just talking," said he, "go over to these hillocks; but I fear your nerves are not strong enough."

"And what shall I see among these rocks?"

"A corpse; you observe that at this very moment the birds are pecking at it. One of the three ruffians whom I employed to recover your debt has paid for all the others. God is just! The man who fell under the dagger of Peralta was the perpetrator of the outrage on the Paseo of Bucareli. The romance is now complete, is it not?"

"Assuredly; and the sight of the vultures will add to the impression your story has made upon me."

"Come," said the licentiate, spurring his horse, "I see you are getting nervous. To town, then."

We parted on the Plaza Mayor in the hope of seeing one another again, but fortune decreed otherwise; and a few weeks after my installation in Peralta's house I quitted Mexico.

During my absence the gambling-house in the Callejon was closed. On my return, Tio Lucas informed me that the licentiate had returned to Spain. Since that time I have made many ineffectual attempts to procure some information about him. The only souvenir that was left me of this extraordinary man is the manuscript of Alonso Urbano, now in the National Library at Paris.

REMIGIO VASQUEZ.

CHAPTER I.

There is one peculiar charm in the towns of Mexico, and that is the perfect straightness of the streets, along which the eye wanders till the point of sight terminates in the blue hills of the country. In Mexico especially I was never tired gazing upon the mountains which bound the horizon upon all sides. On the east I seemed to hear the murmur of the Pacific, and on the west the hoarse roar of the Atlantic sounding from behind these mountains. The first of these oceans reminded me of one of the most adventurous epochs of my life; and I never could forget that the second washed the shores of my native country. I never looked in that direction without feeling a kind of regret and sadness, which often merged into feverish anxiety. In this state of mind, I grasped at every thing which could afford me a pretext for quitting Mexico. I hastened to shake off the sluggishness which began to weigh upon me, and to abandon myself anew to the dangers and emotions of a wandering life— a sure remedy against home-sickness.

One evening, on reaching home, I learned that a stranger had called during my absence. The unknown had said that his business with me related to a matter of life and death; but, when asked to leave his name, had obstinately refused to give it. He happened to say, however, that he was living at an inn, the *Meson de Regina*, and had gone away expressing great annoyance at not finding me, and promising to return the next day. The strange air of the visitor, the numerous questions he put, the care that he evidently took not to allow his face to be seen by arranging the folds of his blue manga over it, and the large hat which shaded his eyes, combined to give to this visit a mysterious character, which acted very strongly on my imagination. When alone in my chamber, I called to recollection every one whom it might possibly be, but in vain, and I waited anxiously for the next day, which might probably unriddle the enigma; but the morning passed, the day advanced, and the unknown had not made his appearance. I resolved to go to the Meson de Regina; and, having got a description of the stranger, set out for the inn.

Although situated in one of the most central streets in Mexico, the Meson de Regina is only distinguished from other inns on less frequented roads by the greater number of travelers who are always coming and going. There is the same range of stabling, the same barrenness of furniture, the same absence of every comfort. I called for the *huesped*. In any other country it would have been an easy thing to find out the name of the unknown, whose costume I could describe to the most minute details, but it is very different in a Mexican hotel.

"Do you fancy," said the huesped to me, "that it is my business to ask the names of those who frequent my house? I have something else to think of, I assure you; but as for the person you are inquiring after, he set out, not half an hour ago, for Cuantitlan, as his servant, who accompanied him, informed me, and, if you are a swift horseman, you may overtake him, if you are so very desirous to know his name."

"What was the color of their horses?"

"Iron-gray and peach-blossom."

A ride of some hours before dinner could not but be salutary. Before setting out in pursuit of the stranger, I went home in order to ask some more questions of Cecilio, my valet, about my visitant. This lad had been already several years in my service, and his round chubby face, with an air at once hypocritical and simple, reminded me strongly of Ambrosio of Lamela in Gil Blas. As I expected, he gave me a very unsatisfactory description of the unknown. I then disclosed to Cecilio my intention of setting out immediately for Cuantitlan, ordering him at the same time to saddle our horses with all speed. Cecilio tried to convince me that, in an affair of so delicate a nature, it were best if I went alone, but I reiterated my order, and he left the room to execute my commands. As I was going to travel in the country, I donned my Mexican costume, and went down into the court in all haste. I remarked, without surprise, that my *serape* had been attached to the back of my saddle. My pistols were in their holsters; and I also carried a lance with a scarlet pennon, heavily shod with iron, which I was accustomed, when traveling, to have fixed to my right stirrup. A sabre hung from Cecilio's saddle-bow, and a tolerably well-packed valise was fixed to the croup of his horse. I asked him why he was making such preparations, as we were only going out for a short ride; but his only answer was, that the environs of Mexico were infested by robbers.

We set out. The travelers we were in pursuit of could not be more than an hour in advance of us, and the unusual color of their horses would aid us in tracking them easily. I flattered myself that if we pushed on we could overtake them without difficulty in two hours, and if that were beyond our power, a couple of fresh horses would not take long to cover the six leagues between Mexico and Cuantitlan. I thus set out with the intention of returning before sunset. The difference of speed, however, between my horse and that of my servant, forced me to slacken my pace. Two hours had already rolled away without catching the slightest glimpse of the man I was in quest of, and the spire of Cuantitlan had not even come in sight. I almost feared that the inn-keeper had sent us the wrong road, when some muleteers, returning to Mexico, told me that they had met two horsemen, one mounted on an iron-gray, the other on a peach-blossom. We reached Cuantitlan in a short time, and I was directed to the hostelry where the two horsemen had stopped. I had not been long in coming hither, and was at last soon to know what I was burning to learn. I went to the inn which had been pointed out to me, and my foot had no sooner reached the ground than I began questioning the huesped with the air of one who is sure of finding what he wants.

"Are your horses tired?" said the host, when I had finished.

"No."

"Well, that's something, for the travelers only entered my house for refreshment and then left, and it will be fresh horses alone that can overtake them."

And the host, who interested himself as much, if that could be, with the horsemen that passed his house as with those that lived within it, turned his back upon me with the politeness peculiar to his class. I vaulted again into my saddle. A quarter of an hour more, thought I, would explain to me a certain defiant raillery which Cecilio had taken little pains to suppress. To my great mortification, however, the time rolled away; night was coming on, and the shades of evening were falling insensibly around. Night at last fell; and I would have given up this long-protracted chase, had not wounded self-esteem goaded me as much as curiosity. A solemn silence brooded over the road we were pursuing. Sometimes I stopped, fancying I heard before me the stamp of horses' feet, and then redoubled my pace with ardor, till the unbroken stillness which reigned around showed that I had been under a delusion. Still, the certainty of being on the traces of the unknown kept up my spirits, for, from Mexico to the place where we now were, not even a bridle-path joined our road. All the probabilities were in my favor. However, after a six hours' ride we required rest, and a twelve leagues' gallop rendered a halt necessary for our horses. It was, besides, time to set about looking for a place to put up, for in Mexico there are two requisites for getting into an inn; the first is, that the inn please the travelers; and the second, that the hour and the travelers please the inn-keeper. Luckily, I was not long in discovering a light in a cabin standing by itself, toward which we spurred our horses. Our host informed us that two horsemen had passed his house about half an hour before we came up, but the night was so dark that he could not distinguish the color of their horses. As he was sure that they must stop a short way off to pass the night, we decided to stay where we were till dawn, hoping to overtake them on the following morning. I considered that if we were off before sunrise we could easily make up for lost time. Unfortunately, Cecilio did not rise next morning till late, and the sun was high in the heavens ere we found ourselves on the road. I had, however, gone too far to recede, and, besides, I had now a definite aim to pursue. Cecilio did not view the case in the same light as myself, and it was with a slight feeling of despair that every now and then he informed me of the number of leagues we had traveled since we left Mexico. But, though seen by so many people, the travelers seemed to slip from me as if by magic at the very moment I was flattering myself that I had overtaken them. I had already passed through the rocky defile of the Cañada, and had left behind me the hacienda of St. Francisco. During my journey I had inquired at every *rancho*, and at all the ordinary halting-places, and every one concurred in saying that two mounted travelers, one on an iron-gray, the other on a peach-blossom, could be only a short distance in advance.

"These two travelers are surely a brace of devils," said Cecilio, sadly, "or two great criminals at least, as they seem to stop to rest nowhere."

Without replying, I continued my route, for I did not wish to have the worst in this contest, and a kind of phrensy began to take the place of my former curiosity. For the second time since leaving Mexico the sun set behind the hills that lay before us, and still there was no hope of attaining the object of our journey. Our horses, jaded by a ride of twenty hours, were beginning to be fatigued; and it was with a lively satisfaction that I perceived, by the last gleams of departing day, the red walls of the *hacienda* of Arroyo Zarco.

CHAPTER II.

The Hacienda of Arroyo Zarco.—The young Mexican Lady.—The young Spanish Nobleman.—Don Tomas Verdugo.

The hacienda of Arroyo Zarco is a vast and imposing building, built partly of brick and partly of large stones, situated almost at the entrance to the extensive and fertile plains of Bajio. The place, however, where this hacienda rises, is far from presenting the smiling appearance which characterizes the basin bearing its name. It stands on a flat, barren plain, where grow a few melancholy-looking stunted trees, one or two of which shade the back walls of the building: a little brook of bluish-looking water, the fountain-head of which is not far off, gives the name of Arroyo Zarco (blue rivulet) to the hacienda. A large square court, ornamented on its four sides with stone arches like the cloisters of a convent, forms a kind of vestibule to the apartments of the family. The rooms devoted to travelers are under these galleries. Stables, large enough to contain with ease a whole regiment of cavalry, make up two or three other courts. It was the only place at which I could put up within six leagues, and here I hoped to find the travelers I was in quest of, provided I had not taken the wrong road.

"We have come thirty-two leagues since yesterday," said Cecilio, taking my bridle, with a sigh, "and if your lordship persist in continuing the pursuit, perhaps it will only be prudent and advisable if I return to Mexico to dissipate the uneasiness that will probably arise there on your account."

"The duty of a good servant is to accompany his master every where," was my reply; and, going up to the stable-boy, I began to put some questions to him regarding the travelers who had arrived before us. From him I learned that about forty travelers had stopped at the hacienda in the afternoon, and, for want of better information, I was obliged to content myself by a personal inspection of the stables. I ought to have gone there at first without making any inquiries; and, as there was still some daylight, I directed my steps to the courts. A great number of horses were munching their provender in their stalls, and, from the joyful eagerness with which they ate, I could see that they had come a long distance; but I could hardly contain myself for joy when I distinguished side by side, like two faithful companions, the iron-gray and the peach-blossom. This was but the beginning of success; for, to complete the discovery, I must examine nearly sixty travelers, for there was almost that number of horses in the stables. This, to speak the truth, was almost impracticable—dangerous, perhaps, in one respect, and ridiculous in another.

As I was going along the lobby which led to my room, where I intended to rest a short time previous to resuming the pursuit, a coach, drawn by eight mules, and escorted by three horsemen armed with muskets and sabres, came rattling into the court-yard. The arrival of a carriage at a Mexican inn is always an event of some importance; it bespeaks travelers of distinction, or, better still, the presence of females, whom, though they may not perhaps be young, the excitement of travel invests with a thousand illusory charms. While the three horsemen who formed the escort, and the two coachmen who conducted the team, were wrangling with the huesped, the court all the time filled with strange figures, one of the horsemen alighted and advanced respectfully to open the carriage door. A man of a certain age descended first, a younger person followed, and, before any one had time to offer her their hand, a young lady hurried out after them. She wore a costume adopted by several rich *rancheras* when traveling, an attire which suits equally well the carriage or the side-saddle. She carried in her hand a hat with a broad brim; and her manga, richly ornamented with silk velvet and gold lace, could not hide entirely her fine flexible figure, and bare, sunburned arms. Her uncovered head left exposed her beautiful black hair; and her eyes, as black, and not less brilliant, gazed around in the free bold style peculiar to Mexican women. She seemed evidently seeking for some one in the group that surrounded her; but when she saw the unknown faces which greeted her, she veiled them modestly under her eyelids.

Night came on, and the young lady had retired to one of the chambers of the hacienda when another traveler entered the court-yard. The new-comer was a young man, evidently about five or six-and-twenty, tall and well made. Though poorly clad, his dress was unstudiously elegant, and a fine black mustache heightened the dignity of his appearance. The predominant expression of his countenance was at once haughty and sad, but his face was remarkable at times for a singularly winning sweetness. A little mandolin hung round his neck, and at the pommel of his saddle dangled an old rusty rapier. The lean and somewhat scraggy horse he rode was followed by another ready saddled and bridled. I could not help feeling a touch of pity for this poor young man with the melancholy face. The famine-stricken appearance of both horses and master, showed but too well the hardships which they had endured in common—long journeys executed upon little or no food, and entire days passed probably without sustenance of any kind. Like the other travelers, the cavalier called the huesped; but, instead of addressing him in a loud voice, he stooped from his saddle and whispered in his ear. The huesped, in reply, shook his head; a cloud passed over the face of the unknown, he colored slightly, looked sorrowfully at the unharnessed carriage, twitched his bridle, and left the hacienda.

It was now time for me, however, to look after my own business. The joy of Cecilio, when he found that the two horses of our travelers were in the stables of the inn, was changed into despair when I communicated to him my orders.

As I could not interrogate sixty travelers, I ordered him to saddle our horses at midnight, and station himself along with me in the court-yard near the gate. In this way not a single traveler could leave the place at any hour of the night without my knowledge. This point arranged, I left Cecilio plunged in melancholy reflection at the prospect of a night to be passed in the open air, and hastened to the kitchen, which, according to the custom of the country, served also for a dining-room.

In this vast hall, travelers of every kind—traders, military men, *arrieros*, and servants, were seated round a number of tables placed near the fire. I sat down like the rest, and, during the whole time of my meal, kept my ears open to catch the conversation that was going on. I did not, however, pay much attention to it, as it consisted only of stories of robbers, storms, impassable torrents—favorite topics of conversation with all travelers. Weary at last of listening to a series of questions and answers in which there was nothing interesting, I asked the landlady, in a loud voice, about the two horses, the colors of which I mentioned, that were then in the stable. I was more fortunate at first than I hoped. I learned that one of the individuals was the Señor Don Tomas Verdugo, who had arrived about an hour before me; but, being pressed for time, he only waited till he got a relay of horses, and then departed, leaving at the hacienda the two horses he had brought with him till his next arrival.

"Although it seems strange that you can have any business with him," added the landlady, "I know that he will stay two days at Celayo, and you will find him at the *Meson de Guadalupe*, where he is accustomed to put up."

I was very anxious to elicit some more information, but the wary hostess kept herself very reserved, and I quitted the kitchen very much disappointed to learn that I had still a forty leagues' ride before meeting my mysterious visitor, but delighted to find that I knew his name, and had a certain aim to pursue. After countermanding my order to Cecilio, as it was not late—and sleep is a long time in visiting a stony couch, especially when one is very much fatigued—I went and sat down at the outer gate of the hacienda, a few paces from the high road.

The country round lay as still and silent as if it had been midnight, and the moon shone brightly overhead. In the horizon the hills began to put on their nocturnal russet. Upon the whitened plain, the moisture from the earth, condensed by the coldness of the night, looked in the distance like a tranquil lake, and from among the vapor towered aloft some aloes which grow upon this rocky soil. In this mournful solitude, in an inhospitable country, where a thousand dangers surround the traveler, especially when he is a foreigner, my present enterprise appeared for the first time in its true light—a perilous folly. For the first time, also, since my departure from Mexico, my heart failed me, and I was almost on the point of retracing my steps, when, as I was taking, as I fancied, a last look at the scene, I thought I heard, amid the stillness of the night, the distant sounds of a guitar. This came, probably, from a party of muleteers who had bivouacked at some distance, or some groom who was playing to his fellows in one of the inn stables. Without stirring, I listened to the strains broken by the distance, when gradually, out of the stillness, a vocal accompaniment stole along on the night air. Owing to the profound silence that prevailed, I easily made out the words of the song; it was a Spanish *Romancero*; but the musician, through some odd fancy, had accompanied it with a refrain, consisting of some by-words very much in use among the Mexican people. This singularity raised in me a desire to see the player. At a short distance from the hacienda, and at the foot of a low hill which overtopped it, I observed the flickering light of a fire. One side of the singer's face was brightly illuminated by the blaze, and near him, two horses, tied together by a long cord, were cropping the scanty grass which grew on that stony soil. I advanced quietly, so as not to interrupt the unknown; but the noise of my footsteps betrayed me, and the music stopped all at once. The stranger rose hurriedly; the graze of a sword which he was unsheathing struck my ear. The adventure was becoming less pleasant than I had anticipated. I stopped, then advanced again; and, by the light of the fire, I distinguished the young man whom I had seen in the court-yard of the inn, but whom I little expected to find again so near me.

"Who goes there?" he exclaimed in Spanish, and in a pure Castilian accent.

"A friend!" I cried; "but put up your rapier; I am alone and unarmed."

The moon lighted up the surrounding objects so clearly that the Spaniard was convinced that I had spoken the truth, and he returned it to its sheath.

"Pardon my indiscretion, Señor Cavalier," I said, advancing into the illuminated circle; "I have been drawn to you, I must say, only by a motive of curiosity. If I am not deceived, you are, like myself, a foreigner, and, as such, almost a friend."

In spite of my politeness, the stranger's features still kept an air of haughty defiance. He seated himself, however, and invited me, with a wave of his hand, to do the same. I did so without ceremony.

"I am a Spaniard, it is true," answered my new companion, haughtily; "but, throughout the whole of America, is not a Spaniard at home? It is now my turn to ask pardon of you for deeming you a spy sent by—"

The Spaniard stopped all at once.

"By whom?" I inquired.

"You are welcome," said the unknown, without replying. He accepted a cigar which I offered him, and we began to smoke with all the gravity which characterizes Indian warriors round a council fire. By the light of the moon, aided by that of the fire, I could easily see, what I had before noticed, that the hard privations which the Spaniard had endured had left ineffaceable traces of mental suffering on his brow, but without altering in the least his noble physiognomy.

"Did you compose those verses yourself," I asked, "which I have so indiscreetly interrupted, and whose originality has struck me so much?"

"No; I only adapted them to an air of my own composition for an affair which it would be too tedious to relate to you."

There was evidently an attempt at concealment in this reply, which whetted my curiosity. I resolved to make a confidant of the young Spaniard by telling him the object of my journey, and the many checks I had experienced since my departure from Mexico.

"Our positions are not dissimilar," said the Spaniard, when I had done. "Like you, I am pursuing a nameless object; but thank God that you have been saved from the dangers that I have undergone."

"Tell me about them," I said. "I like a story told in the open air—at night above all, and in the light of a fire like this."

"Be it so," said the Spaniard. "I shall begin by telling you that I am a Biscayan and a nobleman; not by election, like most of my Compatriots, but descended from a long line of ancestors, who recognize Lope Chouria as the chief of their ancient clan. My name is Don Jaime de Villalobos. I bear another name here for common use. My mother has the first rank in my affection, then my father, and lastly my country. You now know me, Señor Cavalier. I am now about to tell you of the affair in which I am at present engaged."

The slight air of superciliousness with which he began his story was not displeasing to me; it was like a continuation of the Romancero of which the young nobleman had been singing a verse a short time before. He continued with more simplicity.

"Unfortunately, I was born poor, though of noble blood. More than once during my infancy have I been awakened from sleep by the rude ice-wind which whistled without obstruction through the ruined manor-house in which my mother and I dwelt. As a compensation, God gave me a good appetite, which made me forget the cold. I shot up apace; my noble birth interdicted me from all manual labor and servile employment; and to leave my mother, who was now growing old, and take service in the army, was a step which was not in accordance with my inclination. However, I could not long remain a stranger to the civil war which was then raging in the Basque Provinces. Don Carlos, you are perhaps aware, often forgot to pay his officers and soldiers, and all that I gained in his service was the honor of being a creditor of his noble highness. Returning to my maternal abode, I was grieved to find it more dilapidated than ever, and to feel still more the anguish which rent my mother's heart, for I saw her sinking day after day under the double burden of old age and poverty. One evening a peddler came and demanded hospitality of us, and as he only asked for shelter, we granted it. His wandering life had enabled him to pick up all sorts of news, and I learned from him that one of our neighbors had made a wealthy marriage in New Spain.

"'What a capital thing it would be,' said he, 'if a young nobleman like you could be so lucky in that land of gold and silver, where the ambition of all the women is summed up in the couplet,

"'Canrisas de Britaña,[25]

Y maridos de España.'

"In my present position a rich marriage was the only resource left me, and I resolved to go to the New World and seek my fortune. I communicated my hopes to my mother. The payment of a debt gave me the means of procuring a passage in a ship from Bilboa; and full of hopes of being able to bring back a fortune to my mother, which was my only ambition, I set sail. I arrived at Vera Cruz a year ago, and visited the churches assiduously, the only place where the fair inhabitants delight to show themselves, but not one deigned to give me the slightest countenance. At night in the deserted streets I watched long, but to no purpose, for none appeared. I knew well that if I did not announce my presence under a window, I ran a risk of spending my nights as fruitlessly as my days. I had then recourse to music, and purchased a mandolin. Unluckily, though a passable musician, I was not poet enough to compose a good serenading song, and was forced to tack on to an old Romancero a piece of a wretched ballad that I remembered—the miserable bit of doggerel which had incited me to quit the old manor-house. I was engaged in singing that when you interrupted me."

The Spaniard here began to smoke with the air of a man who is resolved to do his duty conscientiously.

"And you are not much older than a boy," said I, much surprised at the abrupt conclusion of Don Jaime's story.

"An old maid, a sort of duenna, who had worn linen of Brittany for many years, had no objection to me on that score. You understand my object in coming here was to get a young, rich, and beautiful wife. Had the duenna been rich, for my mother's sake I would have married her, but she was neither rich nor young, and had never been pretty."

"'Tis a thousand pities," said I; "you are half a century behind, Señor Don Jaime. Fifty years ago every chance would have been in favor of a cavalier of your figure and appearance. Now I am afraid that time is past."

An almost imperceptible smile broke upon the lips of the Biscayan, but I could not guess whether it was caused by the compliment I had paid him, or pity for the incredulity I had manifested.

"Since you are in the indulgent vein, and I in the indiscreet one, Señor Don Jaime, allow me to ask you this last question—Have you supped to-night?"

The brow of the Spaniard lowered. I feared I had abused rights acquired on such a slender acquaintance as mine; but his noble self-respect never gave way. He was, besides, too much of a gentleman to blush because he was poor.

"I have," replied he, with a gracious smile. "May I have the honor of offering you a portion of my supper?"

The Spaniard tendered me a cigarette.

"What! was that all your supper?"

"A cigarette! fie on it; it is, in truth, somewhat too meagre a repast for the last descendant of the Counts of Biscay. I have consumed more than a dozen of them, and have not made a very good supper."

This seemed to have exhausted the patience of the poor nobleman. He said nothing for a few moments, and then, with an air of calm dignity, exclaimed,

"Señor Cavalier, I have granted you the only thing it was in my power to bestow in this world—my hospitality, such as it is. Enjoy yourself at my fire as much as you please; but, after a hard day's journey, you will pardon me if I betake myself to rest. May God bless and protect you!"

The Biscayan threw some sticks upon the fire, wrapped himself up in his cloak, and, after bidding me good-night with a wave of his hand, lay down. I threw my eyes mechanically around. More fortunate than their master, and half hidden by the icy fog of evening, the two horses cropped the short, withered grass which grew on the stony plain. My heart swelled, and a deep feeling of respectful sympathy took possession of me at seeing this deep misery so nobly supported.

"Señor Don Jaime," said I, with a broken voice, "I thank you for the hospitality you have shown me, and, in return, I should be both proud and happy if you would take the use of my chamber in the *venta*."

The young traveler started and sat up; his eyes sparkled in his pale face. He seemed to hesitate for a moment; he then held out his hand.

"I accept your offer," he said; "you will do me a service I shall never forget. I must now tell you, in confidence, that I had vainly solicited that accommodation from the huesped, for which I was too poor to pay, but which on this night, and this night only, I would thankfully have paid for with my heart's blood."

This reply was an additional mystery to me; but I had now become Don Jaime's host, and that prevented me from asking any questions. We took the two horses by the bridle, and, without exchanging a word, returned to the venta.

FOOTNOTE:

[25]

Chemises from Brittany,

And husbands from Spain.

CHAPTER III.

The Elopement.

After my new companion had been installed in my chamber, I went out under pretense of seeing that the horses were taken care of, and ordered Cecilio to fetch from the kitchen a supper sufficient for two persons. The Biscayan, after some ceremony, seemed quite willing to accompany me in my repast. I had already made a good supper, but, for politeness' sake, I took a small portion to bear him company, my guest meanwhile doing justice to the viands, and quite lost in wonder at my abstemiousness.

"How can I help it?" said I, in explanation; "this is my first run through the country, and I have not yet got accustomed to their infernal cookery."

And while Cecilio, standing behind my chair, opened his eyes wide on hearing me say that I had but newly come into the country, I could not help admiring the prodigious appetite that had been developed by a fast of twenty-four hours.

"Now," said I, when the dishes were all cleared, "if the neighborhood of a young and charming lady, whose chamber is next to mine, does not hinder you from sleeping, I fancy you will do well to imitate me." And I muffled myself in my cloak, and lay down on the floor.

"Not a bad idea," said the Spaniard. "But, before going to sleep, perhaps you would like to hear an air on my mandolin."

"Use your freedom, but pray pardon me if the melody set me asleep."

In spite of the hard and cold couch on which I was reclining, in a short time I heard nothing but a confused murmur of broken notes, and then consciousness forsook me. I awoke with a start, under the impression that a strong chilling draught was setting full upon me. The long, thin candle which had been stuck to the wall of the chamber was throwing its last dull, smoky glare around. The Spaniard had disappeared. I was alone; and the chamber door, which had been left open, had allowed the cold night air to enter and awake me. A dead silence reigned through the hacienda, broken only by the distant crowing of the cock. I listened, surprised at the abrupt disappearance of my companion, and rose and shut the door, and, while doing so, threw a hasty glance into the court-yard. From amid the darkness I thought I discerned two black profiles half hidden by a column. One of them was that of the Biscayan, whose voice I could distinguish, although he spoke low; the other was unknown to me; but in the sweet tone, and in the accents, though prudently concealed, I could not doubt for a moment but that it was a woman. I had seen enough. I repaired to the door and pushed it open. At the grating of the rusty hinges, a slender form disappeared like a shadow behind a distant pillar. The Biscayan came up quickly to me.

"No apologies," said he; "you have, without knowing it, made yourself master of a secret which would have been yours sooner or later. It is better, then, that you know it now. Besides, I was just speaking of you. Is it not to you I owe one of the happiest moments of my life? Have I not still need of a new proof of that friendship which henceforth will be so valuable to me?"

Don Jaime then, in a few words, gave me the particulars of a romantic attachment which had arisen six months before in the shady walks of the Alameda; that, owing to the want of fortune on his part, a union could not be effected; that all attempts at flight had been defeated by watchful vigilance, which had never been relaxed till the time when the father of her he loved for her beauty alone, before knowing of her wealth, set out to visit one of his haciendas in the interior of the country. To assist in the attempt at elopement, Don Jaime had brought two horses with him; but at the third stage, at Arroyo Zarco, the poor young man, who had followed the carriage at a distance, was deprived of this last resource, as the huesped would not admit him within the walls of the building. Thanks to our lucky meeting, he had obtained admittance, and was now quite ready for a start to Guanajuato. Once there, Don Jaime intended to intrust the daughter of the *haciendero* to the care of a distant relative of his, who would conceal her in a convent till, the pursuit being slackened and the marriage concluded, he could set sail for Spain. Unluckily, a new obstacle presented itself. How could we quit the inn without awakening the suspicions of the huesped, and how hide the direction of our flight and keep up appearances? Don Jaime had thought that I might be able to accompany them, leaving my valet at the venta, while we accommodated ourselves with his horse. Donna Luzecita (the lady's name) could pass easily for Cecilio, and the landlord, seeing as many pass out as had entered in, could conceive no suspicion.

The Biscayan regarded me with a look of such melting eloquence, that I was on the point of throwing myself, heart and soul, into this new adventure; but, on reflection, I deemed it proper to refuse. Don Jaime sighed, and left me. He returned in a few minutes, accompanied by the young lady. A rebozo, worn in the Mexican manner, was passed round her head. Through the folds of her silk veil you could discern a bandeau of jet black hair encircling a brow empurpled with a modest blush, and under the arch of her black eyebrows two eyes modestly veiled by their long lashes.

"What should I not owe you, Señor Cavalier," said she, in that harmonious voice whose silvery tone had so charmed me some minutes before, "if you would consent to help us in our extremity! At any rate, a refusal will never change my unalterable resolution."

I must confess that her look and simple words had almost brought me over to her side. I only stammered out some commonplace about duty and prudence.

"Your presence," added the Spaniard, "can prevent one misfortune; for I love her so much that, rather than see her torn from me, I would stab her to the heart."

Proud and grateful for this burst of passion in her lover, the lady raised her eyes, which had been hitherto cast to the ground, and gazed steadily at the Spaniard with one of those sharp, piercing looks of love which her Creole impetuosity could not retain. It was thus she desired to be loved. Then, holding out to me one of those hands which God seems to have modeled expressly for Mexican women—"You consent, don't you?" said she.

Every moment was precious. Twelve o'clock had struck, and I could not pain her by another refusal. To carry our saddles and valises to the stables, and prepare the horses for the road, was the work of an instant. The darkness in the stables was very great, and it was only by the light from our cigars that we could distinguish our steeds. In the court-yard the two coachmen were sleeping near their mules.

"Halloo! friend," cried one of them, yawning, "are you for the road so early?"

"I have a long way to go," I replied; "but you needn't stir; the cock has not yet crown."

The snoring of the coachmen, who had dropped asleep an instant afterward, was soon mixed with the chorus of noises that proceeded from the stable, and by groping about we managed to finish our business without any new interruptions. We arranged that the better of the two horses which Don Jaime had brought with him should be reserved for the use of the daughter of the haciendero. One thing only remained to be done—to instruct Cecilio in the part he was to play in our absence. I went to his bed-chamber. His organ of wonder had been largely exercised during the night, but the surprise which now awaited him was still more astonishing than any of the others. The poor fellow was sleeping with his hands clenched, when I, with some difficulty, awoke him.

"Wilt thou[26] listen?" said I to him, when he was fully awakened. "Thou must sleep soundly till ten o'clock in the morning. If thou art unable to do so, at least remain in thy chamber. Reasons of the most important nature demand that thy presence in the venta be not even suspected till that hour. Thou must then slip unperceived out of the hacienda; and, in order that thou may'st do that the more easily, I am going to take away thy horse. Take the road to Celaya, and rejoin me at the venta of the Soledad, where I shall wait for thee."

"I shall execute your lordship's orders," said Cecilio, bowing sadly, and seemingly quite disconcerted at this new inconvenience.

My two companions were in the saddle on my return. Don Jaime appeared to shudder in the cold night air; and his beautiful companion, her head concealed by her thick silk veil, and her shoulders covered with a manga with the lining outside, seemed completely disguised except to a very experienced eye. The convulsive agitation of her bosom, however, and her stifled sobs, betrayed her violent emotion. I well understood the sentiments which agitated her, and I could not help casting a melancholy glance in the direction of the chamber in which the father of Donna Luz slept. In that trying moment, the Castilian generosity, so inherent in Don Jaime's character, showed itself in a remarkable manner.

"Luzecita," he said, in a choking voice, "you have not yet advanced too far to recede—it is your father you are leaving."

Recalled by the voice of Don Jaime to the thought that was uppermost in her mind, the lady trembled, and the two for a time seemed alone in the world. Taking the hand of the one she loved, and carrying it to her lips with the passionate submission of an Eastern slave,

"I have no father now," she said, in a voice at once firm and sweet; "lead on."

On hearing this my last scruples vanished, and we set out. We traversed the court in silence. The huesped was sleeping on the ground close to the gate. I touched him with the point of my lance without speaking; he started up with the mechanical promptness of a man accustomed to be roused at all hours of the night.

"For the road already?" on receiving the reckoning. "And this cavalier also, with his two horses?"

"Yes," I replied; "this cavalier, my valet, and myself, must be at the hacienda of San Francisco before daylight."

"A pleasant journey," he cried, on opening the gate, which soon closed behind us. We at first followed the road to Mexico, so as to tally with the false direction I had given to the huesped; we then turned bridle all at once in the direction of Celaya, making a wide detour to avoid passing near the hacienda. A damp, icy fog covered the plain as far as the eye could reach; the night-wind tore aside the curtain of mist from time to time, and showed us the surrounding country covered with hoar-frost. A few paces distant appeared the watch-fire of the Biscayan: it looked like a star just about to expire. Our horses made their way rapidly through the mist, the breath that issued from their nostrils playing about their heads in immense volumes.

Although not sharing in the feverish impatience of my two companions, I could not help feeling a kind of emotion when I compared the uncertain issue of the event into which they had blindly rushed with the thick vapors which enwrapped in darkness the road and the objects around. We were not long in placing a considerable distance between us and the venta. We then slackened our pace; a grayish glimmer began to light up the objects around us: in the east, and behind the hills, which were still enveloped in mist, a few pale rays heralded the approach of the sun.

"Let us stop here a minute," I said to the Biscayan, "to breathe our horses. In the mean time, I shall alight to listen if there are any pursuers behind us."

We had now covered a distance of almost eight leagues without exchanging a word, this being one of those cases in which a full heart places a restraint upon the tongue. With my ear close to the ground, I listened anxiously to catch the sound of the approach of horsemen: no noise, no echo came from the earth. We were in a vast desert plain. The slight agitation I had felt during our long gallop was succeeded by a soothing calm; I seated myself on the grass, and invited my companions to do the same. This moment of passing security brought out a burst of sentiment which had been restrained during the long gallop. As the hoar-frost immediately disappears when the first beams of the sun have reddened the grassy plain, so anxiety fled from the hearts of the two lovers, and gave place to confidence and delirious exultation. Scarcely had the lady alighted, than, obeying an irresistible impulse of her Mexican nature, she strained in her arms him who would henceforth stand to her in place of the whole world. The faded, melancholy face of the Spaniard seemed all at once lighted up with animation; but the rapture inspired by these caresses was too much for him; he turned pale, staggered, and fell to the ground with his eyes closed. Donna Luz rent the air with her shrieks.

"Don't be afraid," I said; "joy never kills."

I laid him gently upon the grass; Donna Luz knelt by him, and bedewed him with tears. Don Jaime soon revived and came to himself, while the young Creole, turning about, hid her face in her hands with that strange mixture of modesty and passion which lent an additional charm to her beauty.

"You must come with us no farther," said the Biscayan to me. "You have risked enough in our service, and I will abuse your kindness no longer; but, before parting, I have another favor to ask of you: it is that you take my cloak in exchange for yours; it will aid my disguise more effectually."

I consented to his request.

"You will gain little by the bargain," said Don Jaime, with a smile; "but you have done me a great service. Since you are not bound in any particular direction, you may perhaps come to Guanajuato. I shall remain a fortnight there, and you can easily find me out, and I shall be but too happy to express to you once more the gratitude which I shall feel for you all my life."

The parting moment came. We assisted the lady to her saddle. Don Jaime then mounted. Untying the mandolin which hung at his saddle-bow,

"Take this," he cried, "and keep it as a remembrance of me. For a long time this instrument and hope were all my possessions; now, instead of hope, God has given me the reality."

The tears stood in his eyes. He shook me by the hand a second time. Donna Luz paid me with a smile more than she owed me, and the pair galloped away. I followed them with my eye for a long time involuntarily, thinking that there was much between the cup and the lip. The morning mist soon hid them from my sight.

FOOTNOTE:

[26] In Mexico it is the custom for masters to "*thou*" their valets.

CHAPTER IV.

Florencio Planillas, the Mexican Miner.

Left alone in the midst of the desert plain of Cazadero, I remained, I must confess, a considerable time in a state of great uncertainty. Being far distant from any habitation, I was debating within my own mind whether I should not turn bridle and regain the hacienda of Arroyo Zarco; but the sun shone so cheerily upon the plain, and the morning air was so refreshing, that my discouragement and hesitation disappeared like the mist upon the hills, which had now put on their usual bluish appearance. I continued my route. A gallop of barely two leagues would take me to the venta of the Soledad, where I had ordered Cecilio to await my coming. The landlord, on seeing me come in with a guitar slung across my shoulder, took me for a music-mad tourist that had come in the very nick of time to amuse him, and spoke of his love for music with the air of a man who was desirous to hear my performance. I refused, however, point blank, and hastened to take possession of the most retired room in the venta. Cecilio did not make his appearance till nightfall. He had nothing new to tell me. At midday, when he escaped from the hacienda, there was not the slightest stir. This information calmed me about the fugitives, and freed me from anxiety on their account. I resolved to pass the night in the inn. My poor valet, who had traveled on foot a distance of thirty miles, was hardly able to stand upright; and, for my own part, I needed to husband my strength, that I might resume on the following day that pursuit which seemed to be getting interminable.

Next morning, at an early hour, we were in the saddle and on the road to Celaya, where we expected to meet Don Tomas. It was a two days' journey, and these two days were marked with as many odd occurrences as had signalized the first part of this singular excursion. In all the inns at which we stopped Don Tomas had preceded us only by a few hours. At last I arrived at Celaya, and alighted at the Meson de Guadalupe at the very moment that Cecilio was mentally registering the seventy leagues we had traveled since we left Mexico, with this consoling reflection, however, that, according to the intelligence we had received, we were now approaching the end of our journey. Unhappily, I was once more balked. At Celaya, as at Arroyo Zarco, I missed Don Tomas by half an hour. Don Tomas, on leaving Celaya, had taken the road to Irapuato. We set out for that place. In the solitary inn of this small market-town no one had seen him. They knew him, however, for the host told me that Don Tomas owned and inhabited a solitary house at the foot of the Cerro del Gigante (Giant peak).

"Where is the Cerro del Gigante?" I asked, not without an apprehension that it might be a hundred leagues away.

"It is the highest peak of the range of mountains," replied my host, "which overhangs Guanajuato. If you set out from here at dawn of day, you will be there in the evening."

Irapuato is ninety-two leagues from Mexico. To reach Guanajuato I had still twenty leagues to travel. It occurred to me that Guanajuato was the town to which the Biscayan nobleman had conveyed Donna Luz. Besides the certainty of there meeting Don Tomas, I had the hope of learning the fate of a man in whom I already felt an interest as intense as if he had been an old friend. This double consideration determined me.

"Well," said I to Cecilio, "we must go and wait upon Don Tomas in his own house, which he seems in a great hurry to reach."

The road to Guanajuato winds through a ravine of interminable length called Cañada de Marfil, and it was far on in the afternoon before we reached that city, whose steep streets we traversed rapidly in the direction of the Cerro del Gigante. The road that we followed on leaving the town was cut with ravines and full of ruts. I was not long in regretting that I had entangled myself in such a defile as this, especially as night was coming on, and we were on an unknown road. As we advanced the scenery became wilder and more desolate; the noise made by the runnels of water which bounded over the rocks on either side, and the cawing of troops of crows which hovered over head, were the only sounds which broke the stillness around.

"Ah! señor," said Cecilio, approaching me when I had halted for a moment to recall to my recollection the instructions I had received, "this gully seems a real cutthroat place, and I hope nothing worse will befall us than wandering all night long in this labyrinth of mountains, where the cold cuts into one's marrow."

I was not insensible to the cold which began to prevail in this deep valley, and I threw over my shoulders the manga that the Biscayan had given me in exchange for my cloak. I began to share in my servant's fears; but I judged it better to keep my anxiety to myself, and continued to advance, certain besides of being in the right road, although it was becoming rapidly darker and darker. Abrupt precipitous rocks, with whitened crests, rose before and on each side of us. Already the mountains were throwing their long shadows across the valleys; the evening mist was mounting in light flakes from the deep bottoms in which the brooks purled to the mountain tops that the sun was touching with his departing beams; and the Giant Peak, which seemed to me so near, rose always at the same distance, encircled with a purple halo, overtopping the neighboring heights with an appearance of gloomy majesty, as if placed there as the guardian of the mysterious treasures inclosed in the bowels of the Sierra.

"You know the proverb, master," continued Cecilio: "those who go to seek wool often come back shorn. Something tells me that we have got ourselves into a terrible mess. Who can this Don Tomas be whom every body on the road knows, but whom we can never catch? Some bandit chief, I fear, who has his own reasons for not showing himself; and I think," he continued, in a low tone, "that these gorges are not so solitary as they seem. Mother of Jesus! did you not see the gleam of a musket-barrel among those branches up there?"

I carried my eyes involuntarily in the direction pointed out by Cecilio; it was nothing but the wind agitating the thick branches which crowned the crest of a precipice, and I could not see far on account of the fog. I affected to laugh at my servant's fears, when I thought I heard a sound resembling the click of a gun-lock. Our horses could advance but slowly, owing to the rocks with which the bottom of the ravine was covered. I quickened my pace, however. All at once a flash burst forth over our heads, the whiz of a ball shot past our ears, and the report of a gun echoed through the ravine, accompanied by a dull sound, as if the ball had been flattened against the rocks.

"Ah! the scoundrel," cried a voice, which seemed to come from the top of the precipice, "I have missed him."

My first impulse was to close my eyes, in the expectation of hearing another report. An instant passed in terrible anxiety, during which the echoes reverberated among the rocks. I then raised my head to seek for the place from which the shot had been fired, but the fog lay so thick on the heights that I could distinguish nothing. A strip torn off the pennon of my lance, which was within two feet of my body, clearly proved that I had been aimed at.

"'Tis lucky I escaped that shot," said I to Cecilio; "but come, let us climb the rocks on both sides, and lay hold on the scoundrel who is seemingly so sorry that he has missed."

"But," cried Cecilio, who was not at all pleased with the task I had assigned him, "there is no indication whatever that they aimed at you; besides, I won't leave you. It is the duty of a good servant to be always at his master's side."

I gained the top of the rocks before him. As far as my range of vision extended, I saw nothing but the distant hills deeply bathed in violet, a few fields of maize whose heavy heads swung slowly backward and forward, and some deep gorges in the Sierra, denoted by deeper tints of color. The country round had a sad, melancholy look in the gray of the evening that was creeping over all. It would have been imprudent to have turned, so I continued my march. In a short time I perceived in the distance a building of considerable size; no smoke rose above the roof. Indeed, it seemed quite deserted. It had probably been at one time a work-shop. I was confirmed in this opinion by the dilapidated state of the walls, and the large holes in the tiling. Just when Cecilio was alighting to assure himself that the place contained no inhabitant, a horseman issued from a by-road, and came galloping up with a carbine in his hand. He stopped suddenly on seeing me, and continued to look at me for some seconds with an air of fear and visible distrust. All at once he burst into a loud roar of laughter.

"You are not, then, Remigio Vasquez?" he inquired.

"I don't know him," I replied.

"Ah! Señor Cavalier, pardon me; I fancied it was Remigio Vasquez I was firing at."

Again the fellow laughed loudly, but added, in a tone of regret,

"*Caramba!* to say that I missed at twenty paces, when I had covered you too; but a sudden movement you made saved your life. Ah! but I am indeed sorry."

"Of having missed, no doubt. No more of that, if you please. The hour and the place seem quite suitable for my taking my revenge by blowing your brains out."

"For what?" cried he, slightly alarmed. "I thought you were my enemy; I was deceived. I fired at, and missed you. The one quite compensates for the other; and, for my part, I would not harm you the least in the world."

The unknown appeared so convinced by the force of his own argument that I could not help laughing. I then asked if I were far from the Cerro del Gigante.

"A good carbine could carry a ball there quite easily; but, from the windings of the ravine, it is a two hours' march from here; and, as the night is coming on, and the road rather difficult to find in the dark, I offer your lordship a night's lodging under my roof, to show you that I bear no malice."

The dilapidated appearance of the house promised only a very sorry shelter, but the offer seemed frankly enough made, and I was, besides, one of that class of unencumbered travelers with whom robbers only exchange salutations on the road. I made no difficulty, therefore, in accepting the offer, and dismounted. The unknown led me through a vast hall, whose roof was much broken in many parts, and, while he was assisting Cecilio to unsaddle the horses, I could see by the tools lying about the place that I was in one of those metallurgic work-shops (*haciendas de beneficio*) where the silver extracted from the mines receives its last treatment. My host was not long in returning;

he lighted a miner's torch, and then told me to consider myself at home. Misery seemed to have taken up its abode in this ruined building, and I could not help remarking to myself that there seemed little likelihood of getting here even the slightest refreshment. I seated myself opposite to my host, and tried to listen patiently to the explanations he was giving me about the uses of various instruments which I had never seen before; but as time passed, and there seemed to be no likelihood of any thing being placed on the table, I said frankly,

"I am very hungry."

"So am I," he returned, gravely, without stirring.

I feared I had not been explicit enough.

"At what time do you ordinarily sup here? For my part, I can sup at any hour of the evening when I am as hungry as I am at present."

"Any hour is convenient enough for me; but to-day I have had no supper."

This reply astonished me. Luckily, Cecilio had supplied himself with some yards of dried meat.[27] I was able then, our respective positions being reversed, to offer a frugal repast to the singular amphitryon with whom chance had brought me acquainted, and he needed no pressing to make him accept it.

"It appears to me," I said, after we had finished, "that there is a certain person called Remigio Vasquez in the world who is far from being a friend of yours; what ill has he done you?"

"None, till a little ago; and I fired at him (that is, at you) to-day purely from precaution, and to prevent him from ruining me."

Florencio Planillas, that was my host's name, then entered into long details about his own affairs. He was one of those obstinate miners who have all their lives struggled to grasp after merely visionary illusions, and who, like the unlucky gambler, fancy themselves constantly on the point of becoming possessors of millions without ever being able to learn those rude lessons of experience which their unhappy obstinacy prevents them from acquiring. His history was that of many others. Once proprietor of a rich silver mine, then of a flourishing *hacienda de beneficio*, he had seen the thread of silver fail in the *borrasca*,[28] and the want of capital had forced him to suspend his metallurgic operations. According to Mexican custom, a mine once abandoned becomes the property of the person who proclaims the failure of the former proprietor. This proclamation was a perpetual source of annoyance to Florencio Planillas both day and night. His restless, perturbed spirit saw a rival in every one, ready to deprive him of his property, and he had been told that an individual named Remigio Vasquez had arrived the night before at

Guanajuato, with the avowed intention of profiting by the suspension of his works, and claiming them as his own. It would prove a rough blow to Florencio to be deprived of a property which had enriched him before, and very probably might do so again. The Mexicans are very generally in the habit of deciding such cases by the knife. He had therefore vowed the death of Remigio Vasquez. "I never saw him," he added, on finishing his recital; "but his appearance has been so exactly described to me that he can not escape. I spent this whole day at Guanajuato trying to discover him, but in vain, and on my return, deceived by the darkness, by a certain vague resemblance you bore to him, and, above all, by the cloak you wore, I thought you were the person that had come to dispossess me of my rights, and it was only on closer inspection that I discovered my error. I do not say, however, that I am sorry I missed you; but after this I'll use the knife. *El cuchillo no suena ni truena* (the knife does its work silently), as my friend Tomas Verduzco says."

"Verdugo, you mean," said I, interrupting him.

"Do you know him?" cried Florencio, with a laugh. "What a capital joke! But you don't transact business with him, I think."

"What joke are you referring to?"

"*Hombre!* don't you know that his true name is Verduzco, and that he is called Verdugo[29] (executioner) because he is obliged sometimes to see justice done to himself in what he calls his affairs of conscience?"

This peculiarity in the character of the man on whose heels I had been treading so closely was not the most agreeable thing in the world, I must confess; but I wished to get some more information about him, and accordingly inquired how long it had taken Don Tomas to acquire this formidable surname.

"On my word," replied Florencio, "that's one of those matters of which one does not like to keep a too exact account—probably he does not even know himself—but perhaps you will form a bad opinion of Don Tomas from what I have told you. The Señor Verduzco is no egoist; his neighbor may have the use of his knife at a time; and, provided you give him solid reasons (with a strong emphasis on solid), he is always ready to render one a service."

"The devil he is!" I cried. "Don Tomas must be a most inestimable character, and I am quite impatient to make his acquaintance."

In spite of this gasconade, the intense desire that I had shown to see Don Tomas was dispelled as if by magic; but, having gone too far to recede, I determined to make my way, as I had intended, to the Cerro del Gigante. The night passed without any incident occurring except that I was forced to lend my host a part of my manga to stop up a hole in the roof that admitted the cold, and I took leave of him in the morning with many thanks for his munificent hospitality, which had been shown by his appropriating to himself three parts of my supper and the half of my cloak. Moreover, not many hours before he had tried to shoot me.

I mounted, and proceeded in the direction of the Cerro del Gigante. Armed with my lance, whose torn pennon bore witness to the danger I had run, escorted by Cecilio, and having the guitar of the Biscayan nobleman thumping on my back, I bore no uncertain resemblance to the wandering knight of La Mancha in search of adventures, attended by his trusty squire. This mission of mine was one of the most delicate kind, for now I had no doubt whatever but that we were on the traces of a Mexican bravo, and I had been following him for the last six days. I was quite convinced, however, that I had done nothing to get myself involved with Don Tomas.

The *bravï* of Mexico, like their compatriots in other countries where this formidable profession is exercised, begin at first by putting those to death to whom they become indebted at the gaming-table. It was, then, a point of the very greatest importance to establish my identity fully in the eyes of a fellow of this stamp, as I might probably, if this were not done, get a stab intended for some other person. This consideration deciding me above all, I repaired to the Cerro del Gigante, and in a short time arrived at a very pretty house at the foot of the mountain. A purling brook, shaded with sycamores, ran close by the door. My host of the preceding night had described the place to me too minutely to allow of my missing it. I addressed myself to a groom, who was rubbing down a beautiful horse at the gate, by inquiring if the Cavalier Verduzco could be seen at present.

"No, señor," replied the man. "He had scarcely arrived here last night ere he was sent on business of the utmost importance to Guanajuato, which he can scarcely finish in less than three days; and when he comes home, he may require to depart again immediately."

"Where is he going next?" I asked.

"I don't know," said the man, dryly. I made no more inquiries, wheeled my horse round, and rode off.

FOOTNOTES:

[27] In some parts of Mexico butcher-meat is cut into strips, dried in the sun, and sold by measure, like ribbons or cloth.

[28] An appellation given to a mine when it has become unprofitable.

[29] A sharp poniard.

CHAPTER V.

Assassination of the young Spanish Noble.

On returning to the town, I inquired which of the three or four hotels in Guanajuata was the cheapest, convinced that it was only in one of that description that the Biscayan was to be found. I was right in my conjecture, for the first person I met on alighting in the court-yard of the posada was Don Jaime de Villalobos. He was just going out when I presented myself suddenly before him, and I had scarcely dismounted ere he pressed me in his arms, according to the manner of his country. For my part, I listened with interest to his adventures after our separation. He told me that he had arrived at Guanajuato almost four days before me, and that his utmost wishes had been realized. A priest, who had been gained over by the relative of Donna Luz, had married them without difficulty, and since that time his young wife had been hidden in a convent, where he saw her every day, until he could take such steps as would allow them to leave Mexico. One circumstance only caused him a little alarm: he believed that he met in the streets, the night before, one of the servants who was in the train of his wife's father at the venta of Arroyo Zarco.

"But as I fancy that I see every where the appearance of spies and robbers," he said, gayly, "it is more than probable that I am deceived, and that they are seeking me at a greater distance than where I really am. And you," added he, "have you laid your hand on Don Tomas Verdugo yet?"

"No; and, from all I have learned about him, I am more anxious to avoid him now than I was to meet him before." And I recounted my adventure in the ravine with Florencio Planillas. "Your cloak," I added, "served me a bad turn, for it is similar to one that the informer against Florencio wears, one Remigio Vasquez."

At the name Don Jaime turned pale, and cried,

"What! was it Remigio Vasquez that the scoundrel had in mind to shoot? and do they accuse him of a crime which he never contemplated? Ah! my presentiments have not deceived me."

"Why?"

"Remigio Vasquez is the name I bear here."

This unexpected revelation caused me to shudder. Perhaps, even now, that villain, whose knife was at every one's service, might have been sent upon the Biscayan's track to satisfy the vengeance of the injured father. I told him what my opinion was upon the matter, and insisted upon his staying within doors for a few days; but the Spanish nobleman had now recovered all his former courage.

"No," he said, "Luzecita waits me at the convent. Not to go to see her would plunge her into the deepest grief. No one can escape their destiny."

We talked together a short time longer. As he insensibly lapsed into a gloomy mood, I tried to jest with him upon our actual position.

"As for me," I said, "I shall be more prudent than you. I am going to bury myself in the deepest mine I can find, and it will be a terrible thing if this horrid Verdugo meets me eighteen hundred feet below ground."

We separated, Don Jaime to the convent, and I to visit one of the most easily accessible mines in the neighborhood. As I was crossing the square on my way to the outskirts of the town, I fancied I distinguished the well-known face of Florencio Planillas at the door of a pulqueria. Delighted at having this opportunity of undeceiving him as to the intention of Remigio Vasquez, or rather Don Jaime, I went up to the door, in spite of the repugnance I have for these Mexican cabarets, where both men and women sit drinking that abominable liquor prepared from fermented *pulque*.[30] Whether Florencio had seen, and wished to avoid me, I know not; at any rate, he disappeared into the shop. The life of Don Jaime doubtless depended on the interview I was going to have with Florencio. I stepped over some drunkards, quite intoxicated, who were lying, clothed in rags, across the doorway, and entered the pulqueria. What a fantastical appearance met my eye! The walls were covered with frescoes of the most incredible nature, representing ancient grotesque personages, pictures of drunken brawls, of murder, of love, of giants, dwarfs, and cavaliers, accompanied with the most startling devices, and all surmounted with this clinching inscription: (*Hoy se paga, mañana se fia*)—*Pay now, credit afterward.* Large open vats, filled with a milky liquor, from which exhaled a horrible smell, were placed all round the room, and the publican was busily engaged ladling it out with a calabash for his customers, among whom I soon recognized Florencio.

"Ah! Señor Cavalier," cried he, advancing with the glass in his hand, "allow me to offer you—"

"No, I am not thirsty; but I have some good news for you."

I tried then to tell him that he had been falsely informed when he had been told that the person who was trying to dispossess him of his mine was Remigio Vasquez. It was a long time before I could make the obfuscated drunkard understand the purport of my visit, and undeceive him with regard to the Biscayan.

"You see that I am delighted," cried he, when he had at last made out the meaning of my words.

"For poor Remigio's sake?" I said.

"No, for my own sake. I don't fear his information," he replied, with a drunken frankness; "but if that change my intentions regarding him, Remigio Vasquez's affair is not a bit improved. I mean to say—(and, swallowing what remained in his glass, he seemed to be trying to collect his thoughts)—I mean that it is capital for—for—"

"For whom?" I exclaimed, losing all patience.

"Ah! caramba, for our intimate friend, the respectable Don Tomas Verdugo, as your lordship styles him."

And the miner was not slow in telling me that the bravo would receive a considerable sum from the injured father, as he had been told, to avenge the insult offered to his outraged family.

"And where is Don Tomas?" I inquired of Florencio. "I am sure that I can undeceive him as well as yourself."

"I think I know where he is at present," replied Planillas.

"Well, why do you wait here? Let us set out immediately in search of him."

"I would like well enough to be off; but, you see, I can't quit this place without paying my score, and I have not a single tlaco about me."

"That needn't detain you. Call the publican."

"Truly," said Florencio, with much effrontery, "yesterday evening you partook of my hospitality; if you clear my expenses to-day, we shall be quits."

The publican immediately appeared, and I inquired how much Florencio owed him. The miner tipped him the wink, and the other immediately said, "Two piastres." This was far too much, and the drunken scoundrel would very likely gain a piastre and a half by it; but time was precious. I yielded, and we hastened in pursuit of Don Tomas. Unluckily, the tottering legs of my companion but ill seconded my efforts, and I was obliged to proceed very slowly. In this manner we traversed a considerable part of the town. Every now and then the drunken rascal stopped before a house, saying he was within, but he was invariably mistaken. We at last stood before a dark, steep, wet alley, at the end of which you saw the dusky light which issued from a garden.

"Are you sure you are right this time?" I asked anxiously of Florencio; "for time is passing, and poor Vasquez is in danger of his life."

"He is there, assuredly," stammered my companion; "for I could never forgive myself if I had arrived too late, and any misfortune (here his eyes became bathed in maudlin tears) were to happen to Don Tomas. Such a worthy man as he is, too!"

After this burst of sensibility, which failed signally in its object, Florencio plunged into the lane, and I remained alone, for I thought that we could no longer proceed together. I walked about in the street, a prey to anxiety easy to comprehend, counting the minutes, which seemed centuries, and expecting every moment to see this Don Tomas, who had not been out of my thoughts for so many days, appear before me; but time passed, and he did not make his appearance. An hour was spent in this manner, and at last I decided on going to the house myself. I walked through the dark alley, entered the garden at the other end, and the first thing I saw was a man stretched on the ground. This was the unhappy Florencio, who was snoring as if he would burst his nostrils, and had forgotten every thing in his drunkenness. I retraced my steps, resolving to trust to myself only; but it was a long time before I found myself in a part of the town I knew. I got to my hotel with some difficulty. Cecilio met me at the gate.

"Ah!" cried he, on seeing me, "what a dreadful misfortune has happened! The young cavalier that you met this morning had a quarrel fixed on him by a passenger in the street, and they have carried him to his own room. He is dead, there's no doubt of it."

Such an occurrence is so common in Mexico that no unusual stir was visible in the hotel as I mounted the stairs to go to Don Jaime's room. The poor young man, uncared for, untended, appeared to be sleeping the most tranquil sleep of all, upon a bench of stone, with a bloody sheet thrown over him. The fresh air which struck his face as I lifted the cloth caused him to open his eyes, over which the glaze of death was already stealing.

"I know who you are," he said; "it was you who succored me when I was in want, and you will remain by me till the last, I am sure. Thank you."

The Biscayan gave me his clay-cold hand.

"My hand is burning hot, is it not? A few minutes ago *she* pressed it between both of *hers*. Good God! what will she say when she never sees me again?"

"Never fear," I replied. "Tell me where I can see Donna Luz."

The Biscayan whispered her address into my ear.

"Now," replied he, "it is useless. My hours are numbered; she will come too late! When I am gone, don't tell her that she was the cause of my death. Inform her only that my last thought was of her."

Some rambling, unconnected words now escaped from the poor Spaniard—his mother's name, his country's, and his dear wife's, for whom he had paid the penalty of his life. While the exterior world was gradually fading from his eyes, the sweet and holy impressions of childhood, the first imprinted on the heart of man, and the last to leave it, still threw a few bright beams athwart the thickening darkness of his thoughts. All at once, turning himself to me, he exclaimed, in a clear, distinct voice,

"You will go and see my mother, won't you? Be it a year after this, or even ten. Say this to console her, that I died worth millions, but not that I breathed my last on such a bed as this."

I bowed in token of assent, and Don Jaime employed the little strength that was left him in telling me where to find his house, near Vergara, in Biscay. I promised to fulfill this last request. A vague, meaningless smile now played upon the dying man's lips, that moved only in a prayer he put up in which his mother's name was mentioned. These were his last words. I wiped away the foam that covered his lips with a corner of his cloak, and closed the eyes, which were wide open and staring. At this moment somebody touched me on the shoulder. I turned about. A man whose entrance I had not noticed stood behind me. By his staff I saw he was an alcalde.

"Well, Señor Cavalier," said he, "you would give something, I know, to have satisfaction for the death of this young man. I am convinced you would; be calm—the eye of justice sees it all."

"When it is too late," I said, in a low tone.

"Is he a friend—a relation—a brother perhaps?" asked the alcalde.

I knew Mexican law too well to allow myself to be taken in by this appearance of compassion and interest, and said nothing.

"Well, I am waiting for your declaration," pursued he, with an engaging air.

"My declaration, Señor Alcalde, is this" (and I inwardly asked pardon of the corpse lying before me for the lie I was about to utter): "I declare that I don't know, nor ever have known, this young man."[31]

The disappointed alcalde was not long in leaving the room.

"Ah! Señor Cavalier," said the huesped, who had witnessed the whole scene, "you are a foreigner, it is true, but you did not come into the country yesterday."

I pretended not to comprehend the compliment he had paid me, and threw a last glance at the poor Biscayan. His face wore that aspect of serenity and peace which often appears on men who have died a violent death. A quiet smile played upon his lips. Though only commenced a few days before, the short connection I had had with Don Jaime was now closed. As regards the mysterious link which bound me to Don Tomas, that was not broken for some time afterward.

A year had passed since the death of the Biscayan. I had quitted Mexico. Besides the promise I had given Don Jaime, a less romantic motive, one quite personal, led me into Spain. The embers of the civil war were then fast dying out. The diligences which plied between Bayonne and Madrid, and the towns between those cities, had stopped running in consequence of the Carlist bands which infested the Basque frontier. I reached Bilboa, and it was only at great expense that I could procure a pair of horses and a guide. This man, who was to leave me at Vergara, from whence I could reach St. Sebastian, had himself served in the Carlist ranks. From Bilboa to Vergara is almost thirty miles. Throughout this wide extent of country, the people in the villages, fearing invasion, had emigrated in bands, and the road, dangerous even at its best, would have appeared very long without the stories of my guide. We arrived at Vergara at nightfall; the townsmen were fast deserting it. A Carlist band had announced its arrival. My guide could go no farther, his pass not permitting him to leave the town. A league farther on the horses would be seized and himself arrested.

"I must leave you," he said, "but I am very sorry for it. I know my old comrades well; and may the holy Virgin keep you from falling into their hands."

"My nationality protects me," I exclaimed; "I fear neither Carlist nor Christino."

"Your being a Frenchman will not avail you, for—for—for—" The good man, hesitating for a while, added, "For you will probably be hung offhand."

This did not startle me much; I knew, if my life were in peril, I should find a secure retreat in the house of the mother of poor Don Jaime, who had once been a Carlist officer. The mountaineer, who could not account for my coolness, shook me by the hand and said,

"You are a brave fellow, by heavens! and I hope they will shoot rather than hang you."

The ex-Carlist quitted me. I left my valise at an inn, and, after learning the direction of the castle of Tronera, a place which every body seemed to know, set out on foot. It was about three quarters of a mile from the town. The castle of Villalobos, as I expected, was a gloomy enough place, and the wind was whistling in the angles of the crumbling turrets with a noise which sounded to me like the drums of a Carlist band. Flocks of swallows were darting in and out of some apertures in the loose tiles on the roof. The shutters were all closed; some scaffolding, however, raised at different parts of the building, showed that repairs had been begun, but had been interrupted. The castle seemed deserted. I knocked at the door. Some seconds elapsed, and a woman, clad in black, appeared. I desired her to announce to her mistress that a stranger had arrived from America, and was the bearer of some important news.

"Alas!" replied the woman, "the poor lady died six months ago, and I am looking for her son every day."

"He is dead too!" I exclaimed.

I then learned that, some time before my arrival, the mother of Don Jaime had been presented with a considerable sum of money. As no letter had accompanied the remittance, she concluded that the unknown benefactor must have been her son. This sudden change in her fortune had a fatal effect upon her. When on her death-bed, she had ordered the money to be laid out in rendering the castle worthy of the residence of its young master, and had died thanking God that he had allowed a gleam of prosperity to shine at last upon the old race of Villalobos.

I had fulfilled my promise, and did not remain long at the chateau. It is needless to add that, contrary to the warning of my guide, I finished my excursion without meeting even the shadow of a Carlist band or Christino detachment.

FOOTNOTES:

[30] The sap of the aloe, which is first as sweet as honey, but by fermentation becomes stinking, sour, and heady.

[31] By professing relationship, or even acquaintance, with one who has fallen by assassination, you render yourself, in Mexico, bound to defray the expenses of justice.

THE MINERS OF RAYAS.

CHAPTER I.

The Hand upon the Wall.—Desiderio Fuentes, the lucky Miner.—
Don Tomas Verduzco.

Hardly a century ago, Guanajuato was a town of very little importance. Before the sudden change in its fortune, which resulted from the rich yield of silver in the Valenciana and Rayas mines, the mining industry of Mexico had concentrated its activity in the works of Tasco, Pachuca, and Zacatecas. The title of *ciudad* (city) had been borne by Zacatecas since 1588, while Guanajuato, though founded in 1554, did not attain that rank till seventy-eight years later, in 1741. It was not known that the mountains inclosing it on all sides, and on the slope of which it was built, held within their stony bosom the *Veta Madre* (Mother Vein), the richest lode of silver in the world. The situation of Guanajuato is, besides, doubly advantageous. The city is situated at once in the richest mining district in Mexico, and in the best cultivated part of the fertile plains of the Bajio.[32] It is thus the inhabitants call that large extent of country, about eighty leagues in circumference, which is bounded toward the side of Guanajuato by the Cordillera.

Alternately parched and inundated, the Bajio presents at all seasons an aspect singularly picturesque. During the rainy season, the winter of those favored climes, the sky, which loses its blue without losing its softness, floods the plains with fertilizing torrents. For several hours a day the Bajio is a vast lake, studded with tufts of verdure, with blue hills, with groups of white houses and enameled cupolas. On this sheet of water the green summits of the trees alone reveal to the traveler the capricious meanderings of the inundated road. Soon, however, the thirsty soil has imbibed the moisture through the innumerable cracks that eight months' drought has left in its surface. A layer of slime, deposited by the heavy rains and the torrents from the Cordillera, has enriched the impoverished earth. The heavens are clear and cloudless as before. The springs, freed from the crust which obstructed them, gush out more abundantly from the foot of the *ahuehuetl*.[33] The Peruvian-tree, the gum-tree, the golden-flowered *huisache*, amid whose blossoms the scarlet-plumed parrots scream, shade and perfume the now consolidated roads. The songs of muleteers and the bells of mules resound in the blue distance, mingled with the shrill creaking of cart-wheels. It is the time when the Indian laborer returns to his toils. Like the shepherd in the Georgics, with his leathern buskins, his short tunic, and bare legs, he lazily goads the oxen at the plow. And such is the fertility of this soil, that splendid crops cover the ground which the plow has scarcely furrowed. Still, it is not in the rich plain alone that nature has been most indulgent to the happy dwellers in the Bajio. Over the fertile valleys in the vicinity of Guanajuato, the Cordillera rears its metalliferous crest, whose sides are veined with lodes of gold and silver, and which delivers to the mattock of the miner the immense treasures of the Veta Madre.[34] The striking contrast that is visible between the laborer and the miner is nowhere so strongly apparent as in this part of the Bajio. Humble and submissive, the Indian husbandman is at every one's mercy. The miner, haughty and independent, takes a higher rank; and this claim is justified, we must admit, by the importance of the duty he performs. Obliged to submit to labor which yields him only limited results, the husbandman finishes his work in silence, while the pickaxe of the miner resounds, so to speak, to the end of the world, and is constantly adding, at every stroke, to the riches of mankind. Prosperity is not long in coming to the indefatigable miner. The slopes of the hills, the ravines, and the summits of the mountains swarm with a dense population, among whom the lucky finders of a new lode scatter their hard-earned money with thoughtless liberality, and squander in one day the earnings of six months. From the French miner Laborde, who lavished thousands upon Cathedrals, down to the meanest *peon*, the history of this bold workman has been always the same. Fortune is the only god he worships. He goes to his dangerous occupation as if specially sent thither by Divine Providence; and this proud thought is favored by the laws of the country, old privileges according the title of nobility to the worker in the mines. Even at this day he can not be dispossessed by his creditors of his mine, if he can afford to work it. It appears that there is a tendency to respect the descendants of a privileged race. Besides a knowledge of metals to guide him in his search, the miner must be endowed with a number of rare qualities; from that vigorous strength indispensable to one who has to raise heavy burdens, and support all day, on scanty wages, the enervating fatigue of under-ground work, down to activity and pliancy of limb, united with undaunted resolution and coolness. These qualities, it must be owned, are never found in the same man without corresponding defects. A capricious and undisciplined being, the miner only employs all his tact and energy if interested in the success of his enterprise. Sometimes, after toiling for a month, during which he has hardly earned enough to live upon—in a week, or even in a day, he recompenses himself for his long privations. The miner then thanks Dame Fortune. He scatters his gold with a lavish hand, and returns to his work only after all his gains are exhausted. At times he enriches himself by secretly pilfering the ore which really belongs to the proprietor of the mine, and the miners are but too expert at this species of theft.

It was in the midst of a population like this that I found myself at Guanajuato, after the dangerous and useless search recorded in the preceding chapters. I did not wish to let this opportunity escape me of observing upon this theatre of action a class of men, of whom the *gambusinos*, or gold-seekers of the Sonora, give one only an imperfect idea. After spending a day in repose, which the many painful events I had encountered rendered necessary, I went out next morning to visit the mines in the neighborhood of Guanajuato.

While crossing the great square, and keeping myself on my guard, my attention was arrested by an unusual object. Nailed against the wall, and under a small pent-house, was a human hand cut off by the wrist. I stopped my horse to assure myself that it was not a plaster cast. A moment's examination was sufficient to convince me that it was indeed a human hand, once strong and muscular, but now blanched and withered by the wind, the sun, and the rain. Under the pent-house some half-burned candles told that pious souls had been touched by this strange exhibition, which seemed destined to perpetuate the remembrance of some bloody deed. After seeking in vain upon the wall an explanatory inscription, I continued my journey; but, during my short stay, a horseman had approached, and seemed determined to keep close by me. At any other time I would have accepted with a bad grace the company of the unknown, but I had come out, you must remember, in quest of a guide. I stopped my horse, and put some questions to him. The stranger bowed courteously.

"You are a stranger, Señor Cavalier," said he, with a smile.

"How do you know that?" I replied, a little astonished at his abrupt way of beginning a conversation.

"The curious way in which you gazed upon that withered hand sufficiently convinced me that you have not been long in the town, and had not much time to lose. I must say that, for me, who am looking out for a companion, our meeting is a lucky one."

I was not quite sure if I ought to accept with much cordiality the companionship so familiarly thrust upon me. He seemed to observe my hesitation, and exclaimed, with a certain degree of haughtiness, "You do not know me, and I am unwilling that you should for a moment suppose that you have got to do with some of those poor devils who are always ready to offer their services to the first stranger they meet. My name is Desiderio Fuentes. I am a miner; and, in the profession I exercise, there are some days on which fortune is unkind, and others on which you amass so much money that you do not know how to get rid of it. I am in the latter condition at present; and my invariable custom, on an occasion of this kind, is to procure some jolly companion who can share in my pleasures. If I can't get one, I take up with the first cavalier of good appearance I meet, and I confess that I have never had occasion yet to blame Fortune for the comrade she sent me."

This frank declaration reassured me completely. I told Desiderio, however, that I could not accept of his cordial offer. I had come to visit the silver mines in the immediate vicinity of Guanajuato, and was unwilling to waste in his company the time that I intended to devote to such a purpose, supposing always that he would not serve me as a guide. Desiderio preferred doing this rather than relinquish my society, being but too happy to escape from his own thoughts, were it only for a few hours. This bargain made, we spurred our horses, and a few minutes afterward got clear of the town.

On the road my guide informed me that he had made a lucky hit the night before, and that he could take his *far niente* for several days to come from the proceeds of a *partido*.[35] He added that it would be a delightful recreation for him to visit the mines in the neighborhood as an amateur, and he desired me to choose the one I had a mind to visit, premising only that he would rather not go to the Valenciana, as he happened to have a quarrel with one of the administrators. He wished to keep away from the Mellado, because he owed some money to one of the workmen there; and as for the Cata, certain misunderstandings of recent date caused him to avoid it with the greatest care. In spite of the apparent liberty of choice he had granted me, I saw no other way of accomplishing my object but by going to inspect the Rayas— the only one open to me. The precautions which Desiderio Fuentes was forced to take did not say much in his favor. My new friend was evidently very quarrelsome. He had certainly no love for paying his debts, and in his misunderstandings (*désavencias*) his knife had doubtless played no unimportant part. I began to entertain but a very indifferent opinion of my companion. One expression especially that escaped the miner caused me to reflect.

"My first impulse is always very good," he said, "but I own my second is detestable."

We had now come to the extremity of a ravine whose precipitous sides had till now obstructed the view. A beautifully level plain lay stretched before us. Long strings of mules, laden with ore, were slowly making their way to one of those metallurgic establishments known in Mexico as a *hacienda de platas*. High chimney-stacks, from which volumes of smoke and leaden vapors rolled, now appeared; the stone *patros* also, on which the fluid metal is poured a day before its formation into ingots. The noise of the hammer pounding the argentiferous rock, the clattering of the mules' hoofs, and the cracking of whips, were mingled with the hoarser sound of the falling water that moved the machinery. I had stopped my horse to gaze on this animated scene, but my attention was soon attracted elsewhere. A few paces distant, but half hidden from us by a hollow in the road, I espied two men dragging along with ropes the carcass of a mule. Having arrived at a place where Desiderio and I could alone see them, one of them stooped over the dead mule, and seemed to examine it curiously, casting at the same time a suspicious glance around. The moment he caught sight of us, he flopped down on the carcass that he had been dragging a minute before, while his companion immediately disappeared in a dense thicket of low trees and brushwood.

"Well, I thought I was right," said Fuentes. "It is my friend Planillas; but what the devil is he doing there?"

At the name of Planillas I shuddered involuntarily, and, preceded by Fuentes, made my way directly to the place where the man was seated on the mule. I hoped to obtain some information from the friend of Don Tomas Verduzco as to the part the bravo had played in the murder of my friend Don Jaime. Planillas, his elbows on his knees, and his head on his hands, appeared overwhelmed by violent grief. The noise of our approach drew him at last from his abstraction, and he looked up at us, but with an expression of uneasiness rather than of sorrow.

"Ah! señores," cried he, "in me you behold the most miserable man in all New Spain."

"You are doubtless thinking," I replied, "of the young cavalier whom Don Tomas assassinated two days ago, and whose blood is on your head, since you might have saved his life by stopping the hand of your friend—of that Don Tomas who had been paid to kill him, you told me."

"Did I say that?" cried Florencio; "then, by the life of my mother, I lied. I am a terrible liar when in drink; and you know, Señor Cavalier, I had drunk a great deal that day."

Florencio paused, visibly embarrassed. Fuentes thereupon asked him why he was in such a state of grief when we came up, and why he persisted in taking the carcass of a mule for a seat.

"This mule is the cause of my sorrow," replied Planillas. "Although I was tenderly attached to her, I had sold her in my misery to the hacienda de platas you see in the valley below. I got employment in the work-shops to be near her; but, alas! the poor beast died this morning, and I have dragged her to this lonely place in order to mourn over her undisturbed."

Planillas again plunged his head between his hands with the air of a man who will not be consoled; then, doubtless, to turn the conversation, "Ah! Señor Cavalier," he said, "that is not my only misfortune. Yesterday a fight took place between the miners of Rayas and those of Mellado, and I was not there."

"I see nothing so unfortunate in that."

"Nothing unfortunate!" vociferated Planillas. "Ah! it was not one of those vulgar encounters that one sees every day; and you would never guess how it terminated—by a shower of piastres which the miners of Mellado poured upon their adversaries to prove the superiority of their mine. Ah! the beautiful eagle piastres!" he added, with a broken-hearted air; "and I was too late in the field."

I could better understand Planillas's grief for this last disappointment; but I should have doubted this excess of arrogant prodigality on the part of the Mellado miners had not Fuentes confirmed, with proud satisfaction, the truth of the tale. My companion would again have questioned Planillas, of whose lamentations he appeared suspicious, but a sudden cracking of branches in the brushwood behind us attracted his attention. A little thick-set man, a sort of dwarf Hercules, with a somewhat stern expression of countenance, stood before us. He saluted us politely, and sat down on the ground beside Planillas. His mouth tried to smile, but his glance, sinister and piercing as that of a bird of prey, belied the feigned gayety. We were silent for a few moments. The new-comer was the first to speak.

"You were talking just now," he said, "if my ears did not deceive me, of one Don Tomas. Could it be of Don Tomas Verduzco you were speaking?" He said this in a soft and silky tone, that contrasted strongly with the evil expression of his countenance. This simple question, coming from a man who had at once inspired me with the strongest repugnance, sounded very much like an insult.

"Precisely," I replied, exerting myself to keep cool; "I accused Don Tomas of the murder of a young man whom he did not even know the night before."

"Are you sure?" said the man, with a sinister glance.

"Ask this wretch!" I replied, pointing to Planillas.

On hearing this, Planillas bounced up as if he had been touched by a spring. He appeared to have recovered all his assurance. "I never said any thing of the kind. But your lordship," cried he, in an ironical tone, "is surely not acquainted with the respectable Don Tomas Verduzco, since you speak so in his presence."

I looked at the man thus denounced to me, and whom I now beheld for the first time. Imagination placed before me the bleeding body of Don Jaime, his agony, his last moments, and his happy future, all cut off in an instant by the knife of the man before me.

"Ah! you are Don Tomas Verduzco—" I could not finish. A sort of faintness came over me, and, without accounting to myself for what I was about to do, I cocked one of my pistols. At the click of the lock the stranger's face became livid, for Mexicans of the lower classes, who will not wince at the glitter of a knife-blade, tremble at the sight of a fire-arm in a European hand. He never stirred, however. Fuentes threw himself between us.

"Gently, señor! gently, Cascaras! how you take the customs of the country!"

"The deuce take that Planillas," said the stranger, with a forced laugh; "he is always playing off some joke or other. But the idea of passing me off as Don

Tomas is too absurd. Has your lordship any interest, then, in this Don Tomas?"

My passion appeared to me ridiculous, and passed away as by enchantment.

"I do not even know him," I replied, somewhat confusedly, but with all my former coolness. "I can not tell how he has got mixed up in my affairs; but I think I owe it to my safety to show no mercy to such assassins when chance throws them in my way."

The stranger muttered some unintelligible words. I thought the opportunity a good one to get rid of my new friend Desiderio, whose companionship was becoming somewhat burdensome to me, so I saluted the group and rode off; but I had not counted on the idleness of Fuentes, for, before I had gone a hundred yards, he had overtaken me.

"I was perhaps wrong," he said, "to interfere in this affair, and to prevent you from lodging a bullet in the head of that ill-looking knave; for, judging from the revengeful look he cast at you, I presume the first stroke of a knife you will receive will be from his hand."

"Do you think so?" I replied, rather startled at this unpleasant prediction.

"I yielded, in truth, too readily to my first impulse," continued Fuentes, who seemed in a reverie. "What if we went back?" he said. "You might then resume the affair at the point at which you left it, and, in case of need, I would help you."

It was quite clear that Fuentes regretted having let slip this nice opportunity for a quarrel. I dryly refused his offer, and thought to myself that, decidedly, his second impulse was worse than his first.

"You won't! Well, it's no great matter. After all, who cares for a knife-thrust more or less? I have received three in my time, and am not a bit the worse."

I did not deem it necessary to make any reply to this remark, which did not place my guide's character in a very favorable light, and cut short his revelations by asking him some questions about the mine whose buildings were coming gradually into sight as we approached.

FOOTNOTES:

[32] Literally, bottom of a valley.

[33] The name of a species of cedar, whose presence almost always indicates the vicinity of a hidden spring. In Indian, *ahuehuetl* means lord of the waters.

[34] The Veta Madre, wrought by the four mining companies of Valenciana, Cata, Mellado, and Rayas, was discovered by the French miner Laborde, and has yielded, between the years 1829 and 1837, ore to the value of almost six million two hundred and fifty thousand pounds sterling.

[35] The miners are said to be in *partido* when a share of the proceeds is given them as wages. In this case the employers furnish them with tools, gunpowder, and candles.

CHAPTER II.

Description of, and descent into, a Silver Mine.—The Miner's Chapel.

When a mine is first begun, it is always left open to the sky, and the mineral is extracted by following the vein that contains it; but, as the mine gets deeper, two obstacles present themselves: the extraction of the ore becomes more costly, and the workmen are not long in meeting with hidden springs, the waters of which, unless removed, would drown the mine and stop the works. To provide against this danger, shafts are sunk, at the bottom of which a working gallery runs, that follows the vein of metal. The depth of the shaft depends upon the lode, which sometimes stretches so far down into the ground that two or three working galleries, one above the other, are obliged to be constructed. In the richest mines little paths of communication are added to these principal arteries, besides other works to assist in its exploration.

The ore and water are raised out of the mines by means of machines called *Malacates*, placed at the mouth of the shaft. Large bags, some made of the stringy bark of the aloe, others of ox-hide, are fixed to the ends of ropes wound round an enormous drum, the former for raising the ore, the latter for the water, and these are constantly passing up and down the shaft. The motive power is given by horses, which are kept constantly at the gallop.

Besides the grand shaft (*tiro general*), the mine of Rayas has two others of less importance, one of which reaches a depth of nearly eight hundred feet. The tiro general, remarkable for the diameter of its shaft, which is thirty-four feet, and for its frightful depth, almost twelve hundred feet, communicates with three principal galleries, one above the other, and these shafts and galleries, together with their accessories, form the most complete series of gigantic workings that are to be found in the country. The exterior appearance of this mine is, however, far from giving one an idea of the constant activity which prevails within it. Some paltry wooden sheds, covered with tiles, which protect the malacates, or shelter the workmen; a few buildings of mean appearance, the offices of the administrators or overseers, and two or three whitewashed houses, huddled together without any regard to order on the neighboring mounds, scarcely convey to the visitor any notion of the wonders he is going to behold.

It was about midday when I arrived with my companion at the opening by which we were to be admitted into the mine. We dismounted, confided our horses to the care of one of the miners, and entered. Desiderio carried in his hand a huge torch. I stood for a short time at the mouth of this vast laboratory, thinking on the millions of money it had been the means of putting into circulation. My guide, his cloak thickly covered with gold lace, that appeared, as the light of the torch fell on its velvety folds, to be seamed with golden links, looked like the lordly genie of this subterranean kingdom. We descended for a long time a series of steps, every one of which had the dimensions of a terrace. Amid the profound darkness, which the torch dispelled but feebly, we made a series of turnings and windings, changing every minute our temperature and direction, and sometimes mounting an inclined plane only to descend it. In about a quarter of an hour I perceived in the distance some wandering lights, then a few gigantic shadows appeared on the moist walls of the vault. I still kept on, and soon found myself in a square which the piety of the miners had converted into a chapel. In the centre rose a low altar, ornamented with wax tapers, which burned before an image of a saint. A man, who seemed to be praying fervently, was kneeling upon the steps of the altar. He was the first human being I had seen since entering the mine.

My guide touched my arm.

"Take a good look at this man," he said, in a low tone. The suppliant miner was entirely naked. Without the light of the flambeau, which allowed you to see his gray hair and angular features, you would not have thought he was an old man, so much youth and vigor seemed still to possess his nervous members.

"Why?" I inquired of Desiderio.

"This man," said he, "is no stranger to the history of the hand upon the wall that you gazed at with so much curiosity this morning; and, though that history is as well known to me as to him, perhaps from his lips it would have an additional interest, as his son was concerned in it."

I fancied that I had at last found an opportunity for shaking off Desiderio by insinuating that the narrator would probably go more into detail if he were telling the story to me alone. This time he took the hint.

"I am neither irritable nor quarrelsome," cried he; "but your lordship seems very desirous to get rid of his devoted servant."

"I must protest against the meaning you put upon my words."

Fuentes seemed to be calming down.

"Come," said he, with an air of raillery, "I will renounce my desire of accompanying you through these subterranean abodes, seeing you wish it. Besides, I must find out the meaning of the comedy played this morning by Planillas upon the carcass of the mule. You must visit the mine without me;

and I shall tell you what I have learned about this fellow after you have come up the grand shaft, for, to crown your achievement, you must be drawn up by means of the malacate."

I was in such a hurry to be quit of this personage that I promised all he asked, without remarking the ironical smile with which he welcomed my reply. At this moment the miner had finished his prayer. Fuentes exchanged a few words with him in a low tone, and walked rapidly away. I felt relieved.

"Señor Cavalier," said the new-comer to me, "my comrade Fuentes has made me acquainted with your desire to know the story of my son from my own lips—about him who was the pride of the corporation of miners. This desire does me honor; but at present I can not accede to your wish. I am on my way to fire a charge in the mine. If I am still in being after that operation, I shall be with you in two hours, and place myself entirely at your disposal, for I love the brave, to whatever nation they may belong."

"And who told you I was brave?" I asked, with an air of astonishment.

"*Caramba!* a man who visits a mine for the first time, and who, as Fuentes tells me, has a strong desire to make the perilous ascent by means of the *tiro!* Well, we shall go up together, and on our journey I shall tell you the story. I shall meet you, then, in two hours at the bottom of the last gallery, close upon the grand shaft."

I could scarcely have avoided this pompous eulogium; but I could not help feeling a certain sinking of heart at the very thought of being forced, as it were, against my will, to make this difficult and dangerous ascent. I was again indebted to Fuentes for this new annoyance. However, I promised to meet the old miner at the time appointed, and, being alone, I profited by my independence so far as to examine at my leisure the new world into which I found myself transported. I had the torch which Desiderio had left with me, and walked about at my pleasure. Above me, fancifully hollowed out in the living rock, and studded with brilliant spangles, stretched vaults of unequal grandeur, some sustained by wooden props, others letting their sharp points descend, like the pendant of a Gothic lamp, till they threatened to fall and bruise one to pieces. A few tiny streamlets, which flowed along the bottom of the rough pilasters, gleamed brightly as the light of the torch fell upon them. At a distance, large drops of water escaped from the fissures in the rocks, and fell on the stony soil with the dull, regular beat of a pendulum. Before me several dark squares opened; the noise of footsteps reverberated in the sombre caves, and died away in the distance. Various lights from time to time struggled through the deep gloom; these were the miners passing and repassing, with a rush-light stuck behind their ear, looking like the gnomes of the magicians, who, with a light on their forehead, watch over the hidden treasures of their masters.

I advanced with all caution; for, left without a guide in this labyrinth, I did not know which way to go. I soon heard in the distance the dull sound of the pickaxes with which they were hewing away the rock, mingled with mysterious noises which seemed to come from a lower gallery. These sounds, though very indistinct, served to guide me. Since entering the mine, I had seen only those passages in which the ore had been all extracted. I was now impatient to behold a spot in which the miners were actually at work. Such a locality is called the *labor*—that is to say, the place where they are following the vein of silver. A dusky, obscure glimmer indicated that the proximity of the place was not far off; and I soon reached the orifice of a shaft not very deep, from which a strong light proceeded. I descended it by means of a wooden ladder placed zigzag. I hesitated at first to trust myself to this rickety ladder; but, emboldened by the shallowness of the shaft, I ventured to descend, and arrived safely at the bottom. A passage about five feet wide, and six hundred in length, conducted me along this underground hive, the air in which was as hot and stifling as if it had left the mouth of a crater. Lost in the midst of this crowd of workmen, who were too busy to notice my presence, I could examine at my ease the fantastic tableau which there met my eyes. A number of candles, stuck to the walls, threw a dull, confused light upon the miners, the greater portion of whom, up to their waists in water, were attacking the living rock with vigorous strokes of their *barretas*. Others trudged off loaded with sacks of ore, the weight of which brought their muscles into tension, while the lighted rush-light which they carried upon their heads shone full upon their bronzed bodies, trickling with sweat, and their long floating hair. The sharp sound of the pickaxes striking the rock— the splash of the stones in the water—the voices of the miners—their shrill cries, and wheezy breathings, seemed at times to shake the very vault. The reddish glare of the candles reflected in the water—the dust—the vapor, which filled the place like a mist—the coppery veins which ran in all directions through the rock, all combined to increase the singularity of the spectacle.

After spending there a considerable time, I resolved to make my way to a lower gallery, at the end of which I was to meet the old miner. The ascent I was to make from that place did not seem so perilous as I at first imagined, and I should, besides, be saved going over the same ground. I requested one of the miners to conduct me to this place, as I feared to lose my way in the maze, the paths crossing and recrossing each other in all directions. I began, also, to feel the necessity of breathing a purer air, and followed my new guide with pleasure.

I went down an inclined plane so long that the joints of my legs knocked together, and arrived at last, worn out and breathless, at the extremity of the last gallery, which formed a right angle with the grand shaft, whose black mouth yawned right at my feet. This shaft was carried down still lower. The miner had not yet arrived. To a solitary workman, who seemed to have been forgotten in these vast catacombs, was assigned a most dangerous and frightful task. Close at hand, another shaft full of water was in process of being slowly emptied by means of an enormous bag of ox-hide attached to the cable of the malacate. When full, it was raised by means of the invisible machine twelve hundred feet above; but, being violently drawn in an oblique direction toward the axis of the grand shaft, the bag, distended with water, was in danger of being cut against the sharp rocks, had not the workman deadened the impulse it had received from the first motion of the malacate. On a narrow space between the two pits, in the midst of almost utter darkness, the peon held on to a double rope passed round the cable, whose two extremities he held in his hands; then, as he was pulled with a fearful rapidity to the mouth of the gulf, he let go all at once one of the ends of the rope, and the bag struck the opposite side of the rock very gently; but, had he made one false step, or let go the rope a second too late, he would have been dashed down an almost unfathomable abyss. I regarded the unhappy wretch who, every quarter of an hour during the whole day, hazarded his life for scanty wages with a feeling of pity and commiseration.

The bag had already ascended and descended four times; that is to say, an hour had elapsed, and not a single person had yet appeared. I must confess that, at the sight of the dark, gloomy shaft which I had to ascend, I felt my spirits sink somewhat; and as the old miner did not make his appearance, I pardoned him in my heart with a good grace, when, through the thick darkness, the cable of the malacate came in sight. A feeble glimmer lighted up the damp walls, and a voice, which was not unknown to me, called out,

"Halloo! friend, is there not a gentleman waiting here to go up by the tiro?"

I had scarcely answered that I was ready than a packet fell at my feet. I untied mechanically the cord which encircled it. The parcel contained a vest, trowsers of thick wool, a leathern baton, and a kind of plaited rope made of the bark of the aloe. I asked in some terror if the vest and trowsers were quite sufficient to deaden a fall of twelve hundred feet. As for the leathern baton and the plaited strap, I guessed their use at once. The workmen near me described the use of each of these articles. The woolen clothing was to keep me from being wet by the water, which shot forth in fine rain at certain places in the shaft. I was to attach myself to the cable by means of the plaited strap, and the baton was to prevent me from being dashed to pieces on the rock by the oscillations of the rope.

"Make haste!" cried my invisible guide; "we have no time to lose."

I put on the clothes with all speed, drew the cable toward me, and grasped it firmly with my hands, crossing my legs likewise over it. The peon passed the strap twice or thrice round my body and under my thighs, so as to form a kind of seat, tied the two ends firmly to the cable, and placed the baton in my hands. He had scarcely finished ere I felt myself lifted from the ground by an invisible power. I spun round three or four times, and, when I recovered from my astonishment, found myself already swinging over the gulf. A little above my head I perceived the legs of my guide, who was grasping the cable tightly. Although he carried a torch, I could discover but imperfectly his copper body, half naked, which, at certain moments, gleamed like Florentine bronze. However, I could make out his words quite well.

"Am I well enough tied to the cable, do you think?" I asked, seeing that not a single knot or roughness in the rope could prevent the strap that bound me from slipping to the bottom.

"Well, I suppose you are, unless the peon has done his business ill," replied the miner, in a calm tone; "but, should that not be the case, you can grasp the rope with your hands with all your might."

I clutched the cable convulsively. Unfortunately, I could hardly compass it with my two hands.

"How long shall we be in going up?"

"Twelve minutes commonly, but in this instance half an hour—a favor which I have obtained solely on your account, to allow you more time to observe the wonders of the mine."

"And does any accident ever happen in the ascent?"

"Pardon me. An Englishman, who happened to be ill bound to the rope, fell almost from the top to the very bottom, and so suddenly and quietly that a fellow-workman of mine, who was his guide, had not remarked his disappearance till he was at the top of the shaft."

I thought it best to ask no more questions. When I considered that five minutes had elapsed since the first movement of the malacate, I ventured to look above and below me. The shaft seemed to be divided into three distinct zones. At my feet a thick darkness dimmed the horror of that gulf which no eye could fathom; white tepid vapors rose slowly from the dark bottom and mounted toward us. Around me, the guide's torch lighted up with a smoky glimmer the green walls of rock, cut and torn in all directions by the pickaxe and the wedge. In the upper region a column of thick mist pressed round the circle of light produced by our torch, and shut us out completely from the light of day. At this moment the machine stopped to give the horses breath.

I clutched the cable anew as if it were slipping from me, and shut my eyes to avoid looking downward.

"This halt is especially for you," said my guide. "I had forgotten that I was to tell you a story, and this affords me time."

Without waiting for my reply, the miner commenced a recital whose incidents and minute details could not, in a dangerous ascent like this, fail to be deeply engraven on my memory. The attention I gave to the narrator kept my mind from dwelling upon the dangerous position in which I was at the moment, and this cessation of thought I would have welcomed at almost any price.

CHAPTER III.

Story of the Passer of the Rio Atotonilco, Osorio.—Felipe.—The young Miner.—A Duel in the Mine.

"You are perhaps aware," said the miner, "that in passing from San Miguel el Grande[36] to Dolores, the traveler is obliged to cross the Rio Atotonilco. In the rainy season the passage of this river can not be made by any but those who know the principal fords. The stream is about sixty yards wide at the place where the road to San Miguel meets it. The impetuosity of its waters, and the heavy, imposing noise of its yellow waves, produce an involuntary terror in any one who requires to cross it at this place. On the opposite bank, a few cabins, formed of branches, shelter a few wretched families, who make a scanty living by piloting the passengers across by the fords, with which they are acquainted. Often, when the traveler on the other side sees the poor half-clad people wandering upon the bank, and throwing themselves into the water, he hesitates, turns his bridle, and gallops off. A sad event proved that too little confidence can not be placed in men who will not be contented with the scanty living they pick up at this dangerous employment. Some years ago, an old miner of Zacatecas, who had rendered himself obnoxious to justice, and had quitted that province, came and established himself among the passers of the Rio Atotonilco. This man, whose strength and prowess rendered him formidable, was marked as having a singularly unlucky hand. Once or twice, the travelers whom he had engaged to convey across had been ingulfed by the waters of the river. One stormy night, believing himself alone, and seeing a traveler on the opposite bank, the passer crossed the ford to tender his services. He was observed by one of his comrades who had followed him, but who had hid himself among a thick clump of osiers on the brink of the river for the purpose of watching all that passed. The passer, having crossed the river, soon reappeared, followed by the cavalier, whose horse he led by the bridle. When half way across he mounted behind, and, a few seconds after, the splash of some one falling into the water was heard. One only of the horsemen remained in the saddle. This man reached the opposite bank at a considerable distance from the hamlet, and was soon lost in the darkness. The witness to the crime was a young man whom the passer had, a few days before, brutally ill used, and he was now seeking an opportunity for revenge. Thinking he had found it, he threw himself into the water, swam after the sinking body, and soon succeeded in dragging the unhappy man to the other bank, whom, by his tonsure and dress, he guessed to be a priest. Overcome with fatigue, the youth fainted. When he recovered his senses it was broad daylight, and the body of the priest was gone—carried off, doubtless, by some charitably-disposed persons who had been passing. That circumstance did not check the young man's eagerness to make his deposition before the alcalde of the nearest village; but, though a pursuit was set on foot, it was unsuccessful."

My guide checked himself at this moment. As if we had arrived in the region of clouds, a mist enveloped us, which gradually converted itself into a fine and almost impalpable, but soaking rain. The torch sputtered, and gave forth a very feeble glimmer. The water ran off the bronzed body of the miner in streams. The machine again stopped, and I felt a new sinking of heart, similar to the feeling one has on the deck of a laboring ship, when he thinks that every moment he is going to the bottom. A short and terrible apprehension increased the fear of immediate danger which had come over me. I fancied that the strap which bound me to the cable had slipped, and I was sliding downward. I gave a convulsive shudder.

"Has the strap got loose?" cried the miner; then, looking downward, and seeing me always at the same distance from him, he continued, with imperturbable calmness: "A short time after the disappearance of the passer, about whom the strangest stories were noised abroad, a new miner came to work at Rayas, which is about a dozen leagues from Rio Atotonilco. He said he had served his apprenticeship in the neighboring state of Cinaloa, and by his good-humor and liberality (for he appeared to have other resources besides his daily pay) soon gained the friendship of all his fellow-workmen. My son Felipe was the one he attached himself to more than any of the others. There was, however, between him and Osorio (that was the new miner's name) a complete dissimilarity in age and disposition. Felipe was a rough, unpolished workman, jealous of the reputation he had acquired, and haughty as a miner ought to be; for we have no need of ancient privileges to distinguish us from the vulgar, our profession ennobling the right that is granted us. Osorio, on the other hand, who was twice the age of Felipe, seemed to look upon labor as a burden, and passed his time in thrumming a guitar and preaching insubordination to the *mandones* (overseers). However, their friendship might have been of a lasting nature had they not both fallen in love with the same woman. This was the first time that they ever had a sentiment in common, in spite of their intimacy, and this was what produced the first quarrel. They continued, however, in spite of these differences, to pay their attentions to the fair damsel; for, though she preferred Felipe, she could not give up Osorio's music and merry good-humor. The frequent absence of the latter gave a great advantage to Felipe. During one of Osorio's times of absence, a report spread abroad that the Cathedral of Guanajuato had been burglariously entered, and that a monstrance of massy gold, adorned with precious stones, had disappeared from the place in which it was usually put. This sacrilegious theft struck the clergymen of the town with horror; but all their exertions to discover the daring robber were in vain. In the absence of Osorio, Felipe had succeeded in gaining the first place in the affections of the maiden to whom both had been paying their addresses. Her parents resolved to marry her to him, as it would tend to cut short the incessant quarrels that were ever taking place between them. The wedding was to take place in a short time, and all the friends of both families assembled at the young woman's house to celebrate their betrothal. Brandy and *pulque* flowed profusely, and music enlivened the feast, when an unexpected occurrence brought every thing to a stand-still. A man stood in the midst of the guests; that man was Osorio. Every one knew his violent disposition, and his sudden appearance caused all to tremble. Felipe alone remained cool, and waited, knife in hand, the attack of his rival; but he, without putting his hand to his belt, advanced into the circle, and apologized for having come without an invitation; then, taking a guitar from one of the musicians, he seated himself on a barrel of *pulque*, and began to improvise a bolero. This unexpected event caused a general surprise, and the merriment was redoubled. The party, interrupted for a moment, became more boisterous, and it broke up to assemble again on the eighth day afterward."

Here the narrator paused. We were gradually approaching the mouth of the tiro, as I could discover by the light shining through the fog which still enveloped us; besides, the higher we got, the gulf below appeared more frightful.

"Do you know what distance we are from the bottom of the mine?" cried the guide. "Five and a half times the height of the towers of the Cathedral of Mexico."

To confirm this assertion, the miner drew from his belt a bundle of tow steeped in pitch, which he lighted at his torch. My strained eye could scarcely follow it as it slowly descended the pit like a globe of fire, till it gradually became small as one of those pale stars whose light scarcely reaches our earth. The voice of the miner, who again began his recital, turned my mind away from this reflection.

"From that night on which Osorio showed himself at the betrothal, Felipe was annoyed in a thousand ways by some unknown hand. On the very next day a blast was fired close to him, and covered him with fragments of rock; another time, when he was at a considerable height in one of the galleries, the rope to which he was suspended broke suddenly. These attempts being unsuccessful, vague assertions began to be bruited abroad, accusing poor Felipe as the thief who had stolen the monstrance. The brave young man was unwilling to recognize in Osorio the author of these foul calumnies. His eyes could hardly have been opened to the evidence that he was his calumniator, had not a young miner, who constantly watched Osorio, and who had lately entered the mine, apprised Felipe of the snares that were laid for him. Felipe resolved to seek his revenge. On the evening of the day on which the marriage was to take place (for all this had passed in less than a week), Osorio and Felipe met in the subterranean galleries of the mine. Felipe reproached Osorio with his treachery; Osorio replied by recounting the injuries he had suffered; the two then drew their knives. They were alone and almost naked; their *frazadas* were their only shields. Osorio was the stronger, Felipe the more agile; the issue of the combat was therefore uncertain. All at once the young miner of whom I have spoken threw himself between the two combatants. 'Allow me,' said he, to Felipe, 'to punish this sacrilegious robber; my claim is anterior to yours.' Osorio gnashed his teeth and threw himself on the young miner, who stood grimly on his defense. The two then began to fight by the light of Felipe's torch, who had now become a spectator instead of an actor. With their frazadas wound round their left arms to hide their lunges, they commenced the combat. Perhaps the struggle would have been a long-protracted one had not the young miner adopted the following stratagem: he took such a position as allowed the covering on his arm to sweep the ground; then, behind the veil which masked his movements, he slipped his knife into his other hand, and gave his adversary a mortal wound. Osorio fell. He was drawn up by the grand shaft in a *costal*.[37] By chance a *padre* happened to be passing the mine at that moment. They besought him to come and confess the wounded man; but scarcely had the dying man and the padre looked at one another than a cry of horror broke from the priest. The holy father had recognized in the wounded man the passer of the Rio Atotonilco. Osorio discovered in the priest the man he thought he had drowned, but who had escaped as if by a miracle from almost certain death. After that, by the investigations of justice, many mysteries were cleared up. The passer of the Rio Atotonilco, the sacrilegious robber, the miner of Zacatecas, and also of Rayas, were one and the same person. The garrote did justice to the crimes of this wretch, and it was his hand you saw nailed to the wall in the grand square of Guanajuato. I must now tell you what became of Felipe. The providential recognition of the victim and his assassin was soon noised abroad, and a few hours afterward a band of alguazils appeared to arrest the miner who had stabbed Osorio. Unluckily, on that day Felipe had quitted his work sooner than ordinary. I do not know by what fatal mistake he had been pointed out as the murderer of Osorio; perhaps it was an additional token of good-heartedness on that caitiff's part—at any rate, the alguazils came to seize him. The victorious combatant had escaped, and I need not tell you that this mortal enemy of Osorio's was no other than the young man whom he had ill used, and who was a witness of the crime he had committed on the Rio Atotonilco. Had Felipe remained under ground, the alguazils would not have ventured into the inner workings of the mine, for the miners would not have suffered any injury to be inflicted on a comrade in their *fueros*. The alguazils perceived the young man in one of the courts of the mine buildings, and immediately set off in pursuit. Felipe saw he was lost;

but he resolved to die a miner's death, and not suffer himself to be dishonored by the touch of the bailiffs. Having arrived at the brink of this very shaft quite out of breath, 'I will not be insulted as if I were a vile lépero,' he cried; 'a miner is more than man; he is the instrument whom God delights to employ!' Then, with pale face and gleaming eyes, he leaped over the balustrade surrounding the shaft, and disappeared in the black gulf which now yawns beneath your feet."

The miner paused, and the light of his torch grew dim. High above our heads, at the mouth of the shaft, appeared the first gleam of daylight, like the pale blushes of early morning. The impression which the miner's story had made upon me was so great that I could not help trembling in every limb.

"It was very nearly ten years ago," said the miner, in a hollow voice, "since Felipe threw himself down this abyss, and I have never ascended the shaft since, and that has been often, without having a strong desire to cut the cable."

And the madman brandished a large knife, as if he were preparing to carry it really into effect. I would have called aloud for assistance, but, as in a frightful dream, my tongue refused to perform its office. My hands even refused to grasp the rope. Besides, what good would it do me? the cable was going to be cut right above my head. I threw a mournful look at the pale light which was tinging the green walls of the shaft, and listened to the indefinite noises which told me we were slowly approaching the haunts of men—the dusky daylight appeared so beautiful—the confused noises above seemed such delightful harmony. At this moment a peal of subterranean thunder burst up under my feet, and the mine roared through its many mouths like a growling volcano. The compressed air being inclosed in this enormous siphon, a powerful blast, equal to that of a strong whirlwind, shook the cable like a silk thread, and we received several severe bruises against the rocks. The torch was blown out; but, luckily, the terrible knife slipped from the miner's hands, and went whirring down the shaft.

"*Cascaras!* a new knife gone, worth two piastres," cried a voice, which I immediately recognized as that of Fuentes. I had scarcely pronounced his name ere a great shout of laughter burst forth right above me. It was Fuentes indeed, who had come down to serve me as a guide, and play the part of the old miner. The extreme eagerness I had shown to get rid of him prompted him to this kind of revenge.

"Do you know, Señor Cavalier," he remarked, "that you are not easily frightened? In a situation such as would have tried the nerves of the bravest man, you did not even condescend to shout for help."

"Certainly not," I replied, with an impudence which surpassed his own; "you see you have only made yourself ridiculous by trying to frighten me."

The malacate now stopped; we had finished our ascent. Desiderio was first unloosed, and I waited my turn in feverish anxiety. When the strap which bound me to the cable had been untied, I could scarcely keep myself from fainting outright. I soon recovered my senses, however. I pressed the earth with a kind of rapture. Never had Nature seemed so beautiful, so resplendent, as on that day.

In the interval that passed while our horses were getting ready, Fuentes, who had resumed his gaudy dress, stood silently by, and I took care not to be the first to speak. My foot was already in the stirrup when an old man came up to me. I could scarcely recognize, in the person whose dress vied in richness with that of Fuentes, the old miner whom I had seen a few hours before kneeling at the altar.

"You will pardon me for having broken my word," said he to me; "but my work detained me longer than I expected. You must have heard the explosion in the mine: it took place not half an hour ago."

"True," I replied. "I have been also told a touching and very mournful story."

"My boy behaved nobly," replied the old man, raising his head proudly; "and you can tell in your own country that the miners are a race by themselves, and that they know how to prefer death to dishonor."

I have seen the gold-seekers in the state of Sonora, and could not help admiring the kind of grandeur which characterizes their physiognomy, for every thing in the desert takes the largest proportions; but in the towns the type of the miner was far from exercising upon me a like fascination. The whimsical and capricious character of Fuentes, and the immorality of Planillas, had brought about this disenchantment. The story I had heard, while it helped to make up my mind partly about the class, proved that the miner had not quite degenerated: the vices of Planillas, and the oddities of Fuentes, like the dark shades in a picture, disappeared before the austere figure of that old stoic who had bidden me farewell with such haughty expressions, and I forgot Osorio only when I called Felipe to remembrance.

FOOTNOTES:

[36] A small town near Guanajuato, celebrated for its manufactures of zarapes, which almost rival those of Saltillo. Dolores is a market-town, still more celebrated for having been the cradle of Mexican independence.

[37] A kind of basket formed from the filaments of the aloe.

CHAPTER IV.

Rencounter with Don Tomas Verduzco.

I fancied a favorable moment had at last arrived for taking leave of Fuentes, for whom I entertained no good feeling, though a regard for myself caused me to conceal it.

"What!" said he, "are you going to town? I am going there also; and you will find it more cheerful to have a companion by the way."

We set out. Daylight was fast ebbing away, and it was doubtful if we should reach Guanajuato before nightfall. Desiderio kept up a continual flow of talk about the sayings and doings of the miners, and what an excellent profession he belonged to; but I took no interest in his conversation, and inwardly imprecated the bore whom I could not shake off. All at once he stopped, and struck his forehead with the palm of his hand.

"*Voto al demonio!*" cried he. "I have forgotten the unhappy devil for these two hours, and he may have bled to death by this time."

"Whom do you refer to?"

"Planillas, to be sure."

Almost at the same moment Fuentes went off at a gallop. I had now got a capital opportunity of ridding myself of him; but my curiosity prevailed, and I hastened after him. When we had arrived at a place not far from where we had that morning met Planillas plunged in grief, sitting on the carcass of the mule, Desiderio paused, and made a gesture of surprise.

"I don't see any body," I said.

"No more do I, and that's what astonishes me. True, he must have been tired waiting. It is very shabby of him; and another time I won't believe him. However, it is more than probable that some charitable person has removed him, for he had excellent reasons for remaining there till the sounding of the last trump."

"What has happened to him?"

"Look!" said Fuentes, pointing to the earth dyed in blood, and to the mule which the vultures were then preying upon. The miner added that, in the morning after leaving me, he had returned to ask some questions of Planillas, whose crooked morality made him an object of suspicion. Not finding either him or the mule at the place he had left them, he had followed their traces, and having arrived at the spot where we now were, found poor Florencio lying on the ground almost insensible, and bleeding profusely. He had then learned the truth from the lips of the wounded man. The mule, which

Florencio and his companion were dragging to a solitary place, had died, it is true, in the hacienda de platas; but Florencio had never seen the animal till that day, and the cause of his tender solicitude was, that its flanks contained a number of silver ingots which Planillas had stolen and hidden there, so that the clerk of the mines might not discover them. The stratagem had been successful; but when they came to divide the spoil, after having drawn it to a still more solitary spot, a quarrel arose, and the result was, that Planillas got nothing but a couple of stabs from the ready knife of his neighbor, which had placed his life in great danger.

"You can guess the rest," continued Fuentes. "I could not help being sorry for the fellow, and went away, promising to send him assistance. I can't tell how it is, but I completely forgot the poor devil."

Fuentes was right in not boasting of his second impulse. As for this reckless indifference to human life, I had seen too many similar instances in Mexico to be at all astonished at it. I rode sadly back to Guanajuato, still in the company of Fuentes, who did not fail to stop me at the little pent-house in which the hand of the sacrilegious robber was exposed. This memorial of a barbarous justice reminded me that I had observed some imperfections in the miner's story.

"If I understood you aright," I said, "of the three persons, actors and witness, who were present at the duel between Osorio and the young miner, two are dead, and the third escaped. How comes it, then, that you can speak so positively about actions of which no person could have informed you?"

"Very simply," replied Fuentes. "I had forgotten to tell you that it was I who killed Osorio; it was I who witnessed the deed on the Rio Atotonilco. Don't think, however, that I am an utterly heartless bravo like that Don Tomas, surnamed *Verdugo*.[38] I have given, it is true, more than one stroke in my time; but in Mexico one must see a little justice done to one's self. Were you not yourself on the very point of killing a man this morning? And don't you think that a similar case might perchance happen to me?"

I shuddered at this rude speech, which reminded me of the danger I ran by remaining any longer in Guanajuato. The man whose life I had threatened that day was, I had no doubt, the murderer of Don Jaime. It may be easily imagined that I felt some degree of satisfaction in finding myself safe at the door of my hotel.

"Ah! you live here?" said Fuentes, grasping my hand; "I am very glad I know; I shall call on you to-morrow, and we shall have a pleasant day together."

"Well, to-morrow," I said. We parted, and I entered the inn.

My valet Cecilio waited on me with as much impatience as curiosity in his countenance. He had been long obliged to make himself acquainted with all the particulars of my life, but seldom had he been necessitated to follow me into such a maze of disagreeable incidents. I interrupted his questions by ordering him to have our horses saddled at midnight, as I wished to avoid both Fuentes and the treacherous designs of Don Tomas.

"After this," said I, "we shall travel only at night; it is better for the health."

By traveling at night and sleeping during the day, I reasonably hoped to baffle all pursuit. However, grown bolder by success, I returned to my ordinary habits; and when I came to the venta of Arroyo Zarco, it was midday before I arrived, after having passed the night at San Juan del Bio, and journeying almost the whole day. In this last stage of my excursion many sorrowful remembrances crowded into my mind. The plain, the venta, alike reminded me of Don Jaime. It was while musing sadly on this young man, so prematurely cut off, that I found myself, almost without knowing it, at the very spot where he had lighted his fire. Of so many dreams of love and fortune, what was left behind? A corpse three hundred miles away, a few burned sticks, and some ashes which the winds of the plain were scattering about! The supper-hour approaching, I went to pass away an idle hour, if not at the common table, at least in a room where all the travelers, and they were numerous on that day, were generally accustomed to take their meals. The company consisted, as it had done before, of a curious mixture of all classes of Mexican society, but I had no end in view as I had then, and accordingly seated myself in a corner after looking around me with a careless eye. I thought for some time on the cruel isolation to which foreigners are subjected in those countries inhabited by people of Spanish extraction, when the hostess pronounced, almost at my ear, the name of a person that made me start.

"Señor Don Tomas," cried the hostess, "here is a foreigner who was inquiring after you a fortnight ago, and whom I was telling you about just now."

I jumped up. In the man whom the hostess had addressed, and which a secret feeling in my own mind convinced me was the person, I recognized the sinister companion of Planillas. A cold shudder ran through my whole frame. I looked at the by-standers, but I could see on their countenances only that expression of apathetic indifference which makes a comedy or a tragedy a matter of mere moonshine to them. Almost immediately, and before I was able to prevent it, I was strained between two strong muscular arms. I disengaged myself without any ceremony, but he affected not to perceive the repugnance with which he had inspired me.

"Ah!" cried he, with an impudence seldom to be met with, "how happy am I at meeting here a cavalier who has won my entire regard! What! were you inquiring after me? In what can I serve you?"

"It was all a misconception on my part, I can assure you; but, if you have not forgotten your visit to the *Secunda Monterilla*,[39] you may perhaps recall to your memory your object in coming there."

"Do *you* live there? You can then boast that you have come more than two leagues in search of me."

"I have gone two hundred and forty to meet you," I answered, "and find you here at last."

The bravo replied by the same constrained smile I had seen his face wear the first time I met him. "I was seeking for a foreigner with whom I had been engaged to do a little business, and an error that I now recognize alone conducted me to you; but I know you now, Señor Cavalier, and will not commit the same blunder a second time. I only need to see a person once to remember him ever after. I never forget faces, even at the end of twenty years."

These last words were accented in such a way as to leave me in no doubt of the ruffian's meaning. I said not a word, but the bravo seemed to have repented of having shown any resentment. Turning to the hostess, and in a tone of rough gayety,

"Halloo, *Patrona*!" cried he; "you have doubtless supplied this cavalier, whom I hold in particular esteem, with the best fare your house affords?"

"I have supped," I said, interrupting him, "and I must only express my perfect satisfaction with our hostess's arrangements; besides, I am not hungry."

"Well, we shall drink to our unexpected meeting. Patrona, bring us a bottle of Catalonian brandy."

I was quite at a loss how to decline this forced invitation that prudence was urging me to accept, when Captain Don Blas P——, or rather lieutenant, for he held the former title only by courtesy, rose from the table, and advanced to welcome me.

"You are one of us, captain, I hope?" said the bravo.

The captain accepted his offer; but, emboldened by his presence, I formally refused.

"I am much jaded and tired," I said, "and would rather go to my room. Captain Don Blas, if your road lies the same way as mine, I should be happy to profit by your company, and to-morrow at break of day we might pursue our journey to Mexico together."

Don Blas excused himself at not being able to agree to my proposal by stating that certain very important business would detain him all next day in the neighborhood. He then sat down opposite Don Tomas, before whom the hostess had already placed the bottle of Catalonian brandy.

"Good-night, then, señores," I exclaimed. "I hope your slumbers will be as refreshing as mine."

I settled my bill, and, disguising my precipitate retreat under an air of haughty defiance, quitted the room with measured steps, the bravo all the while regarding my motions with indirect glances. I reached my room, fearing more the oily silkiness of Don Tomas than his anger. I found Cecilio sleeping on our saddles.

"Listen!" I said, awakening him. "Saddle our horses immediately without any noise; then bring them round to the back of the venta, and wait for me there. In a quarter of an hour I shall be with you."

That time had hardly elapsed when I quitted the hostelry without being observed. My flight at this time formed a striking contrast to that which I had shared so cheerfully with Don Jaime. I need not say that we covered the distance between Arroyo Zarco and Mexico still more rapidly than on our departure: the parts only were changed. The man before whom I was flying was that very person I had been pursuing so long. Thank heaven, the issue of this adventure was not tragical, as I feared at one time it would have become.

FOOTNOTES:

[38] Lit., poniard.

[39] The street in Mexico where I lived.

CAPTAIN DON BLAS AND THE SILVER CONVOY.

CHAPTER I.

Threatened Insurrection in Mexico.—Stealthy Movements of Troops.—General Don Antonio Lopez de Santa Anna.

The day was approaching on which I was to leave Mexico for Vera Cruz, to embark for Europe. For several years before this a Yankee company had established a line of diligences which ran between several of the largest towns; wagons, also, for the conveyance of heavy goods, competed with the picturesque caravans of the *arrieros* on all the principal roads. Ought I to give up my habit of solitary traveling for no other reason than the quickness of transit between Mexico and Vera Cruz? I must then renounce the hospitality of the venta, so pleasant after a long ride—the siesta under the shade of a tree—the friendly connection of horse and rider, and all the enlivening contingencies of solitary travel. I must confess that I could not look upon this innovation, due to the foreigner who had brought Vera Cruz within four days' journey of Mexico, without some degree of abhorrence. I felt that, under the influence of more rapid communication, the ancient appearance of Mexico was beginning to alter. I groaned and chafed like an antiquarian who sees rude hands defacing some rare and ancient medal. The establishment of this new kind of conveyance in Mexico had been attended with annoyances of a most dangerous character. Well-organized bands of robbers turned the innovation to account, and not a diligence passed without being pillaged. The remembrances of my ancient relations with the Mexican *salteadores*, ordinarily so courteous to every traveler unencumbered with baggage, rendered the prospect of a similar humiliation very disagreeable. The pillaging part of the business was not a thing at all to my mind; besides, the idea of passing several days in a close carriage, drawn by four swift steeds, and bounding over a Mexican road rutted by heavy rains, and covered with large pieces of rock, was a mode of traveling not at all in accordance with my habits and tastes.

A mere accident caused me to decide what course to follow. Several merchants in Mexico, profiting by one of those political lulls so rare in the republic, were about to send a rich convoy of silver (*conducta de platas*) to Vera Cruz. Some muleteers were loading their mules with sacks of piastres, inclosed in little wooden boxes, in the great court of one of the houses in the street of Monterilla, where I lived. The sight of these preparations had drawn a great crowd of spectators around the gate, myself among the rest. When the mules had received their precious burden, they all instinctively huddled together in a corner of the court. A score of *mozos de mulas* (stable-helpers) kept up a running fire of oaths while at their work. Under the archway of the court the *arriero*[40] brought matters to a close by signing the bills of lading, and invoking the Virgin and all the saints to give him a safe and successful trip, every now and then stopping to scold the helpers. In the street, the multitude speculated on the possibility of such a rich lading surviving the perils of a long and dangerous road, while the greatest part of the spectators in tatters did not take the least pains to conceal their real sentiments.

"*Canario!*" said a lépero, covering a breast seamed with scars with a cloak almost torn to ribbons, "if I had only a beast like the one that cavalier has between his legs!"

And he eyed a horse, black as jet, which a *ranchero* was riding. The animal, tightly reined in by his rider, champed his bit furiously, and threw the foam to the right and left. I could not help admiring the beauty of the horse, and remarking at the same time the firm but easy seat of the cavalier, who seemed to manage his steed only by his own will, a quality possessed in the highest degree by the gentlemen of Mexico.

"Well! what would you do if you had, Gregorito?" asked one of his companions.

"Canario! I would accompany the conducta to a spot on the road I know well; and though, as you are well aware, I am no braggart, I should count myself very unlucky if one or two such loads did not fall to my share."

"One or two loads, Gregorito!" said the other, in a tone of surprise.

"Yes, three loads at most. You know I never had very much ambition, but the horseman there seems to have even less than I."

The ranchero, in appearance at least, looked on the whole convoy with disdain, but what was passing through his mind it was impossible to tell from his face.

Meanwhile a squadron of lancers, designed to serve as an escort, had great difficulty in keeping the crowd out of the court, among whom Gregorito was one of the most modest in the expression of his desires. The fluttering rags of the léperos, and the waving pennons at the points of their lances, formed a curious contrast. The loading was at length completed, the last mule left the court, and the detachment formed up to accompany the convoy. The crowd gradually melted away, and at last only the ranchero remained, who appeared to be counting the mules with care, besides eyeing attentively every individual *mozo*. At last the ranchero began to put his horse in motion. At this moment the lépero Gregorito approached him, and begged him to allow him to light his cigarette at his. A long and animated conversation, in a low tone, took place between the two men, but I paid little heed to an incident which appeared to me so insignificant. I left the place, and went home.

The sight of the convoy awakened in me a desire which I was not long in putting into execution. The departure of the convoy, whose escort I could easily join, would furnish me with the only opportunity I should ever have, not only of escaping the ennui of a diligence, but also of satiating my curiosity by exploring, in perfect security and by short stages, the long route between Mexico and Vera Cruz. The loaded mules would travel but slowly, and I could easily rejoin them, even though they were at several leagues distance from Mexico—thanks to the proved swiftness of my horse—so as to allow me a couple of days even to bid farewell to my friends. I began in all haste to make the necessary preparations for departure. My first object was to procure a horse for my servant. He had been so ill mounted during our long journey while searching for, and flying from, the bravo, that his horse had broken down entirely after we re-entered Mexico, and I had ordered him to replace it by another. As for my own steed, one of those I had brought with me from the hacienda of Noria, he nobly justified the name of *Storm* which I had given him; the strength and vigor which his free life in the desert had produced rendered him fit to endure the hardest fatigues.

Cecilio went about the business immediately. I told him that economy was to be considered in the purchase, but the fellow did not conform too scrupulously to my instructions. A few hours afterward he came to tell me that a *picador*, one of his friends, had a horse to dispose of which seemed to come up to my standard. In a few minutes, a sorry hack, of a dun color, with hanging head and tottering legs, that apparently had escaped from the bull-ring, came slowly into the court. I almost screamed when the picador, with matchless effrontery, asked ten piastres for the miserable brute; but, considering that the only time on which we needed to travel rapidly would be in joining the convoy, and that afterward short stages would be the rule, I consented to the purchase. The picador and Cecilio, seeing my impatience, began to expatiate on the noble qualities that lay hidden beneath the miserable skin of the wretched beast, and I paid the knave the sum he demanded, knowing well that my honest valet would partake in the plunder with the picador.

All my preparations being made, I determined to set out next morning; but a series of unforeseen events retarded my departure for several days. The time for sending this rich convoy of silver to Vera Cruz appeared to have been ill chosen. A dull, vague feeling of uneasiness weighed on all men's minds. The most alarming symptoms of an imminent political storm were apparent. Even on the very day after the convoy had left Mexico, it was universally regretted that a lading so valuable had been exposed to the dangers of a long road at this conjuncture, and several circumstances, it must be owned, justified these fears.

General Don Anastasio Bustamente—after losing in Europe, in learned retirement, the remembrance of his country's misfortunes—had returned, and assumed the presidency of the republic. If disinterestedness and probity, joined to ardent patriotism, were sufficient to govern a great state, Bustamente was the man for Mexico. Like almost all the generals who have attained to power in Mexico, it was in the war of independence that he showed what he was capable of performing. A devoted friend and partisan of the Emperor Iturbide, he had taxed Santa Anna with the blackest ingratitude in commencing his military career by revolting against the one who had raised him from obscurity. This was the commencement of that personal enmity which still subsists between the two generals. During the time I was at Mexico, Santa Anna could not be prevailed on to forgive Bustamente for having forestalled him in the presidency. For three years Bustamente had been subjected to many trials. Two years had scarcely elapsed since the taking of Vera Cruz by the French, and already the emptiness of the public treasury had compelled Congress to impose an additional duty of fifteen per cent. upon imports. Commerce languished by this measure. The decision of Congress only augmented its sufferings. A general bad feeling began to gain ground in the state, which, to all accustomed to the march of political events in Mexico, seemed likely to be employed to the disadvantage of the existing government. Events were not long in confirming the justice of these forebodings.

The reader may not, perhaps, have forgotten a certain lieutenant Don Blas, whom I had met at the venta of Arroyo Zarco, and had left seated at table with the bravo, Don Tomas Verduzco. The slight degree of acquaintanceship which I had with this officer never occurred to my mind without recalling to memory the mysterious relations which seemed to exist between him and a man who I had every reason to believe was my mortal enemy. Since my last meeting with Don Tomas I had been under a continual apprehension, but too well justified by the known antecedents of this ruffian.

I had, I believed, taken every precaution against an attack which would, according to all appearance, be made in the dark. Besides, I had conformed to the rules of the strictest prudence by restricting myself only to short walks from my place of abode. The porter of my house was an old soldier of the wars of independence, a brave and honorable man, who never showed more vigilance than when he was intoxicated. The result was, that the house could not have been better guarded. I was, it is true, the first victim of this excess of precaution on his part, for it was not without the greatest difficulty that, on one occasion, I prevailed upon him to unlock the iron chain that held together the two leaves of the entrance gate.

The Angelus was still sounding from all the churches in Mexico when, returning from a gallop on the Paseo, I rode through the streets, as I fancied, for the last time. Night was coming on when I gained my lodging, and it was not without a longer parley than ordinary with the old porter that I succeeded in gaining admittance. Leaning against the wall to steady himself and keep up appearances, the brave man, with a bayonet in his hand, contented himself by jerking his thumb over his shoulder in the direction of a soldier, who, seated on one of the stone benches of the vestibule, rose up eagerly at my approach. A peakless shako, too small for the head it covered, tottered on the top of a dense thatch of thick yellow hair. A uniform coat of thick cloth, and a pair of trowsers as large as the shako was small; shoes, whose upper leather had long parted company from the sole, not only allowing the toes to be seen, but also ventilating on the most approved principles the wearer's feet, and a complexion of a bright copper color, all served to stamp the man as a lépero who had been torn away, by the exigencies of the service, from following his profession of sleeping in the sun on the pavement. However, a sort of picaresque and arrogant bearing about the fellow showed that he was not insensible to his profession, and to the splendor of his military dress. The soldier, who was the *asistente* of Don Blas, had been sent by him with a letter to me. I recognized, in fact, his handwriting. The note ran thus:

> "MY DEAR FRIEND,—I have just read with much emotion, in a French novel that you lately lent me, a story of two friends, who, when in need, aided one another with their purse and their sword. As I require some money at present, I should be obliged by your sending with the bearer, in whom I have every confidence, an ounce of gold, which I shall restore to you on the first opportunity. I can tell you that this will be a service with which the country will be as well pleased as your devoted friend and servant,
>
> "Q. S. M. B.,[41]
>
> > "BLAS P——.
>
> "P.S.—On reflection, if you will bring the ounce of gold yourself, it will be better; and, to imitate the devotion of those friends whose story has made such an impression upon me, I offer you my sword."

I thought, as the lieutenant did, that the ounce of gold would have a greater chance of coming into his hands if I carried it myself.

"Where is your officer?" I inquired of the soldier.

"At the Guadaloupe gate."

"It is a pity," I said, "that the oracion has sounded, as we can not now ride thither."

"If it is the intention of your lordship to accompany me, as my captain said you might," the messenger replied, "he recommended you to go on foot."

In spite of the great honor that would accrue to me by rendering this service to the Mexican nation, I could not hide from myself that I would have the worst of it in this chivalrous exchange of purse and sword. However, the desire of knowing from the mouth of Don Blas how much I ought to fear the resentment of the bravo with whom chance had brought me acquainted, determined me not to allow this opportunity to escape. I took time only to throw a cloak over my shoulders, and hide my pistols under my coat. I then set out, followed by the soldier. Still, I took care, while passing through the town—which became more and more solitary as we approached the suburbs—to walk in the middle of the road, as well to see all who were approaching, as to avoid the angles in the wall that might shelter ambuscades. I arrived without accident at the Guadaloupe gate, sometimes smiling at my terrors, sometimes shuddering at some sudden noise. The night was very dark, and the July rains were already announced by a thick fog, the moisture of which rendered the pavement slippery.

"Shall we soon be there?" I asked of the soldier, when we came to the gate.

"Immediately," he replied.

A drizzling rain succeeded the fog. We soon arrived at a road which ran between the lakes, without the soldier showing any signs of having reached the end of his journey. A thick mist, which hovered over the water, hid the two snowy peaks of the volcanoes which cap the Cordilleras. At last I perceived at some distance the lighted windows of a small house, and very soon a confused sound of voices reached my ear. Arrived at the house, the soldier tapped with his bayonet, and the door opened. He entered first without any ceremony, and motioned me to follow him. Under any other circumstances, I should have seen nothing very extraordinary in this invitation; but my ideas having been running on ambuscades for the last month, I hesitated about penetrating into such a cut-throat looking place. A voice that I knew put an end to my hesitation: it was that of the Lieutenant Don Blas, who was conversing with his *asistente* about the result of his mission. All my fears then vanished, and I entered. At the same time Don Blas sprang to meet me, and pressed me in his arms with all a Mexican's warmth. After the first compliments had passed, he led me through a room (crowded with men of all grades), a kind of vestibule, into a spacious hall, where some individuals of a higher rank sat round half a dozen tables, drinking and gambling. They all appeared to be military men, judging at least from their mustaches, and Don Blas himself bore no other insignia of his rank than a round jacket, decorated with a sort of epaulet on each shoulder, denoting only the brevet captain. We sat down at a table by ourselves. The men looked at me in a way that was not altogether pleasant or comfortable.

"He is a friend," Don Blas said, hastily; "he won't betray us."

I had the best of reasons for being discreet on such an occasion, and made no remark upon the words of the lieutenant. We were served with an infusion of tamarind with a strong dash of brandy in it; I then asked him, "How comes it that you did not, in person, ask for the favor you expected from me? You would have saved me a long walk, and a return home alone in the dark."

"I am going to reply to your question," said the lieutenant, stretching out his hand for the ounce of gold, and putting it into his pocket. "The reason why I have given you so much trouble is that I am kept here as a kind of pledge for the money I owe; as for you, you will return home at daybreak in the company of your very devoted servant."

"Does that mean that I am to be kept here as a kind of pledge also?"

"Not at all; but certain affairs will happen, two hours hence, which will prevent you from returning. At present I can tell you nothing farther."

Such a disclosure as this opened a wide field for conjecture; but I wished, at the moment, to obtain some information regarding an affair which touched me more nearly.

"You were good enough," said I to the lieutenant, "to place yourself at my disposal in exchange for the small favor that I was able to render you, and doubtless you will be happy to learn that a very important conjuncture makes it necessary for me to ask the assistance of your valorous sword."

A cloud came over the hitherto smiling face of Don Blas, and I fancied that the lieutenant never thought that he was so soon to be taken at his word. However, he promptly recovered himself, and cried, "Play is an unfortunate thing! Caramba! my sword is in pledge with the rest of my accoutrements; but what have you done to need the loan of mine?"

"It is your strong right arm, and not your sword, that I require," I replied, smiling at the evasive subterfuge of the lieutenant. "The sword of the Cid would be useless in my hands against an enemy so formidable as—"

"Speak lower," said Don Blas, interrupting me and twirling his mustache; "my rash bravery is well known here. All are aware that danger electrifies me, and it might be feared that I had lent for another motive the weight of that arm which belongs to my country alone."

The hectoring air of the officer made no impression upon me; but I had no wish to turn what was intended only for a joke into something more serious. I desired only to know if the bravo had made me the subject of conversation after my departure from the room on that night I happened to be at Arroyo Zarco, and it eased me not a little to hear that he had asked not a single question about me.

At this moment the gallop of a horse rang on the stone causeway, and almost at the same moment a young lad, about fifteen years of age, bounced into the room. By his military cap—a kind of beret, ornamented with a profusion of gold lace, as well as his uniform—I immediately discovered that he was a *cadete* (cadet).

"Every thing goes on swimmingly, gentlemen," cried he; "the colonel is coming to receive his general's commission. This evening his division reached Cordova. Valencia is advancing. In three days we shall be masters of Mexico, and then I shall be *alferez*!"

All in the room sprang to their feet; and I asked the lieutenant, by a motion of my eye, what I should do.

"Do you still wish to leave?"

It was evident that I was witnessing the first act of some new revolution which was about to take place, and that I was a spectator of some of those little scenes which serve as the prelude to some grand event.

Among the numerous causes which have tended to exhaust the public exchequer in Mexico, and contributed to isolate the country from European progress, the most deplorable and the most striking are, without contradiction, those which prevail in the military executive. In a country whose geographical position effectually preserves it from all rivalry with neighboring nations, the army was, it may be said, disbanded at the declaration of independence, but in a short time afterward it sprang again into existence. Unhappily, the heads of the new republic only looked to that power as an instrument for executing its own ambitious designs. Since then, a warlike mania has seized a people that had been pacifically disposed for three hundred years, and gradually the army had become accustomed to decide upon and settle all political questions. The result of this warlike transformation is well known. To-day the pettiest Mexican officer fancies himself called on, not by a political conviction, but only by his own ambition, to protect or to overturn the established government. It would seem, as one might say, that an article of the Constitution gives to every one the right of becoming a colonel.

Accustomed since infancy to trample under foot all civil institutions, the cadet, transformed into an officer almost before the age of reason, and the soldier of fortune, to whom a long series of *pronunciamentos*, in which he has taken part, has given a commission, have both in view the same design, a rapid promotion by the same way, that of insurrection. Liable to be broken at every instant by a sudden change in the government, the officers have no hope of obtaining a higher grade but by their swords. Then, according to the fortunes of civil war, the officer who has fought his way to a higher rank, or who has seen the banner under which he fought leveled with the dust, has no more chance of getting his pay from the new government than he had from the old. He thus constitutes himself a creditor of the state till some stray bullet closes his account forever, or till the time when he can dip his fingers into the public purse, and become a permanent debtor of those who have outstripped him in his career. However, although the vicissitudes to which the country has been subjected are numberless, it is the exception, and not the rule, if the officer arrive at the head of affairs; his life, in such a case, becomes only a continual series of annoyances. Then, a revolutionist by ambition—a gambler by nature—a contrabandist on occasion—a knave by necessity—a *remendon de voluntades*[42] when in want, the officer practices every trade, deals in all sorts of merchandise, and becomes at last more an object of pity than blame; for he knows nothing of business, and his country never has paid him for any service he has rendered her, not even though he may have shed his best blood in her behalf.

The news of an approaching insurrection was doubtless soon communicated to the men in the other room, for a deafening din drowned the general hurrah, in which cries of Santa Anna forever! Death to Bustamente! Down with Congress, and fifteen per cent.! and others, of a like import, were shouted, and which will always find an echo in the hearts of people still too young to know what true liberty is. When silence had been re-established, I questioned my friend the lieutenant about the political movement; but in a hurried tone, "Tut!" he replied; "here you must seem to know nothing. I shall make you acquainted with every thing afterward. For the moment, I have nothing more pressing than to pay my score and go away. You must know that the country is as much your debtor as if the debt had been committed to writing, for its safety is concerned in the liberty of my person."

"About two such debtors I need have no fear," I said, gravely; "but how comes it that a mere civilian has dared to place an embargo on a military man?"

"Alas!" replied Don Blas, in a melancholy tone, "one must borrow wherever one can. The misfortune is, that this inn is kept by an officer, and I only learned that when, enchanted with the credit I received here, I had used the place as if the owner had been a civilian."

That the inn was kept by an officer was not at all astonishing to one, like me, well acquainted with Mexican manners, but that an officer had ventured to give credit to a comrade appeared a piece of the most inexplicable rashness.

"Halloo! Juanito," cried the lieutenant to his asistente. The man soon made his appearance in a costume still more picturesque than the one I had seen him wear an hour before. His peakless shako still trembled on the top of his frightful mop of hair, but he had donned the horseman's jacket instead of the foot-soldier's coat; and it being too short for him, a large portion of his copper skin was exposed to view above the waistband of his trowsers. The fellow was evidently in a bad humor.

"What's the matter, *muchacho*?" asked Don Blas.

"The deuce!" cried Juanito, sharply; "you called me away at the very moment I was going to receive a dragoon's helmet for my shako; and who do you think would be pleased with that?"

"Request the huesped to come here," said Don Blas, affecting not to perceive the rough reply of the soldier.

Juanito wheeled half round, and went out without saying a word.

"That is a man devoted to my interests, and I overlook the liberties he takes in consideration of his devotion," remarked the lieutenant, by way of apology; "devotedness is such a rare thing in this world."

The host was not long in appearing, and I immediately explained to him the position in which the lieutenant stood. The huesped was a man of Herculean proportions, with broad shoulders and a florid complexion. He sported a formidable pair of mustaches curled up at the ends. In a word, he had quite the appearance of a *valento* (bully) of the first class.

"How much do I owe you?" inquired Don Blas; "for it is always a pleasure to me to pay my debts."

"The fact is, if the rarity of the pleasure doubles the value of it, the payment of a debt ought to be a perfect treat to you," replied the host: "you owe me fifteen piastres and a half."

"Fifteen piastres and a half!" cried the lieutenant, jumping up hurriedly; "demonio!"

And, handing the colonel the ounce of gold that he had newly received from me, he received in return change to the amount of four reals.

"Caramba! colonel, you will give me a real more, I hope," said the debtor, in a suppliant tone.

The host turned a deaf ear to this demand, and taking from a press the sword and helmet of the lieutenant, he gave them to him, saying, "Take notice that I charge you nothing for the trouble I have been at in retaining these articles in pledge for two days."

The debt of Don Blas having been thus satisfactorily arranged, he proposed a walk with me upon the road. I unhesitatingly attributed this proposition to the desire of making use of the liberty he had now acquired, but I was soon undeceived. The lieutenant exchanged some words in a low tone with the other officers in the hall, and went out, promising to let them know every thing he saw or heard. I hastened to follow him; for, in spite of the curiosity that possessed me, I could not hide from myself the fact that the place for a foreigner was not in the centre of a band of conspirators, whatever their private opinions on other points might be.

The rain had ceased. A thick mist still covered the surface of both lakes, but their still waters already reflected in their bosom a sky less sombre than before. The volcano of Popocatapetl was still shrouded in mist, while the snow of the neighboring mountain sparkled in the gentle light of the moon. By her uncertain light the *White Woman* (Iztaczihuatl) looked more like one of the pale Scandinavian divinities under a northern sky than an American nymph reclining under that of the tropics. The lights of the town went out one after the other, and a deep silence reigned around. A confused noise, however, like the wind agitating the reeds in the lake, at times came stealing upon our ears.

"Come on," said Don Blas to me; "it is close upon the hour, and I am astonished that I have seen nothing yet."

"What are you waiting for?" I asked.

"You will soon see; come on."

After walking for about a quarter of an hour, the indistinct noise which broke the stillness of the night soon resolved itself into the tramp of a body of horse. The sounds were deadened by the damp air, and the soft, moist earth on which they moved. It was doubtless a troop of cavalry on march. A dark mass was not long, in fact, in advancing.

"Who goes there?" cried one of the leaders.

"Friends!" replied Don Blas.

"*Que gente?*" asked the same voice.

"*Mexico!*" was the lieutenant's reply. He demanded, in his turn, where the division had come from.

"From Cordova," answered the same voice.

The troop passed, and we remained in the same place. A little after, a second troop, and then a third, came in sight, and made the same replies, and afterward continued their march to Mexico. I saw nothing, however, in these men but ordinary travelers, for there was little in their bearing that betokened them as regular troops, when some distant lights sparkled in the midst of the fog, and I fancied I heard repeated *vivas*; this was another band advancing. In the centre, and clearly seen by the light of the torches, rode two officers on fiery horses, in the costume of country gentlemen—half military, half civilian. The superior officer had a physiognomy and mien which struck me forcibly, and awoke in my mind a feeling of curiosity and vague remembrance. He was a man apparently about forty-five years of age, of a lofty and commanding aspect, and swarthy complexion. A high forehead, which his hat but imperfectly concealed, and a rounded chin, perhaps too large for the perfect regularity of his features, denoted obstinacy and resolution; a nose slightly aquiline, great black eyes full of expression, and flexible lips, stamped him with an air of haughty nobility; his strong black curly hair flowed over his temples, and shaded his high cheek-bones. I remarked, also, that his bridle hand was mutilated.

Don Blas made a gesture of surprise, and, scarcely giving himself time to reply to the countersign which was asked of him, bounded toward the officer on horseback.

"Your excellency ought not to forget that we are within a short distance of Mexico," said he, uncovering respectfully, "and prudence requires that you come no nearer."

"Ah! is it you, Captain Don Blas?" said the cavalier, stopping his horse; "I am very glad to see you among us." Then, addressing himself to his cortège, "You know well, señores," said he, "that the pleasure I feel in finding myself once more among you has caused me to forget my own safety; but the time is not far distant, I hope, when I shall come again, and find there," pointing to Mexico, "none but brothers and friends."

After this speech he wheeled his horse half round, and I could see that it was a wooden leg which rested in the right stirrup. A general hurrah followed his last words. The torches were hurled far into the lake, and went out with a hiss, and all again was dark, but not before I had recognized in the cavalier who was conversing with Don Blas the man who for twenty-five years had been the evil genius of Mexico, the cause and fomenter of all its revolutions—in one word, General Don Antonio Lopez Santa Anna.

FOOTNOTES:

[40] A kind of farmer.

[41] *Que sus manos besa.*—Lit., he who kisses your hands.

[42] Lit., Humorer of caprices.

CHAPTER II.

The Colonel Inn-keeper.—Sharp Fighting in the Streets of Mexico.— General Bustamente, President of the Republic.

The lieutenant and I remained alone. I asked him to give me some explanation regarding the scenes of which I had been a witness. He very eagerly gave me some account of the discontent that prevailed among all classes, caused by the import duty of fifteen per cent. It was, in fact, the bad feeling which arose from this that had furnished the pretext for the new *pronunciamento*. The numerous pedestrians we had met on the way to Mexico were part of a regiment of cavalry in garrison near the city. Don Blas had been urged to entice them into the service of Santa Anna, with the promise, if successful, of getting a commission as captain of cavalry. I then comprehended how the *asistente* of Don Blas had shown so much eagerness in procuring a cavalry uniform. Advantage had been taken by the partisans of Santa Anna of introducing the regiment which had been gained over into the town in a civil dress, a thing of very easy execution, as the difference between the civil and military costume in Mexico is very small.

On returning to the inn, the lieutenant recounted all that had passed to the officers assembled, who had taken the initiative with their soldiers. They then adjourned, as the project for which they had been waiting had been realized, and the officers rose to make their way, one by one, into the town. Don Blas and I, like the rest, set out on foot for the same place. The soldiers passed in small scattered bands through different gates.

On the way, I pointed out to the future captain the fears that I entertained about the fate of the convoy of silver, exposed, as it were, to the attack of the insurgents.

"May I ask if you have any interest in that?" said he, sharply.

"None at all; but the pillage of the convoy would entail considerable loss on some of my countrymen."

"There's no fear of that; a powerful but hidden protection is extended over the convoy. An extraordinary courier, that left town this morning, has seen it put into a place of safety. The chief muleteer will wait for the conclusion of events; and the escort has been intrusted to the command of a brave and faithful man. Why, I take as lively an interest in it as yourself."

"And for what reason?" I asked, astonished.

"Because we do not wish a crime to sully the glory of this coming revolution. And, besides, I am to be the commander of the escort of the *conducta*."

I could hardly explain the heat with which the lieutenant spoke of a piece of business that seemed to offer no apparent advantage to him. But, without asking any more questions, I contented myself by telling him of the project that I had entertained of joining the conducta. Don Blas received this news at first very coldly; then, seeing me determined in my resolution, he pretended that it would be no bad thing to have me for a companion on the road. Unfortunately, it was impossible yet to fix a day for our departure; and many dangers, although Don Blas perhaps exaggerated them, menaced the precious convoy.

Twenty-four hours after our arrival in the town, it was rumored that Generals Santa Anna and Valencia were advancing at the head of two divisions, to obtain redress of those grievances which they affirmed they had suffered under Bustamente's government. Events now succeeded each other with startling rapidity. A few skirmishes, and those not of an unimportant nature, had already taken place between the government troops and the factious, who had advanced to invest the *Plaza Mayor*, and had raised a barricade at the corner of the streets San Augustin and Secunda Monterilla. It was learned afterward, to the general consternation, that the garrison in the palace, corrupted by the rebels, had seized the person of the president even in the palace itself. While this conflict was raging I heard nothing of Don Blas, but on the morning of the day that followed these events, some blows, violently struck on the lodge gate of my house, awoke me with a start. A few minutes after, the lieutenant entered my chamber in a pretty plight. A long beard, disordered hair, and a face begrimed with the smoke of gunpowder, proved, or at least seemed to prove, that he had taken an active part in the engagements of yesterday. I congratulated him on his warlike appearance. Don Blas received my praises with the air of a man who knows his own merit, and informed me, with a certain air of importance, that he had come to occupy the terrace of my house with a body of his men, as it commanded the palace square.

"I have chosen your house without even asking your permission," said he to me, "because it is in the neighborhood of the presidential palace, and also to show you how a captain's rank is gained. I hope that you will follow me to the terrace, where my company is already stationed."

"I shall assist at your triumph with much pleasure," I said; "and, if you will allow me to dress, I shall be very happy to take my place near you; only I must keep out of the way of the balls, as I have not the least honor to gain. But you are still in the infantry, I see."

"I have very good reasons for making no change as yet," replied the lieutenant, with some slight hesitation. "In a hubbub like this, a horseman is too much exposed—he is quite useless, I mean; and, besides, how the devil have I the means of purchasing a horse?"

At this moment the door opened, and the helmet of a dragoon was shoved in at the aperture. This helmet covered the head of the asistente Juanito, who, more lucky than his master, had found means, thanks to *monte*, of half transforming himself into a horseman; for all that remained of his former costume was his enormous trowsers, in which he seemed every moment ready to be ingulfed.

"Captain," cried the asistente, "if you don't come immediately and put yourself at the head of your men, some misfortune may happen."

"What!" said Don Blas, "are my fellows so impatient to come to blows?"

"Oh no," replied Juanito, "they are in no hurry for that—rather the contrary; but upon the terrace of the Ayuntamiento, opposite the house of this French señor, stands that great rascal of a colonel you know—the master of the inn who kept your lordship in pledge. He proposes to buy our cartridges of us."

"And my braves have scouted the idea with indignation, I am sure?"

"They did; but that was because he only offered them half price."

"Has this d—d colonel, then, betrayed us?" cried the lieutenant.

"That may be, Señor Captain. I am not in the habit of meddling in other people's affairs. The colonel has perhaps changed his side for very good reasons: who knows?"

The officer started after the impassible Juanito, and I dressed myself in all haste. I was curious to see how, according to the expression of Don Blas, one attained the rank of captain. When I was almost on the last step of the flight of stairs that led to the terrace, I heard the word "Fire" given in a very loud voice. I stopped. To my great astonishment, perfect quiet reigned on the roof. A second command was no better obeyed; and it was not till after a third that a report followed, but so feeble as to show that the cartridges, though only valued at half price, still possessed such a value in their eyes as to prevent them from being prodigally expended.

I opened the door of the terrace with all imaginable prudence, and stole along, protected by a wall which ran round the azotea, and got behind one of the pilasters, which rose turret-like at regular intervals.[43] I had a telescope in my hand.

"What are you going to do with that glass?" inquired Don Bias.

"Why, I never go to the theatre without my glass—not even to a bull-fight. Should I have forgotten it when I am come to secure the best place for seeing the gigantic efforts of the combatants on both sides."

The future captain seemed to look with an eye of envy upon the place in which I found myself in such perfect security. I could clearly discern from my terrace even the quadrangle of the palace and the adjacent streets. The national flag floated no longer from the roof of that building, and the president found himself a prisoner in his own abode. At the opposite angle of the building, through the grated windows of the prison, which formed part of the palace, I espied the heads of the prisoners, who were furious with excitement. The troops which had remained faithful to the cause of Bustamente were ranged upon the grand square, officers went and came, giving their orders, and cannon-wheels rumbled upon the pavement, while the distant booming of the heavy guns, and the white smoke which rose in dense massy clouds behind the houses, showed that, in those streets which were hidden from my view, a fierce engagement was going on. I could make out but imperfectly the places where the combats were raging; but, according to Mexican tactics, the same scenes were repeated on the tops of the houses. The fighting on the terraces was on the same plan as that pursued in the streets below. The roof of the palace was covered with soldiers, forming part of the garrison that had been brought over by Santa Anna. These men kept up an incessant fire against the troops of the colonel, thus placed between two fires; but the close proximity of Don Blas's detachment gave him the most serious alarm.

The lieutenant was just about to command his party to fire again, and probably with more success than on the two former occasions, when the tall colonel advanced to the edge of the azotea to hold a parley; and, forming a kind of speaking trumpet with his two hands, cried out, "*Muchachos!* don't you see how shabby it is of you to fire upon us in this way? *Caramba!* you show little discretion by it. Is it not too bad for two to fight against one? All brave men think so."

"Traitor!" cried the angry lieutenant.

"Traitor! traitor! You are a pretty fellow, on my word, my dear Don Blas! One does not become a traitor for mere pleasure; and your notions of politics appear to be behind the age. Ah! have you got cavalry on the roof?" cried he, pleasantly, observing the gleam of the asistente's helmet in the sun.

"You have made my soldiers the most insulting proposals," Don Blas replied.

"That's true," answered the colonel, "I did. I have not offered them a reasonable price for their cartridges, but I am ready to atone for my fault."

A general hurrah, which burst from the lieutenant's men, showed that he was regaining the ground he had lost.

"The colonel is no bad reasoner, it appears to me," said I to Don Blas.

"His reasons seem solid enough," he answered, with the air of a man who seemed almost convinced; "but my duty obliges me to look on him as an enemy."

Affairs, however, appeared to be drawing to a pacific conclusion, when the colonel added, "It is an understood thing, then, that we do not fire upon each other. Besides, what would your captain gain by shooting me? He does not owe me a single real."

This unhappy allusion, which brought to the lieutenant's mind the disagreeable circumstance that he had been held in pledge for a debt of a few piastres, kindled anew all his former hatred, and he exclaimed, "Death to the enemies of our country! Fire upon the traitors!"

His men were astonished at such an unexpected order, but they were forced to obey, and the two parties began to fire at one another with a want of success only equaled by their obstinacy. The balls passed above my head, and tore through the air with a sharp whiz, similar to that produced by thrusting red-hot iron into water. Carefully squatting down in an angle of the wall, I marked the countenance of Don Blas, and I must say that it did not appear quite at ease, when a fresh discharge was heard, and the lieutenant fell. I ran toward him, but the asistente was before me. Don Blas, lying at full length, gave no sign of life. I saw Juanito shove several of the soldiers imperiously aside, and could not help admiring the fidelity of this man to his master, when, to my great surprise, he thrust his hands into the pockets of the lieutenant's uniform, and drawing them out empty, cried out, with an air of disappointment, "Nothing! not a real! How can we expect to be properly commanded by officers who have not a single real in their pockets? What if he had on cavalry trowsers!"

After such a funeral oration, this devoted servant detached the gold epaulet from the lieutenant's shoulder with the utmost coolness, and appropriated it to himself by way of consolation. Don Blas breathed feebly, opened his eyes, and begged to be conveyed from the scene of action. His orders were complied with, and four men took him up in their arms. I wished to accompany him, to see him laid on my bed till his wound could be examined. He objected strongly to that arrangement; but I insisted, and made them carry him to my chamber.

"This will not do," said Don Blas to me; "powder and shot have no effect on an old soldier like me. Go up again, and watch what turn matters are taking. Victory will be my only cure."

I obeyed, and returned to the place I had left. During my absence the colonel had proposed a cessation of hostilities. It had been agreed to, and when I regained my former position, both parties were exchanging the most courteous salutations with each other.

The most serious affairs, however, were taking place all round us. Reassured by the peaceful attitude of the soldiers of Don Blas and the colonel, I could observe more easily the progress of events. The redoubt established at the corner of the streets of San Augustin and Monterilla kept up continual discharges of grape-shot, and the road was covered with the dead and wounded. Some fell with all the stoicism of the Indian character, others uttering the most heart-rending cries. The latter were principally those whom curiosity had drawn to the scene of strife. Farther off, in the direction of the barrier of San Lazaro, the roar of the cannon was heard without a single pause; while in the street of Tacuba, opposite the palace, a battery, established by the insurgent troops, swept the square, and made large breaches in the wall which surrounded the palace. Masses of rubbish increased rapidly, the iron balconies were torn and twisted like lianas in an impassable forest, and very soon a large portion of the wall tumbled down. Then a man advanced boldly to a dismantled window with so firm a step as to overawe the crowd. I could distinguish in his bold features all the marks of one of those vigorous natures which a kind of predestination seems to push forward for the rude trials of a military life. This man was, perhaps, the best citizen in Mexico. I had seen General Bustamente too often not to recognize him immediately, in spite of the distance which separated us. More grieved, doubtless, at the bloody scenes which then filled the city, than careful of his own safety, the general addressed to the seditious townsmen some words which I could not hear. However, the cannon still roared without intermission; chips of stone, struck from the sides of the window, began to fly about him in showers; but the president appeared not to heed the danger, which was increasing every moment. A new incident drew the general attention. The walls of the prison, torn by cannon shot, had opened in many places, and I could see the prisoners, shouting lustily, creep through the breaches, one after the other, in spite of the storm of grape which swept the square, and disperse themselves through the streets of the town. This completed the anarchy which reigned at this moment over the devoted city.

These sad scenes were beginning to disgust me, when a temporary truce was arranged between the combatants. A deep silence succeeded the booming of the artillery; the time had now come for both sides to count their dead and to remove the wounded. I went to my room, anxious to know how Don Blas was getting on, but he was not there, and the bed on which I had laid him was very little disarranged. On questioning the people of the house, I learned that, at the very moment the truce had been proclaimed, he had been seen to descend the stairs and go into the street. He had probably thought that it would be more reasonable and prudent of him to see after his much-coveted rank of captain than remain quietly in my house. Seeing, then, that his wound must have been but slight, I went out also. In the streets they were lifting the wounded, and carrying them into the houses. As for the dead, their game had been played out, and the pedestrian trod their bodies under foot with the coolest indifference. They were already completely forgotten.

On the very next day, however, the combat recommenced, and blood again flowed in the streets. Beaten without being overcome, the executive annulled the obnoxious law of fifteen per cent. A full and entire amnesty was granted to the insurgents; and, issuing from the gates of the presidential palace, marched, with all the honors of war, a body of the factious citizens, among whom I recognized, with no small dismay, several convicted felons, notorious in the annals of crime. The ruins of fallen masonry which encumbered the streets, the blood that had been every where shed, and the withdrawal of the obnoxious law, were the deplorable results of an insurrection which had brought in its train twelve days of fighting and anarchy.

FOOTNOTE:

[43] Since the time of the Spaniards, these turrets or *almenas* denoted the house of a nobleman.

CHAPTER III.

**Departure of the Convoy.—Victoriano, the Muleteer.—His sudden
Disappearance.—The Convoy is attacked by Robbers.**

I purposed leaving Mexico now that order appeared established and
commerce had returned to its wonted channels. I learned that the conducta
was already in motion. I still held by my purpose of making part of the escort
under the command of the Lieutenant Don Blas; and on the morning after a
day spent in taking leave of my friends, I traversed the streets of Mexico for
the last time, attended by my valet Cecilio.

Upon reaching the open country, the joy that had taken possession of me at
the idea of my speedy return to Europe was slightly tinged by a vague feeling
of sadness. Mexico is still surrounded with lakes as in the time of the
Conquest; but the appearance of these still waters, traversed by a magnificent
road, has been completely changed. The time is gone by when they bore on
their bosom the brigantines of Cortez and the pirogues of the ancient
inhabitants. Partly lessened by evaporation and partly by drainage, the lakes
of Mexico preserve nothing of their former splendor. The distant report of
some sportsman's gun, and the wild songs of the Indians, whose pirogues
may sometimes be seen making their way through the bending reeds, at rare
intervals break the mournful silence which broods over the fields in their
vicinity. Some white aigrets—sitting motionless on the surface of the
water—white as the flowers of the water-lily, a few water-hens, wild ducks,
and huge reptiles which shake the aquatic plants as they pass, and here and
there an Indian angler standing up to the middle of his legs in water, are the
only living beings to be seen in these solitudes. The heavens and the
mountains are alone unchanged; and the same volcanoes, their tops covered
with eternal snow, still shoot up aloft into the air as they did three hundred
years before.

Having arrived at Buena Vista, which commands a view of the whole valley
of Mexico, I stopped to take a last look of the beautiful plain at my feet. In
the midst of a belt of blue hills and small villages, whose white houses
contrasted beautifully with the green of the willows, the lakes assumed, owing
to the distance, something of their ancient glory. Mexico seemed still the city
of the New World. I stopped for a moment to contemplate the distant domes
with a feeling of involuntary dejection. I looked for the last time upon a city
to which I had come with all the curiosity and enthusiasm peculiar to youth.
Mexico was my halting-place when I returned from my excursions in the
country round. It was like a second country to me; for, if infancy has its
souvenirs dear to that state of childhood, youth can not forget the place
where the flower of adolescence has shot up, and withered, alas! too soon. I

looked again at this fertile valley, where smiles an eternal spring; and, to escape from the sadness which possessed me, put my horse to the gallop, and the lofty towers of that city which I was never more to behold were soon quickly lost to my view.

After passing a night at the venta of Cordova, my road lay through the woods of Rio Trio, so notorious for the robberies committed there in broad daylight, and the smiling plains of San Martin, which strongly remind one of those of the Bajio. The snowy peaks of the volcanoes in the vicinity of Mexico were lighted up by the last rays of a sun that sparkled like an expiring beacon-fire when I rode into Puebla. The conducta had passed through that town the same evening. Puebla, the lofty towers of its convents, churches, and cupolas all covered with enameled tiling, looks at a distance like an Oriental town overtopped with minarets. I halted a short time to rest myself, and on the third day after my departure from Mexico descried from a distance the red pennons of the lancers who escorted the convoy.

In the first cavalier to whom I addressed myself after overtaking the escort I could scarcely recognize the asistente of Don Blas. The desires of this worthy lépero on becoming a soldier had been completely satisfied, for, except that he had only a bottine on one foot, a shoe on the other, and no straps to his trowsers, his cavalry uniform left him nothing to desire. In consonance, also, with military discipline, he had parted with his hair.

"Tell me, friend," said I, accosting him, "are you still in the service of Lieutenant Don Blas?"

"Captain Don Blas, if you please—for he has been promised this rank as a reward for his heroic conduct on your azotea; and I have got my stripes also now. I am his servant no longer. He is a captain in a regiment of lancers. You see a detachment of them here."

I proceeded onward, and, in spite of his new uniform, had little difficulty in recognizing Don Blas. The captain was riding gloomily at the head of his troop. I congratulated him on his promotion, and inquired about his wound. He reddened slightly when he told me it had quite healed, and hurriedly asked me if I had counted the cost of traveling with him. I assured him it was my unalterable intention to accompany the convoy to Vera Cruz. Don Bias affected much joy at my resolution, after which the conversation fell quite naturally upon the dangers of the road, the mishaps of which I thought I should escape in his company. The captain shook his head.

"I am not so sure of that," said he. "I fear that you are jumping from the frying-pan into the fire, for the late troubles have increased the number of *guerillas*.[44] And folks say that we shall probably have a hard fight with the highwaymen in the gorges of the Amozoque. The time is gone by when, under a certain viceroy, the standard of Castile, floating above a silver caravan, was sufficient to protect it in its passage."

"I hope," I replied, "that the troop of lancers under your command will make up for the want of the Spanish flag."

"God grant it!" returned Don Blas. "Although I am not blind to the dangers we shall have to run, I shall do my duty in every case."

The long file of richly-laden mules, each having a burden of five thousand dollars in coined money, over every one of which the guardians of the convoy kept an incessant watch, was, in fact, a prize worth striking a blow for. The road to Mexico presents the most striking scenes incident to beauty in landscape, but the thick woods, the deep gorges, and the narrow defiles which we had to traverse might be swarming with robbers. I had scarcely passed a few hours among my new companions ere I began to feel the want of some amusement to dissipate the ennui attendant upon a slow and monotonous march through a desert country. The captain was assuredly a merry companion, but his jokes were trite and commonplace. The stories and songs of a muleteer who took the lead in that kind of entertainment in our little troop were infinitely more agreeable to me. He was a man of about thirty years of age, called Victoriano. He had traveled this road for several years, and had a story for every halting-place. In the evening, under a starry sky, when the mules, relieved from their burdens, munched their maize under the *mantas* which served them for a rack; when round the bivouac fires the sentinels mounted guard over the treasure committed to their care, and the other soldiers slept upon their arms, the captain and I always had a new pleasure in listening to Victoriano, whose unflagging spirit found vent in pleasant stories, or in songs accompanied by the mandolin.

I pitied then the travelers I saw whirled along in the diligence like a flash of lightning, their horses galloping at the top of their speed, while the passengers very likely would be pointing us out to their friends as the only remnant existing of the old Mexican manners. A few more vices, I said to myself, and a few less charms, are the only results of this parody of civilization, which, up to the present time, has destroyed every thing and constructed nothing. On these evenings, round our watch-fire, living at once the life of a muleteer and that of a soldier, I still experienced without alloy, even though on my way to Europe, the feelings incident to life in the Eastern deserts.

Since our departure from Puebla, Acajete, the hacienda of San Juan, Tepeaca, and Santa Gertrudis (for we had deviated from the ordinary route) had been so many resting-places, marked by a certain quiet in which the fatigue of the body is transferred to the mind, and which seems to prove that the happiness of a man consists in physical motion as much as in thought. We had just passed the town and fort of Perote. "Señor Cavalier," said Victoriano to me, "you ought to go to see the fort. I can easily accompany you to the gate, and, upon my recommendation, you will be admitted without difficulty. You can rejoin us afterward at Cruz Blanca, a little village about two leagues from here, where we shall pass the night, and on your return I shall tell you a story about it which made a great noise some years ago."

I took the advice of the muleteer, who, according to promise, introduced me into the fort, the interior of which I ran over at my pleasure in the company of an officer, who was glad to attend me in the capacity of guide. I was about an hour in the place, and, as the sun was beginning to set, galloped at full speed to join the convoy.

I passed over one of those arid and desolate plains, bristling with volcanic scoriæ, known by the name of *mal pais*, upon which a scanty layer of earth allows only a few stunted plants to grow. The wind, blowing in sudden gusts, seemed to moan as it struck the sonorous leaves of the nopal and the clumps of juniper. The wolves also began to howl frequently, and the fog which was falling was so dense and cold that I thought I was long in reaching the watch-fire at which I expected Victoriano to fulfill his promise. However, the fear of losing my way in the fog, which hid the horizon, joined to the roughness of the ground, forced me to slacken my pace, and night had fallen before I arrived at our halting-place—Cruz Blanca. In the small number of houses which composed the village, it was not difficult to find where the conducta had stopped. To my great astonishment, I learned that Victoriano had not made his appearance. This circumstance had alarmed every body. Some accident of a serious nature must have happened to prevent a man, whose habitual punctuality was well known, from rejoining the cavalcade, and every one was lost in conjectures as to his absence, when a stranger presented himself, and requested to speak with the chief arriero. The new-comer was dressed in a well-worn stable-coat, and an apron such as is generally worn by mule conductors. He told us that Victoriano, whose horse had come down, had been much injured by the fall, and that they had conveyed him to Perote, where the utmost care would be taken of him. The unknown added that it was by his express desire that he had come to supply his place till he should be in a fit state to rejoin the convoy. The chief arriero, who had only the number of men strictly necessary, accepted his offer perhaps a little too inconsiderately. The new-comer was a stout fellow of about the same age as Victoriano, but the sinister expression of his countenance did not inspire me with the same feeling of confidence as the arriero.

The next morning we resumed our march, intending to pass the night at Hoya, a little village about five leagues from Cruz Blanca. The journey, though slow as ever, seemed more fatiguing, as Victoriano was not there to enliven it with his stories. Every thing seemed to go wrong after his departure. On arriving at Barranca Honda, about a league from where we had started in the morning, a mule cast its shoe, then a second, and afterward a third. Very long halts were necessary for re-shoeing the animals. Victoriano's substitute acquitted himself as a farrier with great zeal and intelligence, to the great delight of the arriero, who continued, however, to discharge as many oaths as there were saints in the calendar. For my part, I must say that I could not look upon our new companion with the same satisfaction as the muleteer.

"Does it not seem to you," said I to Don Blas, "that this fellow, who shoes the mules so cleverly, might not show an equal address in unshoeing them?"

The captain looked on my suspicions as ridiculous. "I am perfectly disinterested in the matter," I replied, "for, fortunately, none of the precious boxes belong to me; but I can't help regretting the absence of Victoriano."

The convoy put itself again in motion. Still, although it was necessary that the pace should be quickened, the mules appeared to have lost all their former energy, as if some enervating drug had been mixed with their food. Just when we were passing through Las Vigas, the arriero held a sort of conference with the chief of the escort. The former advised that we should pass the night in the village; Don Blas, however, thought it would be better to push on to Hoya, alleging that a delay in a convoy so soon expected in Vera Cruz, especially when the stages in advance were well known, would tend to spread a prejudicial uneasiness. Unluckily for the muleteer, this advice prevailed, and we resolved to push on to Hoya.

There is, perhaps, no part of Mexico in which the difference between the temperature of the plains and that of the more elevated regions is more keenly felt than in the approaches to the Vigas. A few seconds before reaching the village, you were in an instant transported into the vegetation peculiar to cold climates. There the warm breeze and blue heavens were gone, and in their stead a cold north wind blew sharply through the icy vapor which floated around us. Our eyes met only a dull sky, and an arid soil torn up and thickly covered with volcanic boulders. The fog, which at first crept along the surface of the ground, and rolled about in volumes like dust under the feet of our horses, was not long in mounting aloft, and hiding from our view the tops of the tall pines. We could scarcely distinguish one another in the dense mist which the icy wind was driving right in our faces. Deep ravines ran parallel with the road, which was of volcanic formation, and it was a difficult matter to prevent the mules from straggling in a path so hard to follow. I could not help admiring the calmness of Don Blas, the great importance of whose trust absolutely frightened me. As for the arriero, he was in great perplexity, and he galloped incessantly up and down the whole length of the convoy, the sparks flying from his mule's feet at every stroke. The poor man inspired me with a lively interest, for every thing he had in life was at stake; an immense responsibility rested upon him, and he counted and recounted his mules every minute with an anxiety painful to behold. When night had fully come on, Don Blas divided his escort into two bodies. With one he rode at the head of the convoy, and left the other under the charge of Juanito, his ex-asistente. The march was gloomy and silent, the chief noise heard being the tinkle of the bell of the leading mule, the songs of the soldiers, and the clattering of the mules' feet on the stony road. Riding alone on the flank of the convoy, I passed through my mind the various incidents of the morning; the disappearance of our favorite, the unshoeing of the mules, and the dull listlessness with which they now marched, appeared to me, in the midst of the fog which enveloped us, alarming in the highest degree. At the very moment I was asking myself if some treachery was not at work around us, I was joined by my valet Cecilio.

"Señor," said Cecilio, in a low voice, "if you will believe me, we ought not to stay here a moment longer. Something strange is going to happen."

"And where are we to go," said I, "when we can not see two paces before us among these rocks and ravines? But what is the matter?"

"The matter is, señor, that Victoriano has just slipped in among us, and perhaps I am the only one that has remarked his presence; but his coming bodes no good. The story of his accident appears to be only a falsehood."

"Are you sure of it?"

"Yes, quite; but that is not all. About a quarter of an hour ago, I was in the rear, as I have been generally all the march, owing to this confounded beast of mine, when two mounted cavaliers passed without seeing me, as I was concealed behind a mass of rock. One of them bestrode a magnificent black horse, and was otherwise too well equipped for a peaceable traveler."

"A magnificent black horse?" I said, interrupting him, thinking of the ranchero in Mexico who had looked so coolly on the departure of the convoy.

"The other," continued Cecilio, "rode a mule, and had the costume of a muleteer; and, if I rightly understood what they said, Victoriano must be an accomplice."

"And what became of the horsemen?"

"I have no doubt that, under cover of the darkness, they mingled with the escort. It is easy to guess why; and, probably, they are not alone, for these ravines could conceal an entire *cuadrilla* (band). If your lordship will be guided by me, we shall let the convoy go on without us."

"Not at all," I answered; "I must go and tell the captain."

"And who told you, señor, that the captain is not also an accomplice?"

I made no answer. It was not the time for discussion, but for acting. Without considering whether Cecilio's suspicions of Don Blas were well or ill founded, I spurred my horse to warn at least the chief arriero. With some trouble I made up to the rear guard, passed it and some of the mules, the others still forming a long line in front. In the midst of the fog I was guided by the clank of their hoofs on the rocky ground. At last I distinguished the tinkling of the leading mule a few hundred yards in advance. At the same moment I fancied I recognized in the cavalier by my side the sinister countenance of Victoriano's substitute. Some seconds after, the voice of a muleteer rose in the darkness.

"What's the meaning of this?" cried he. "Halloo! Victoriano, is that you? It is, by heavens! and by what chance?"

There was no reply, and the question was not repeated. I shuddered. I thought I heard a stifled cry, followed by a heavy fall. I listened again attentively, but the only sounds were the whistling of the wind, and the echo of the mules' feet upon the stony road. A few seconds after my horse shied violently, as if he had distinguished in the darkness something that had alarmed him. Desirous of clearing up the terrible doubts that harassed my mind, I took out my tinder and steel as if to light a cigar, and to warm me by the exercise it afforded. I fancied for a moment that I was the sport of a dream. By the momentary light it sent forth, I thought I saw some strange figures marching along with the soldiers of our escort and the muleteers. Silent phantoms seemed to have glided mysteriously out of the darkness, and were traveling along with us, some clad in lancers' uniform, others wearing the striped frocks of the muleteers. All at once the bell of the leading mule ceased to sound; in a few seconds it recommenced, but in quite a different direction, and similar sounds issued from the ravines on the left of the road. I had seen enough—nay, too much; treachery surrounded us on every side. But what could one do in the midst of a thick fog, and on a road bordered by ravines? How could one distinguish friends from foes in the deep gloom? Astonished and disconcerted, I stopped my horse; then, at the risk of breaking my neck in the darkness, I galloped to the front of the convoy; it was now too late. A cord whistled over my head and encircled me; my horse made a bound forward; but, instead of being dragged from my saddle, and thrown under the animal's feet as I expected, I felt myself bound to my horse with a terrible tightness. The noose intended for me alone had also enlaced him. My right arm was so tightly bound to my body that I could not disengage myself sufficiently to allow me to draw my knife from my boot to cut the lasso. I dug my spurs into my horse's flanks. The noble animal neighed, and tore forward with irresistible vigor. I felt the lasso tighten till it almost cut me, then suddenly slack. A snap of broken girths, an imprecation of rage, and all at once I found myself free, almost before I could fully realize the danger I had escaped. A vigorous bound of my horse almost unseated me. I kept my saddle, however, and galloped furiously on. Some shots were heard, and a ball whistled close to my ears; at the same moment, cries of alarm arose in the darkness. The repercussion of the firing was fearful, and the confusion indescribable. The mules, deceived by the bells which rang in various directions, ran against each other, and jostled one another in the darkness. The flashes of the fire-arms tore through the fog, and the reports died away among the rocks. By the glare of the musketry you could see the lancers, in their red uniforms, huddled together in confusion, and firing away at random in the thick darkness; the balls went whistling through the air, and the cries of despair of the muleteer were heard distinctly above the din of the tumult.

My frightened horse had carried me far from the scene of combat. I pulled him in immediately and returned. When I rejoined the convoy the contest was over and the bandits had disappeared. Don Blas, who had kept himself very cool during the whole affair, grasped me silently by the hand. I had no time to question him, for a man threw himself between us, a torch in his hand, imploring the captain's assistance. By its light I recognized the discomposed features of the poor muleteer. Some of the soldiers, dismounting, cut branches off the fir-trees and lighted them. We could then survey the sad spectacle which met our eyes. The mozos, among whom Victoriano's substitute was no longer to be seen, watched the poor animals that were standing in groups round the leading mule, whose bell had disappeared. Several mules were bleeding from large wounds: two soldiers, very likely hit by the balls of their comrades, were bandaging their legs with their pocket-handkerchiefs. In a shallow ravine, which the torches reddened with a melancholy glow, a poor muleteer lay writhing in the death agony. This was the man who had recognized Victoriano; he had expiated the fault of having seen too well. The arriero, torch in hand, walked from one mule to another, tearing his hair the while, and wiping off the sweat, which, in spite of the coldness of the night, dropped profusely from his face. "I am lost— ruined!" cried the poor devil, who appeared scarcely to have sufficient courage to ascertain his precise loss with exactness. He commenced, however. Don Blas, who seemed very pale even by the reddish glare of the torches, sat motionless in his saddle. I scrutinized his features as I thought over Cecilio's words, but nothing in his countenance betrayed the painful emotion of a man who, by negligence or misfortune, had failed in the execution of his duty.

"Don't you think," said I to him, "that it would be no bad thing to pursue the robbers who have carried off their booty, and who are every moment increasing their distance from us?"

Don Blas seemed to wake out of his reverie.

"Doubtless," he cried, roughly; "but who told you that they have carried off any thing?"

"Heaven help this poor man!" said I, pointing to the muleteer, who uttered a doleful cry.

"May God pity me!" cried he, "for I shall never survive it. Five, Señor Captain! five are gone!" he continued, in a choking voice. "I have lost in one night the fruit of twenty years' toil! Ah! Señor Don Blas, by the life of your mother, try to recover them for me; the half shall be yours. Ah! why did you advise me to proceed to-night? Why did I listen to you?"

And the poor muleteer, dashing his torch upon the road, rolled in the dust.

The captain being thus forced to make some reparation for the misfortune which he had either ignorantly or designedly caused, picked out a dozen of his best-mounted horsemen, ordered them to cut some pine branches to serve for torches, and to commence the pursuit without delay. I did not anticipate any very successful issue to the expedition, although I had been the first to advise him to it. Persuaded, however, that, though there was little chance of success, there was little risk to be run; desirous, besides, to witness the wonderful sagacity of the Mexicans in following even the faintest traces, I insisted upon accompanying Don Blas and his band. The captain agreed without much difficulty, and we set out immediately for Hoya.

FOOTNOTE:

[44] Bands of robbers.

CHAPTER IV.

Don Tomas Verduzco is shot by Juanito.—Death of Captain Don Blas.

It was a difficult enterprise on which we had entered. Darkness masked the march of the robbers, whose trail it would be almost impossible to follow unless during daylight, as it led over a volcanic soil. We were certain that the stolen mules had not been taken in the direction of Perote. From the place where we now were, the lights in the village of Hoya were easily discernible even through the dense fog which stretched all round us. The news of our disaster could not be long in reaching that place, and the presumption was that the robbers were not to be sought for in that direction. The ground on the left side of the road was impracticable in the darkness, from the large number of sloughs and ravines which seamed its surface. There was no doubt but that the bandits had gained the woody heights on the right which overhung the road, and that the pursuit must be begun in that quarter. A soldier remarked that the light of our torches would betray our presence. We were ignorant of the number of our enemies, who could very easily see us from the lights we carried, and prudence prompted us to hide our motions in darkness. By the captain's order we extinguished the flambeaux, not, however, without casting a glance over the ground we were going to traverse. A steep path led to the crest of a ridge that overhung the road. Three of us, of whom I was one, remained to point out this particular spot. The rest were sent to explore the different paths which were to be met with more in advance. We waited in all stillness the return of the exploring party. Thus passed some minutes. The winds, sighing through the pines which formed a gloomy arch above the hollow road at whose mouth we were stationed, shook upon our heads the condensed mists which fell drop by drop from their sloping branches. At the end of half an hour the horsemen returned. They had seen nothing, but they were certain that no other path than the one on which we were posted led to the high road. If we followed it, we would be sure of hitting the right trail. The soldiers, animated by the hope of a rich reward, were as desirous to begin the pursuit as a pack of dogs to hunt a stag. The captain alone seemed to have no heart for the work, and the orders he gave betrayed a considerable amount of indecision. We began our march, however. Unfortunately, the darkness of the night made our progress very slow. At times, and during a short halt, one of the horsemen alighted and applied his ear to the ground, but not a sound was heard but the sighing of the wind. The rocky ground, carefully examined by the light of a cigar, seemed incapable of bearing even the slightest impress. Guided, however, by an inexplicable instinct, the soldiers did not appear to doubt but that the robbers had passed that way. The gravel soon ceased to crunch beneath our tread; we were now on softer ground. We had at last some chance of discovering the trace of the men or animals which had followed that road. Half of us alighted, and by the light of our cigars, or sparks from flint and steel, began examining with the utmost minuteness every bit of moss or bare earth on the path. Tracks crossed one another in every direction; and at the end of a few minutes, a soldier uttered a cry of joy, and pointed out to us the distinct impress of the two feet of a mule. One of the marks showed that the animal had been newly shod, from the deeper dent made in the soft ground. This was, assuredly, the traces of one of the mules of the convoy that we had been forced to shoe that very morning. At this time we were marching only at random, and our delight at this discovery was intense. The trail was followed till it conducted us to a vast open clearing, a sort of square, from which several paths struck off similar to the one we had followed. There we were completely at fault.

A considerable time had now elapsed since we began our search. The captain, in order to husband our horses' strength in case a new and longer pursuit would be required, ordered a halt. The different paths, which crossed one another in such confusion, could not, he said, be properly examined unless by daylight. The men began to murmur at this unexpected check; but obedience was necessary, and they all alighted. Some large fires were kindled, more for warmth against the freezing cold of the night, and to guard against a sudden surprise, than for the light they afforded. As I took no great interest in the search, I joyfully welcomed the opportunity I had of warming myself at a good fire, and of taking some repose, of which I stood in great need.

After a few minutes' talk, all was silent. The clearing in which we were bivouacked was illuminated throughout its whole extent by the light of our fires. Nothing was heard but the rapid and measured step of the two sentinels we had posted. Several hours rolled away; our fires were just dying out, and day could not be far off, when a cracking of broken branches was heard at some distance. One of our sentinels, his carbine in one hand and a torch in the other, advanced to the place whence the noise proceeded, and soon reappeared leading a mule, which, from its color, and the pack-saddle on his back, was easily recognized as one of those that had been stolen from the convoy. His broken bridle showed that, after having been deprived of his precious burden, they had tied him up in a thicket to prevent our finding him, and that the poor beast had only been able to gain our encampment by breaking his tether. Every body was soon on foot. The woods, perviated every where with paths, unhappily afforded us no new traces, and we much feared that the robbers had divided their plunder, and gone off in a different direction. This thought, which discouraged us so much, produced quite a different effect upon the captain. Up to this time Don Blas had seemed to take no interest in the pursuit, but now he flew into a violent passion, and uttered the most violent menaces against the bandits, whose daring had caused us to lose so much.

"Ah!" cried he, "if chance but throws any of them into my hands, I shall shoot them without benefit of clergy."

Speaking thus, Don Blas walked backward and forward, hitting the ferns which branched out above us with his sabre.

"Whom will you shoot?" I asked.

"Whom?" replied the captain; "why, the first man that happens to fall into my hands."

"That will be a right which it may be difficult to exercise, for robbers on the high road have generally long arms."

"That's my concern," answered Don Blas, with a strange smile; "I will find the means to have the law on my side."

The captain immediately gave the word to mount. The soldiers, delighted at the prospect of regaining their lost time, welcomed the order with acclamation. I must confess that I could not account for this sudden change in the conduct of Don Blas. Why so much zeal after so much coldness? I pleased myself by thinking that hitherto it had been only in appearance, and that the captain had shown so much apathy at first for the sake of propriety, that it might not be thought he was actuated by too lively a desire to gain the reward promised by the arriero.

One of the three paths which led out of the clearing was so narrow, and so little frequented, judging by the appearance of the ground, that, according to all appearance, it could not lead to any inhabited place. The other two were deeply marked with the footprints of men and animals. They would very likely lead to some hacienda, or rancho at least. According to the conjectures of the soldiers, the least trodden of the three paths was that which most probably the robbers had taken. Opinion being divided on that point, the captain ordered us to separate into two parties, and each, taking a particular path, to explore it to the utmost, and two hours after nightfall to rejoin one another in the clearing. Don Blas placed himself at the head of one of these detachments, the other was under the command of Juanito. As for myself, I followed Don Blas, although he did every thing he could to dissuade me from doing so, but I had an instinctive notion that he would not be the man to prefer the most dangerous road. The path we had taken led us toward a wide plain. We soon arrived at an open square in the wood whence several roads diverged. This was a new embarrassment. Our band, however, proceeded in pairs to explore each of these ramifications.

"If this continue," I said to Don Blas, "we shall soon be completely separated from one another, and be liable to be pursued in our turn by those whom we are pursuing."

Still Don Blas did not think that any danger was to be apprehended by this division of our forces. He forthwith proceeded to reconnoitre one of these roads, and I accompanied him. However, when we had proceeded some distance from our companions, his ardor seemed suddenly to cool. He stopped his horse, which was before mine, and proceeded to expatiate upon the beauty of the landscape with the cool indifference of a dissatisfied tourist. The sun had dissipated the mist which had till now enwrapped us. The sky was clear and without a cloud, and a pleasant warmth soon made us forget the sharp and piercing cold of the preceding night. A slight perfume of guava, that the wind wafted along at intervals, was now and then mixed with the sharp and pungent odor of the pines. This was like a harbinger of the beautiful azure sky of the hot regions, and the magnificence of their luxuriant vegetation. We were now separated from the first of our party by several miles.

"I should like to know," said Don Blas to me, after a short silence, "how far the audacity of these brigands would go."

"That is very clear, it seems to me," I replied, "and, since yesterday evening, facts show very strongly how much they are capable of doing."

We had not proceeded far till we met with evidence which proved to us that we were now on the trail of the robbers. Don Blas, seeing some pieces of wood lying on the ground, alighted and picked them up. It was the remains of one of the little boxes in which the sacks of piastres had been packed. He then begged me, in spite of my entreaties, to remain where I was; and, wheeling his horse about, set off at full speed. A turn in the road soon hid him from my view, and I remained alone, without being able to explain the reason of his singular conduct. A painful suspicion, which I had been trying to drive from my mind for some time, now recurred to me with redoubled force. Had Don Blas really any connivance with those robbers, whose presence he wished to seek without a witness? Suddenly a distant shot was heard, which roused me from my reflections. I thought I heard likewise a feeble cry of alarm and distress. I listened, but every thing was calm and silent round me. Prudence urged me to retrace my steps. The captain might be killed; if still alive, dangerously wounded. In these two cases I could be of no assistance; but I resolved to return to procure help. Having come to the place where Don Blas and I had separated from our companions some time before, I discharged my two pistols in succession. I soon had the satisfaction of being rejoined by two of our men, whom I informed in a few words of what had passed.

"The brigands!" cried Juanito; "they are capable of killing my captain for his gold epaulets;" and, to prevent a proceeding so prejudicial to his interests, the sergeant set off at a gallop. The lancers imitated his example, and I followed them, impatient to rejoin Don Blas, but without much hope that Juanito would be deceived. My fears were soon changed to a painful certainty. The captain, unhorsed by the shot I had heard, lay upon the grass, his breast pierced by a ball, but still alive, in spite of the dangerous nature of his wound, and the blood that was flowing from it in abundance. We all hastened to assist him. One of the soldiers stanched the blood, and bound it up very dexterously with our handkerchiefs. While one of the escort went in pursuit of Don Blas's horse, which had escaped, and the captain, with his back to the trunk of a tree, was slowly reviving, I began to examine the ground on all sides. The unhappy man had evidently surprised the bandits at the very moment they were dividing their booty, for broken boxes and bags turned outside in strewed the ground in all directions. Refreshed by a sip of brandy that I caused him to swallow, Don Bias declared that he had seen nobody, and that he had but newly arrived at the place when he was stretched on the earth by a musket-shot. He then added that he knew the hand that had fired the piece. This was too singular a contradiction to provoke a reply. Whether he had said too much, and, being fatigued, wished to say no more, I know not, but he spoke not another word. In the mean time his horse had been caught, and the wounded man affirmed that he thought himself sufficiently recovered to be able to reach the convoy. Still, his strength not being equal to his inclination, it was necessary to lift him on horseback. A soldier mounted behind to support him and take the reins, and we set out on the road to Hoya.

We arrived there about midday. A new incident here awaited us. Scarcely had Don Bias been laid on one of the rough beds, hastily knocked up for him in a cabin in the village, when a detachment of the escort which had been scouring the country round all the morning brought in a prisoner with his hands tied behind his back. His face was blackened, and half concealed by a handkerchief. This disguise was most suspicious, as it is the one usually adopted by Mexican highwaymen. Under this hideous mask I fancied I discerned—a remarkable circumstance—the features of a man who had played a most prominent part in one of the most melancholy episodes of my wanderings, Don Tomas Verduzco. Surrounded by a crowd, he did not discern me. He entreated to be led to the captain; and his voice, though altered by his agitation, was still that of the bravo. I went before the men who were conducting him, and entered first into the hut where Don Blas lay. As soon as he saw the person they had brought him, his pale face became livid, and hatred gleamed in his eyes; he, however, said nothing. The prisoner stood unmoved, and an air of impudent assurance had replaced the expression of stupefaction that was visible a moment before in his countenance.

"What! Señor Don Blas!" cried he; "can I believe my eyes? Are you dangerously wounded? The conducta, it seems, has been pillaged in part, and I am accused of having assisted in that piece of villainy. Good God! it seems as if it were only a dream."

"I fear that it is something worse than a dream," replied the captain, coldly.

"What do you mean by that coldness?" said the bravo, for it was really he. "Your lordship will, perhaps, be less pleased at seeing me than I am in meeting you."

"On the contrary," answered Don Blas, in a voice to which excitement had restored all its former firmness, "I doubt if you are as glad to see me as I am to have you in my power."

"I do not understand you, Señor Captain," returned the bravo, impudently.

"You *will* understand me," said the captain. "If I am pleased at meeting you again, it is only that I may treat you as a highwayman, as a murderer, by shooting you at once, without benefit of clergy."

The look of the captain, which expressed an implacable hatred, added strength to his words; and the bravo, the predominant feature of whose character was evidently not courage, seemed almost to quail under this terrible menace, and he lost countenance for a moment. Seeing, however, that his wound gave Don Blas more assurance, he made a strong effort to master himself, and replied, in quite a firm tone of voice,

"Shoot *me*! That's rather a good joke; but I have more protectors than you think; and, if it is necessary, I will say—Señor Captain, I will say—"

It was now Don Blas's turn to tremble. The captain ordered the bravo to be silent by an imperious gesture; and, signing to Juanito to leave the room, remained alone with the assassin. I am wholly ignorant of what passed between these two worthies, and could only guess what cause had so suddenly changed the opinion of Don Blas with regard to Verduzco. I only know that, after an hour's conversation, the bravo quitted the captain's chamber under the escort of Juanito, who appeared from that moment to treat the prisoner with singular consideration.

The captain's wound did not, however, look so alarming as it did, and a considerable difference could even be observed upon his spirits. After passing two miserable days in the cabin at Hoya, I heard without much surprise that Don Blas thought himself sufficiently recovered to be able to accompany us to Jalapa in a litter, which the chief muleteer had constructed for the purpose. The wounded officer would probably find in that town better medical advice than he could get in Hoya. He could also keep his prisoner in his own hands and under his own guidance.

We had more than fifteen miles to go to reach Jalapa, and, although it was almost two hours after midday before we set out, it was possible to reach that town if we traveled at a quickened pace. This time, a reconnoitring party had been sent on in advance, and every precaution taken to guard against a new surprise. Juanito carried the prisoner behind him. The sergeant and his prisoner chatted as gayly as two friends who were going to the same fête, sharing the same horse. The convoy advanced at a rapid pace. We had now marched two leagues, and had reached San Miguel el Soldado. I then could not help observing that Juanito's horse, probably from its double burden, had lagged behind, and was now far in the rear. Restrained by curiosity from leaving the captive out of sight, I gradually checked the impetuosity of my horse in such a way as to follow Juanito and the bandit at a short distance.

"Caspita!" cried the sergeant, after a long silence, "you have on a capital pair of boots, Señor Don Tomas."

I must remind the reader that Juanito had only a bottine and a shoe.

"I am glad my boots please you," Verduzco replied, "and I would place them at your disposal, but you see I am not quite done with them yet."

"You are very kind, Señor Don Tomas," replied the sergeant, with equal courtesy, "but I mean that I would only borrow them from you when they are of no more use to you. That is always the way I do with my friends, and you are decidedly one. I shall wait, then."

The two horsemen then spoke in a low tone, and I could only catch snatches of their conversation. I was soon drawn away from the distraction into which I had been betrayed by the beauty of the landscape. We were just over San Miguel. From this elevated point the eye wandered over a charming valley, encircled by a belt of foggy mountains. The Naocampatepetl,[45] an extinct volcano, which has the appearance of a square block of stone, is the highest eminence in this range. At the foot of the peak of Macuiltepetl, upon a beautiful carpet of verdure which covers the valley, in the midst of orange-trees in full blossom, of lofty palm-trees, and bananas loaded with fruit, stands the town of Jalapa, set as in a garland of flowers. Placed between the icy fog of the mountains which surround it and the hot atmosphere of the sea-coast, Jalapa is only visited by breezes laden with perfumes. The thick vapors, which hang like a curtain over the plain, lend to it a delicious freshness. Viewed from the top of the hill, where nothing was near but gloomy pines and a stunted vegetation, similar to that of the north, the valley which now lay at my feet seemed more enchanting from the contrast which it afforded.

Day at last came to a close. Macuiltepetl, and the sides of the extinct volcano, began to lose their shades of dusky violet, and already the peak of Orizaba[46] appeared at a distance like a brilliant star. At the bottom of the picture under my eye ran an almost imperceptible white line, which terminated to the right and left in the horizon. This line was the ocean, and it was not without a lively emotion that I contemplated that immense mass of water which laves the shores of France.

While I was absorbed in the contemplation of this enchanting landscape, the convoy had advanced considerably beyond me. I then fancied that the belt which bound the body of the bravo and the soldier together was not so tight as it used to be. This circumstance, remarked also by others, led me to believe that Juanito was conniving at a plan of escape on the part of the prisoner. I asked myself, though it was a business repugnant to my feelings, if I ought not to apprise the captain of the matter. However, I thought that my presence would be a hinderance to Verduzco's attempt to escape, and so preferred remaining where I was. Suddenly the belt, cut by the bravo's knife, divided into two, and the bandit, slipping from the horse's back to the ground, darted off at a run. The lancer was up with him at a single bound of his horse. Juanito applied the muzzle of his carbine to the bravo's head, drew the trigger, and blew out his brains before I could even utter a cry.

"On my word," said Juanito, replacing the carbine in its case, still smoking, "he can't complain that I have not had a regard for his feelings, for I could have got possession of his boots two hours sooner."

Set completely at ease on this delicate point, the sergeant dismounted, and, snatching the objects of his desire, pulled them off the corpse and put them on.

"I knew quite well," added he, "that I would complete my equipment at last."

"My dear Juanito," said I to him, "you are a faithful servant to the captain, although I always suspected the contrary; but there is a mystery wrapped up in this which I do not comprehend, and if you unriddle it for me I will give you a piastre."

"With much pleasure," said Juanito, taking the money; "I wish I could find every day a confessor equal in generosity to your lordship."

The sergeant remounted, and, while walking our horses together, he said,

"What you saw me do was by an order of the captain. To shoot this wicked knave would have been, in the eyes of the law, a crime that would have cost us dear; to place him in the hands of the judges would have offered him a favorable chance of getting off altogether; to kill him, on the contrary, when he was trying to escape, was quite lawful. The attempt at flight, at which I seemed to connive, was only a plan concerted between the captain and me, and the prisoner fell into the snare."

"But why has your captain acted in such a way to a man with whom he had formerly such intimate relations?"

"Ah! that's quite another thing!" replied Juanito. "Before sending Verduzco to a better world, my captain charged me to confess my prisoner. Here is what he told me, and which I will tell only to you, or to those who will give me a piastre for the information. Counting upon the influence which he had in high places, Verduzco engaged to procure for the captain an acting order as commander of the first convoy which left Mexico, the agreement being that he was to allow the conducta to be pillaged on its march, and that afterward the proceeds should be shared between them. Don Blas accepted these conditions; but I must say in his favor that he seemed to have repented of the bargain he had made with the bandit. Now, you know what happened to the convoy; but the best of the joke is, that the successful *coup* was made by another band than that of Verduzco's, who had not reckoned on any thing of the kind. While the bravo was waiting for the conducta beyond Hoya, another body of robbers, better informed, met it before it reached that place. It was by these wretches that the captain was wounded. He fancied that Verduzco had betrayed him, and it was on that account that I received the order to seize the first opportunity that offered to blow the ruffian's brains out."

We spurred our horses to rejoin the convoy. As soon as Juanito perceived the captain's litter, he set his horse to a gallop, and rode alongside for a time. Some minutes passed, during which, bending to the patient's ear, he whispered to him the execution of his orders. Suddenly he ordered the convoy to stop. All pressed round the litter, and I galloped up to ascertain the cause of the halt. A painful feeling, produced by the sergeant's report, had brought on bleeding internally, and when I came up he was already in the last agonies.

The death of Don Blas severed the last tie that bound me to the silver convoy. I resolved to let it proceed without me. The scenes I had witnessed had left a painful feeling on my mind, and I was no longer able to support the company of men whose brutal passions were not satisfied till a crime had been committed. I then halted, and soon saw the cavalcade disappear in the mist, conveying a litter which contained only a corpse, the escort around it holding their lances reversed as a sign of mourning. Night approached. I set out, and reached Jalapa after a slow march, where my sombre and melancholy thoughts were soon replaced by more cheerful feelings.

FOOTNOTES:

[45] In the Indian tongue, the square mountain.

[46] Called by the Indians Citlaltepetl (star mountain).

THE JAROCHOS

CHAPTER I.

Jalapa.

If there is any place in Mexico where the sun shines upon a richer vegetation than that in the valley of Jalapa, there is certainly no part of the country that enjoys a moister atmosphere. A dense, compact mass of light gray vapors always stretches from the summit of the *Cofre de Perote* to the very verge of the horizon. From this dark canopy, which is always charged with moisture, a fine drizzling rain falls, cloudlets of mist roll along the roofs of the houses, the streets are deserted, and Jalapa suffers dreadfully during the greater part of the year for the magnificence of its perpetual verdure; but the sun has no sooner torn aside this cloudy veil, and the deep blue of the heavens and that of the hills has become blended into one, than Jalapa becomes the enchanting town which at a distance it promises to be. The steep streets, which have now put on a very lively appearance, present at every step some charm which is ever varying. The eye is arrested sometimes by the blue and red painted houses which peep out from clumps of guava-trees, of liquidambars and palms—sometimes by the mountains which overhang the town—by the rocks which are completely hidden by a drapery of convolvuli—by the thousand streams which burst from their sides—and by the paths which are soon lost to view between a double hedge of daturas, honey-suckles, and jasmines.

When evening has come a shade falls upon the landscape, but the veil is so transparent that it softens its contour without effacing it. Even the night at Jalapa is quite as beautiful as the day. It is then that life begins to stir in the town. The ground-floor is, in all houses in hot countries, the place of rendezvous for the family and friends. It is in the evening at Jalapa, and at several other towns in Mexico, that the stranger can obtain the best insight into the domestic life and manners of the inhabitants. Every open window then sends forth a welcome ray of light into the dark and silent street, and the traveler can not but hear the joyous merriment that is going on within. In the warm nights of this beautiful climate the stranger can thus share in these fêtes every evening; he can see the Jalapeñas[47] display their charming vivacity without affectation, from the first moment that the fête commences till the flowers in their head-dresses wither, the harp ceases to be heard, and the windows are closed behind their iron bars.

It is always with regret that you leave this charming, warm valley, whether you are going to Mexico through the icy fogs of the frigid zone, or to Vera Cruz through the stifling and unbearable heat of the country between Jalapa and that city. I had deferred my departure from day to day, and two weeks had almost rolled away like a dream since that evening when, permitting the silver convoy to go on in advance after the death of Don Blas, I had entered Jalapa alone. My pecuniary resources were almost exhausted, and I was obliged to set out, taking with me my servant Cecilio and another traveling companion, a young spaniel bitch, answering to the name of Love, an appellation which Cecilio had transferred into a Spanish name with quite a different signification, Lova (she wolf). This dog followed me in all my wanderings; and my horse Storm, who had contracted an affection for her, never galloped with greater animation than when he felt her bounding between his legs or fawning upon his chest.

We soon left behind us the fertile hills of Jalapa, its orange groves and daturas, its plains dotted with bananas and guava-trees, and arrived at Lencero. This name was given to the place by one of Cortez's soldiers who had set up a venta there. In that quarter are still to be found some of these huts called jacales.[48] Lencero offers likewise an additional interest to the curious traveler. Near the hamlet, upon the top of a hill, from which, in a clear day, the serrated tops of the Cordillera and a distant view of the ocean can be easily obtained, rises a little house with red stained walls, ornamented with a modest veranda, and surmounted by a *mirador* (belvedere) of glass. This agreeable retreat is the country house of General Santa Anna.

At some distance from Lencero our road passed through the gorges of Cerro-Gordo, and a dull roar, like the sea-waves breaking on a rocky beach, warned us of our approach to the River Antigua. Seven arches, thrown with great boldness over a deep ravine, at the bottom of which the river flows; the blasted rocks and the filled-up abysses, still attest the ancient grandeur of the old masters of Mexico. This bridge is now called the Puente Nacional.[49]

Vera Cruz is only about forty miles from the Puente Nacional; but since our departure from Jalapa, the heat had become gradually overpowering. Storm snuffed up with delight the burning wind which imbrowned the grass; it reminded him of the hot breezes of the savannas. It was the first time for five years that he had bathed in the rays of a sun similar to that of his distant *querencia*, and his joy was manifested by his wild neighing. Love, on the contrary, her tongue lolling out, and her chest heaving, sought in vain for some drops of dew in the midst of a vegetation parched and withered by the heat of such a sun.

Fatigued by a ride which had lasted longer than I had anticipated, I pulled up for an instant. I had not intended that my halt should be long, as I wished to reach Vera Cruz that evening, leaving my servant to follow next morning if his horse could not keep up with mine; but Fate had decreed otherwise. Cecilio, who had lagged behind, came up at the very moment I was going to start. The sweat was rolling in beaded drops from his burning brow, and his face, ordinarily so calm and placid, wore an appearance of extreme uneasiness. He shuffled up alongside of me. I was doubly surprised. It was the first time that he had ever shown himself wanting in respect, and the effort he now made to keep his horse close to mine was quite without precedent.

"Señor," said Cecilio to me, "if the accounts I have picked up on the road are to be relied on, we have entered the district in which yellow fever is so rife, and I must say that I have strong fears for my personal safety, and, with your lordship's permission, will go no farther."

"Very true," said I, "the yellow fever has haunts peculiar to itself; it is, besides, very partial to stout, healthy people like you; but never mind; you know the road from here to Mexico, and you may consider the horse on which you are at present mounted your own, in lieu of the money I owe you."

Unfortunately, there was a question of wages between the valet and his master which the gift of a foundered horse, fit only for the knackers, could scarcely cover. The former hinted delicately at the difficulty, and wished to be paid on the spot. I had then recourse to an argument which I thought would leave him without any reply.

"You know why I left Jalapa so soon. Now, as there are no commercial houses in these deserts that will accept a bill of mine upon Vera Cruz, you must have patience till we get there."

Cecilio made no reply; but his attitude proved that he did not consider himself beaten. In fact, after riding in silence for about half an hour, he came again to the charge.

"If your lordship would take me to Europe with you," he said, "I should not care about running my chance of the yellow fever. He who runs no risk will never cross the sea, as the proverb says."

I reminded Cecilio that such a voyage was very expensive, and that among those foreigners who had emigrated to Mexico there were very few millionaires, and that the greater part generally went away as poor as they came. "Although," I added, "such men may be looked upon as of consequence here, when they arrive in their own country they are not treated with a like consideration."

This stopped his mouth, and he again lapsed into his former taciturnity. We continued our journey, but he still hung obstinately on my heels. All at once he uttered a cry of joy.

"What is the matter?" I asked.

"I have hit upon a capital way of settling the business."

"Ah! let me hear it."

"I propose to your lordship," he replied, gravely, "to stake your horse Storm against the wages which are due me. As it is impossible for you to pay me here, and you see that I am unalterably resolved to go no farther, your lordship can not refuse to assent to my proposition. If your lordship win, we shall be quits, and I shall then have only the honor of having served you for nothing. If your lordship lose, I shall have the chestnut horse and the favor of God."

At first I was on the point of rejecting with indignation a proposition so extraordinary, but the very idea seemed so extravagant that I laughingly accepted it. We alighted. According to a habit common enough in Mexico, Cecilio never stirred abroad without being provided with a pack of cards; and master and valet sat down, face to face, beneath a clump of trees on the off side of the road. Love stretched herself panting on the sand, while Storm, impatient of delay, pawed the ground with his hoof. At sight of the noble animal, that perhaps, in a short time, would cease to belong to me, I could not help regretting my rashness for an instant, but I had gone too far to recede. Cecilio passed me the cards.

"Your lordship will honor me by dealing them," said he, with redoubled gravity.

I shuddered, and took the pack with a hand not at all steady. Not to prolong my absurd position, I determined that the game be decided in three *alburs*.[50] Five minutes would then settle the question. I put down two cards from the pack. Cecilio chose one, I took the other; then, after laying down half a dozen cards in succession, I won the first albur. Not a frown crossed Cecilio's face; and, for my part, I thought that fortune was going to befriend me for once in my life, but I lost the second throw. The third albur remained, which would decide the affair.

While thus engaged, we had not perceived two horsemen who were advancing toward us. I did not see them, for my part, till they were almost at my side. The sound of their voices caused me to raise my head, and at a single glance I saw in one of the new-comers a perfect specimen of the Jarocho.[51] He wore in all its purity the peculiar costume of this class of men, a straw hat with a broad brim turned up behind, a fine linen shirt with cambric frills, without any vest above it, a pair of blue cotton velvet breeches open at the knee, and falling in a point to the middle of his leg. In a belt of Chinese crape of a scarlet color hung a straight sword (*machete*), without guard or sheath, the sharp and glittering blade of which sparkled in the sun. His feet, which were bare, were held in the wooden stirrup only by the tips of his toes. This Jarocho, his head inclined indolently upon one shoulder, sat his horse in the attitude peculiar to people of his caste, whose easy manner and unconstrained demeanor suited him to perfection. His complexion partook equally of the darkness of the negro and the copper color of the Indian. It was a more difficult matter to define precisely what the other cavalier was, who was habited in an Indian robe, blue pantaloons, and bottines of Cordovan leather, while a rich hat of *Jipijapa* straw[52] sheltered him from the rays of the sun. His face, with a slight tinge of sternness in it, might have become equally well a merchant, a horse-dealer, or a highwayman, and the easy-going horse that he bestrode seemed to suit equally all three suppositions.

Two gamesters at play, wherever they may be, are always an agreeable sight for Mexicans of all classes, and, to my great annoyance, the two horsemen stopped short to look at us. I sat quite motionless with the cards in my hand, and was much confused at being surprised at an occupation so contrary to my habits. As no stake was visible, however, I flattered myself that I would be able to keep up appearances so far as to make them believe that it was only the most innocent pastime; but I had to do with men who are acute judges of human character.

"Might I ask if this beautiful horse is the stake?" asked the horseman in the Indian robe, saluting me, and accompanying his request with a piercing look.

"Exactly so," I answered.

"In that case you are playing high, señor," replied the cavalier; "and if, as I fancy, the horse is your own, I wish Fortune may be propitious to you; but would you not like any body to help you with their advice?"

"I prefer finishing the game as I commenced it. I have always remarked that I have more luck when there is no one by."

The cavalier was too much of a gamester himself not to see at once the full force of my scruples, and, turning to his companion, said, "'Tis as well as it is. Time presses. We must part here, although, if I have time, you may trust on my rejoining you at the fandango of Manantial; still, to speak truth, if certain infallible signs do not deceive me, the north wind will not be long in beginning to blow."

"To-morrow, then, if it is possible," answered the Jarocho; and the two cavaliers separated, the first following the direct road, while the horseman in the Indian robe took a path on the left.

"What the devil has the north wind to do with a fandango in a little village?" I asked, mechanically, of my valet.

"The cavalier in the Indian robe is perhaps afraid of catching cold," said Cecilio, with an affected air.

After this absurd explanation, we again began the game which had been so unexpectedly interrupted. I once more drew two cards out of the pack. One was the *sota de bastos* (knave of clubs). Cecilio chose it. I shuffled the cards this time with a trembling hand. My heart beat. Perhaps I was going to lose the daily companion of five long years. Cecilio wiped away the sweat which ran in streams down his forehead. Suddenly he uttered a cry which pierced to my innermost core. I was just turning up the knave of hearts.

"You have lost, sir!" cried he.

At these words, spoken in good French, I regarded Cecilio with mute surprise. He, meanwhile, stepping up proudly to my horse, put his foot in the stirrup, and was going to spring upon Storm's back.

"Stop!" I cried; "the saddle does not go with the animal." I then ordered him to take the saddle off, and to put it on the back of the other horse. Cecilio executed this order, which would probably be the last he would ever receive from his old master, with sufficient readiness and good will. This done, he mounted that horse which was no longer mine. I cursed my folly, but it was too late. A feeling of pride, however, kept me from showing the remorse I felt; and, to hide my chagrin, I asked Cecilio how he had managed to pick up so much French without my knowledge.

"I have not been behind the chair of your lordship," he replied, "especially when you dined with your countrymen, without acquiring some of the language; and as for making you acquainted with that fact, I was too wide awake. Your lordship, from that time, would have kept your secrets to yourself."

Cecilio was evidently like one of that class of valets who figure so largely in the picaresque romances of Spain. More than once he had reminded me of Ambrosio of Lamela in Gil Blas. His physiognomy had not deceived me. However, in spite of the impudence which he here manifested for the first time, he seemed, when the parting moment came, to suffer considerably. It was natural, in fact, to show some emotion when he was leaving a master who had used him kindly. Moved by this token of feeling on his part, I showed that I was not without some affection for him.

"Cecilio, my friend," I said, "the horse you have won from me would have been yours before many days had passed. Are you grieved because you have been the means of taking him from me?"

Cecilio squeezed out a tear.

"The truth is," said he, "I regret seeing your beautiful saddle on the back of such a sorry brute, and I am ashamed at the miserable appointments that the horse I have won is provided with. But, if your lordship is in the humor, would it suit you to play for the saddle and bridle?"

This was too much. Overcome by this last piece of ingratitude, "Take care," I cried, cocking a pistol, "that I do not take back a horse which you are not worthy to mount."

Cecilio made no other reply to this threat than by spurring his horse and whistling on the Spanish dog, which had looked upon this scene with a painful air of dumb anxiety. I whistled also. Thus forced to choose between two parties whom he had affectionately loved all his life, the poor animal hesitated. He ran up to Storm, and then came back to me with a most pitying expression in his face. The convulsive movements of his body betrayed his anguish, and showed the struggle that was going on within. His limbs shook for an instant; he then gave three convulsive howls, darted from me, and was soon lost in the dust raised by his much-loved companion. I remained alone. My heart was in a storm of rage and grief, and I was even tempted to vent my ill-humor on the miserable hack that fortune had left me, but this weakness lasted only for a moment. I had learned, in the many crosses incident to a life of stirring adventure, the difficult virtue of resignation, and the different phases of this sentimental episode had been accompanied by circumstances so ludicrous that I finished by throwing myself on the grass and bursting into a violent fit of laughter.

FOOTNOTES:

[47] The women of Jalapa are renowned throughout the whole republic for their beauty and grace, and their taste in fêtes, music, and flowers is unrivaled.

[48] These huts are constructed of bamboos, wattled so as to admit both air and light freely.

[49] Before the independence of Mexico this bridge was called Puente del Rey (the King's Bridge).

[50] The game called *monte* is thus divided.

[51] The peasants of the sea-coast and the country round Vera Cruz are so called.

[52] These hats, which take their name from the place where they are made, are often worth from £10 to £12 each.

CHAPTER II.

I arrive at Manantial.—Superstitions of the Jarochos.

The unfortunate occurrence recorded in the preceding chapter caused me to change my route. It was impossible for me to reach Vera Cruz that day, mounted as I was; so I resolved to pass the night at Manantial, a little village which I supposed to be not more than a mile off. I had thus some time before me, and I thought it could not be better employed than in taking a siesta under the shade of the trees, amid the green solitude in which I found myself. It was a spot in one of the most picturesque forests which cover almost the entire country between Puente Nacional and Vergara. Amid these matted thickets, narrow paths, cut by the hatchet, run in different directions, overshadowed by the almost impenetrable foliage of the trees, while a wall of luxuriant vegetation on each side bars every where the entrance of man, and almost that of the fallow deer. The long, pendent branches twist and interlace their tendrils with the boughs of the neighboring trees. The cocoa-nut-tree covers, with its large leaves, its necklace of green fruit; and the Bourbon palms stretch their branches, covered with shining foliage to the ground; the silk-cotton-tree shows its white flakes of cotton just bursting from the dark green pod. In the deep shade of these inhabitants of the forest the friar's cowl abounds with its polished chalice; and at the bottom, as well as the top of this green vault, the gobeas hang their little bell-flowers of variegated colors. Such is the aspect of these woods—an appearance, however, which assumes a different phase according to the hour of the day. At midday the rank vegetation droops under the scorching rays of the sun, from the palm, with its towering crest, to the lowly moss which covers the ground. A hot breeze at that time rushes through the thickets, and appears to arrest every where the progress of vegetation; wild beasts, birds, insects, and plants—all animated nature, in fact, seems to languish under this stifling heat; but when the sun's rays no longer gild the tree-tops, and the vapors rise slowly from the ground, to fall back again in dew, these forests and their denizens, once so silent, start again into life.

Overcome by the powerful influence of the sun, I fell fast asleep without any thought about my horse. The pettiest thief, indeed, would have been ashamed of such booty; and I was, besides, in a district where no stain of dishonesty rested on the character of the inhabitants. The sun was yet high in the horizon when I awoke, but a refreshing breeze was beginning to temper the sultry heat. High up amid the branches of the trees which sheltered me, the paroquets had begun their discordant noises, and their infernal melody was of such a kind as to annoy even the strongest nerves. I got impatient; and, hastily bestriding the wretched animal which supplied the place of my excellent Storm, set out on the beaten path that led to Manantial.

After riding slowly and painfully along for about half an hour, the shrill croaking of the paroquets always paining my ears, I perceived a horseman a little way in advance. This cavalier, attired exactly like one of those who had interrupted Cecilio and me at our game, seemed, like myself, to be quite out of humor. He rode, as all the Jarochos do, with his body inclined more to one side of the saddle than the other. His horse shuffled slowly along, and every now and then he held up his fist to the skies in all the fury of passion. Delighted that chance had sent me a companion in misfortune, I wished to offer him my hearty condolence, and succeeded in that design beyond my expectation. Scarcely had I managed, by dint of hard spurring, to make up to him, than a loud ringing laugh replaced the mental irritation in which I thought he had been indulging a minute before.

"May I ask if you are laughing at me?" I said, abruptly; for, in the bad humor I was in, this hilarity seemed quite out of place.

"At you? No, Señor Cavalier," answered the Jarocho. "But you will excuse me if, at sight of your horse, I bid adieu for a time to all customary politeness."

"My horse is in no worse condition than the *andante*[53] you are on," I replied, almost choking.

"You may think so; but that hack of yours is a mere bag of bones, and it is no small satisfaction to me to find one worse mounted than myself."

The horseman then began to laugh in such a merry, unconstrained fashion, that, tickled with the very absurdity of the thing, I could not help joining him, and we had a good hearty laugh together. The squabbling of the paroquets, struck with the unusual noise, ceased all of a sudden. They recommenced their ear-splitting cries, till at last I discharged a pistol at random among the foliage. To my great surprise, a bird fell at my feet.

"Did you take aim at it?" asked the astonished Jarocho.

"Of course," I replied, sharply; "and this will serve to show you that it is not altogether safe to jest with people you don't know."

At these words the Jarocho stopped his horse, and, straightening himself in his saddle, placed one hand upon his haunch, and pulled his straw hat over his eyes with the other. He then cried out, "*Oigajte, ñor deconocio.*[54] I am of a caste and of a country where words are few, and whose actions are prompt. I did not mean to offend you; but if you seek a quarrel, I shall not flinch. In spite of the disparity of our weapons, I am not afraid to try which of us is the better man."

He hummed a tune, drew his sharp sword from the leathern belt which encircled his waist, and flourished it in the air. I likewise drew my sabre.

The idea of crossing swords, mounted as we were on such sorry jades, was so absurd, that we at last burst into a mutual roar of laughter, which ended the matter. I then hastened to explain to the Jarocho that I had no inimical feeling toward him. He held out his hand.

"I am glad you are satisfied," he replied, "for I should have been very sorry to have an enemy in one so brave as you appear to be, as at present I have a more serious quarrel on my hands."

We then rode along together quite amicably. To turn the conversation, recalling, besides, to my recollection the parting words of the two horsemen at the cross-road, I said, in a careless kind of a tone, "Isn't there to be a fandango at Manantial to-morrow?"

"There is, confound it! I promised ña[55] Sacramenta a bow of red ribbons for the occasion, and there is not a bit to be had in all the neighborhood. At the very moment you joined me I was cursing my unlucky star. Probably you are yourself going to the fandango?"

"Well, I am; but chance alone brought me to think of it, for I had reckoned on sleeping to-night at Vera Cruz, had not an unfortunate occurrence come in the way."

"You will have no cause to regret it, I hope, for *the crowd will be as thick as smoke.* But where will you put up at Manantial? There is no inn in the place."

"With you, perhaps, since you appear to be so desirous to have me at the fête."

The Jarocho bowed in token of assent, and then began to give me an account of the numerous pleasures that awaited me on the morrow. Conversing thus, we reached Manantial. Night had come. A few scattered lights gleaming from among the green foliage announced our approach to the village. We soon reached a little clearing in the wood, dotted with cabins formed of wattled bamboo. This was Manantial. Some men and women, clad in the national costume, were dancing to the monotonous sound of a mandolin, while the mothers were rocking their infants to sleep in hammocks formed of strips of aloe bark. I soon learned the name of my new host.

"Ah! it's Calros,"[56] cried they, in a tone as if his arrival had long been looked for. He paid no attention to the greeting of his friends, who advanced to welcome him, but his eye roved about till it rested on the slender and graceful form of a young girl, whose pretty little feet were twinkling merrily in the dance. Her hair, black as ebony, was ornamented with a wreath[57] of suchil flowers, interspersed with fire-flies, whose pale bluish light encircled her forehead with a mysterious and fantastic halo. Draped in a white robe, whose waving folds were every moment blanched by the pale rays of the moon, Sacramenta, with her bare shoulders and variegated hair, looked like a fairy dancing by night in a glade of the forest, when all around is at rest.

The almost disdainful glance which she threw at him showed me at once the true state of affairs. The Jarocho waited till the dance was finished, and then advanced toward the girl. By the entreating tone of his voice, it was clear that he was excusing himself about the red ribbons he had promised her. I was too far off to hear his words, but the light which streamed from a neighboring cottage showed me the full expression of her features. It was evident that all Calros's rhetoric had been useless, and he remounted, but with a saddened, irritated air. Sacramenta, in shaking her head to a remark of his, allowed one of the suchil flowers to fall from her chaplet. The Jarocho regarded it for some time with an undecided air; and she, marking his hesitation, and while pressing the wreath on her forehead, in a fit of coquetry, raised the flower on the tip of her tiny foot, and presented it to him. The cloudy countenance of the Jarocho was now lit up with joy; he seized the flower eagerly, spurred his horse, and was soon lost in the darkness.

It was quite clear that he had completely forgotten me, but it was as clear that I had no intention of taking up my quarters for the night in the forest.

"Halloo! Señor Don Calros," I shouted after him, "you have left me behind."

"Pardon me, Señor Cavalier," cried he, pulling up; "but there are times when I am hardly master of myself."

"I am convinced of that," I said; "and it is certainly no indiscretion in you to forget a stranger whom you met by the merest chance."

"In my country the stranger is at home every where; but you shall not have my hospitality for nothing, for you must pay me either by doing me a particular piece of service, or assisting me with your advice."

"With pleasure," I answered, "if it is in my power."

The dwelling of the Jarocho, called a *jacal*, was situated at the other end of the village. A small inclosure, in which a few goats were penned, was attached to it. The cabin was divided into three apartments by reed partitions. In one of these, the mother of the Jarocho was preparing the evening meal over a fire whose reddish glow lighted up the whole jacal. The repast consisted of rice boiled in milk, fried bananas, and red haricots from the Tierra Caliente, which enjoy a proverbial celebrity in Mexico. When supper was ended the old woman left the room, wishing me a pleasant sleep.

The distant thrumming of guitars apprised us that the company we had left were still keeping up their merriment. The voice of the Jarocho awoke me from the reverie in which I had been indulging.

"Do you see," said he to me, as we were lying at the door of the cabin, "that fleecy mist which dulls the light of the stars? These are the vapors which, at the end of every hot day, arise from the lakes, brooks, and waterfalls. Do you think it possible that, at the command of a mortal like ourselves, this shadowy impalpable fog should assume the form of a friend who has been lost, or an enemy that has been murdered?"

"I doubt that much," I replied, astonished at this preamble; "I fancied that these superstitious notions were peculiar only to northern climes."

"Here," said Calros, in a solemn tone, "ghosts haunt not the abodes of the living; they love to flit about in the woods, and to frisk among the leaves and flowers. But you smile. Let us talk of something else. Did you see ña Sacramenta this evening?"

"The pretty girl with the wreath of *cucuyos* and the *suchil* chaplet?"

"The same. She is very beautiful, is she not? Six months ago, at a fandango in the neighborhood, a quarrel arose on her account, which was followed by the death of a man. The victim was a relation of mine; and, according to universal custom, it became my duty to avenge his death. I had, besides, an additional inducement in seeking the murderer; he adored Sacramenta, and every one who loves her is my sworn enemy. Twenty times have I persuaded myself into a belief that Sacramenta loved me, and twenty times have I been forced to confess to myself that I was deceived. I feel that I love Sacramenta more than my life—than my honor, perhaps—else I should have been on the murderer's traces long ago; and yet this evening I have even ventured to hope."

"Yes, a mere suchil flower may sometimes work miracles," said I, interrupting him.

"What!" cried Jarocho, "have you the gift of seeing what no one else has seen?"

"I only observed what every body else might have seen, had they chose; but when a man receives a flower from the hand of a girl he loves, he needn't, I think, despair."

"Thank Heaven!" cried the Jarocho, cheerfully. "Yet," he added, with a sigh, "this is not the first token I have had from her; to-morrow the illusions of this night may be dispelled. Ever since ña Sacramenta came to live at Manantial I have suffered the utmost tortures of anxiety, and yet vengeance has not been done on my cousin's murderer. I have tried to forget that duty; unluckily, there are others who do not. The dead man's mother reminds me every day of the charge which has devolved upon me. Eight days ago I met the old woman. I wished to avoid her, but it was impossible. She is looked upon as a sort of witch by the people around. On passing me she cried out, 'The dead have better memories than the living.' I asked her what she meant, although I knew full well. 'You will see him to-night,' she replied. In truth, that very evening," Calros continued, in an altered voice, "I was seated at the same place where we now are, Señor Cavalier; the door was open, and my thoughts were engaged about nothing in particular. I was only listening to the voices in the trees and on the wind; a pale white mist was creeping up to the sky, as it is doing now. All at once a cloud came between my eyes and the stars; it took a human form, and the dead man was before me! I saw him distinctly, right in front of me. I closed my eyes, and when I opened them he was gone. You will now understand why I asked you, señor, who, as a European, must be a learned man, if mortals like ourselves can raise the dead."

These superstitious notions are not at all prevalent in Mexico, and the Jarochos seem to have a complete monopoly of them. I gently hinted that all this was nothing but the result of a diseased imagination.

"I know well," said he, "that the ghost of my deceased relative has not been raised by any human power, but I believe that God himself has sent it to me. I have taken my resolution. I shall not stay in the village a day after to-morrow, although I leave it with a broken heart."

"But is there no way of reconciling your duty with your love?"

"That can only be done by delegating my powers to a devoted friend. A guest makes a part of the family; and in this quality, señor, you might take my place and seek the murderer, who would not hesitate to give you satisfaction."

"That would be too glorious a mission for me, and I fear I should not be successful in the search," I said, modestly; "but I have no objections to accompany you, and aid you in your task."

"That is an offer which I will not refuse," Calros answered. "We shall then set out the day after to-morrow."

This delicate point settled to our mutual satisfaction, we stretched ourselves under a shed which served as a sort of veranda to the cabin. A gentle breeze was beginning to dissipate the heat of the day. The lizards were silent in the grass; and in the savannas, the wild cattle, by their joyful lowing, testified to the grateful freshness of the night. Lulled by the soft murmur of the twittering leaves, I soon fell asleep.

FOOTNOTES:

[53] Local synonym for a horse.

[54] Listen, Sir Stranger.

[55] Abbreviated form of Doña, used in this part of Mexico.

[56] Calros, Charles.

[57] A head-dress greatly in vogue among Mexican females.

CHAPTER III.

The Fête of Manantial.—The Combat.

The name of Jarochos is given to those peasants who live on the sea-board round Vera Cruz. Their costume bears no resemblance whatever to that of the people around them. The inhabitants of Andalusia wear a dress very similar to theirs, and it is the general opinion, from their manners and character, that they are the descendants of the Gitanos of that Spanish province. Their dialect is, like their attire, strange and singular. It abounds in words of the purest Castilian, interspersed with local terms disfigured by a vicious pronunciation, and can not be understood, even by those who know Spanish, without diligent and careful study. They are impatient of restraint, and, consequently, ill fitted for acting as soldiers or sailors, although well versed in the use of arms, and not unacquainted with the dangers of the sea. It is their love of independence which causes them to prefer the wandering life of the herdsman and the horse-dealer, and the *machete* plays no unimportant part in all their difficulties. The Jarocho would rather want the most indispensable part of his dress than be deprived of the long, sharp, glittering blade which he wears in his belt. This sabre is more generally in the hand of the Jarocho than at his side. A small point of honor, or the most futile remark, has often been the means of bringing on the most bloody and long-continued series of combats. They are possessed, however, of some rare qualities, which atone for their defects. The Jarocho is temperate, frank, loyal, and hospitable to the *whites* (by this term he means the higher classes); he looks upon theft with horror; he loves the place of his birth. A stranger to every desire for wealth, he lives contented with a little in the midst of a fertile country where three harvests a year cover the ground, which is sown but not tilled. The inhabitants of the country round Vera Cruz are in general robust and well made. They are strong and muscular; and nature has thrown round their persons an air of elegance in exact harmony with the devotion the Jarocho pays to three things: his horse, his sword, and his mistress.

Seven years before my arrival in Mexico, I once had an opportunity of meeting with one of this singular race; but, from want of familiarity with Spanish, I could not well understand his peculiar dialect.

As soon as I awoke in the morning, I was reminded, by the handsome and elegant dress of my host, that it was the fête-day of Manantial. A twisted fringe, strung with Venetian pearls, and studded at regular distances with little mirrors, ran round his hat; his shirt, of the finest linen, was embroidered in the most beautiful manner; the buttons of his velvet *calzonera* at his girdle were made of solid piastres, and those which ran down his legs of reals and half reals. On his feet were half-boots of Cordovan leather. His *cortante*,[58] polished to the highest degree of brilliancy, hung suspended from his girdle of scarlet silk, and two bows of the same color adorned its hilt. Set out thus to the best advantage, the Jarocho had an air of refinement about him which augured well for his success.

In spite of a degree of satisfaction which shone upon his countenance, Calros could not help twirling the end of his mustache with an anxious expression. His joy seemed to be mixed with an alloy of bitterness. I asked him the cause of it.

"Ah! if you could only free me of my vow of vengeance, I should be relieved of a charge which will embitter, I fear, all my pleasures."

"What! will your oath keep you from drinking, singing, and playing?"

"No, but it will hinder me from knocking a fellow down; and what is a fandango without some little quarrel to enliven it? No matter; one can not have all one's pleasures at once. I shall sing louder, play more, and drink as much as will soothe me for the disappointment."

I doubted much the calming efficacy of Catalonian brandy, but I affected to believe fully in the power of the remedy.

Manantial, like the Jarocho, had put on its holiday garb for the occasion. An unusual stir was visible in the village. At the doors of the cabins, women, arrayed in abundance of muslin and lace, appeared from time to time, decked with gold and coral ornaments, so dear to the swarthy beauties of Southern countries. In a glade, an estrade had been erected for the accommodation of the dancers; little shops had been improvised for the supply of water, *tepache*, and Catalonian brandy; gambling-tables had been set up. In a few hours the Jarochos from the surrounding villages would come pouring in. The sun was shining full upon the spot in all its dazzling brilliancy. The shadow cast by the palm-trees, already a little off the perpendicular, showed that it was two hours past noon. Crowds of horsemen now began to arrive, who, after alighting, tied their foaming steeds to the trunks of the trees or the pillars of the houses. Horses and men were soon mingled together in strange confusion; the cries of the men, the neighing of the steeds, and the tuning of guitars, were now heard on all sides. Circles were speedily formed round the gambling-tables, the *ventorillos*,[59] or the estrade reserved for the female dancers. Here I stationed myself.

The estrade, on which female dancers were alone to figure, was elevated a few inches above the ground. According to a singular custom prevailing in all the villages round Vera Cruz, the men on this occasion are mere spectators of the women's performances. A Jarocho squatted himself down on the ground close to the estrade, and commenced strumming his mandolin. Eight or ten girls answered to his call, and began to dance. I could not help admiring the graceful dexterity with which many of them carried a glass of water on their heads without spilling a drop, dancing, too, all the while with the greatest vigor; or the agility with which they untied, without using their hands, the silk bows attached to their shoes,[60] When this dance, very coldly applauded, was finished, the guitar struck up a new tune, that of the dance called *petenera*.

This time the estrade was quite full, and among the women who advanced to take a part in this measure I recognized, by her graceful mien and dazzling beauty, Doña Sacramenta, whom my host called, in his flowery language, *his dearly-beloved angel on earth*. She was attired in a beautiful dress of transparent muslin. Her rounded arms were adorned in the upper part by the embroidery and lace of her cambric chemise, the rest remained bare. The contour of her fair shoulders was masked, but not entirely concealed, by a gorget of lace very like Arlesian. She wore shoes of the most beautiful satin, and a tress of her magnificent black hair was wound round a tortoise-shell comb mounted with massy gold. Her eyelids, cast down under the fiery glances that were shot from all sides at her, allowed one to see the long silken lashes with which they were fringed. She was not now the calm beauty that I had admired the evening before in the moonlight, but an impassioned daughter of the tropics in all her brilliancy.

The excitement among the spectators, increased by their frequent libations, became greater and greater every minute, but another and a more intense interest was soon awakened in the minds of the crowd.

"Ah!" cried a Jarocho at my side, whose hair was beginning to turn gray, "at the last fandango held at Malibran,[61] Quilimaco lost one of his ears, and Juan de Dios the point of his nose, in a quarrel that arose about a beauty who was not worth a lock of hair compared with that girl there."

"Have patience, *tio*,"[62] answered another; "the beautiful Sacramenta has more than one aspirant in this village, and I venture to predict that, before nightfall, she will have danced the *machete* and *chamarra* for two at least among us."

I did not understand what they meant, but the events that followed soon explained it. Two groups had by this time formed round the estrade occupied by the dancers. In the first, a Jarocho, as richly dressed as Calros, seemed to exercise a marked ascendency. In the second, my host appeared to be the head of another party. Animated by the hope of some quarrel arising between the two factions, the musicians strummed their guitars with redoubled ardor, and a fearful discord filled the air. Just when the dancers were beginning to put themselves in motion, some singers chanted, in a nasal tone of voice, a couplet whose words bore no relation whatever to the present circumstances, and which consisted of a series of proverbs put in verse, almost devoid of meaning, but strongly tinged with obscene allusions. I was then standing near my host, whose eye was following with a jealous attention the least movement of Sacramenta, but she did not deign to bestow upon him the slightest glance.

"You see my hard fate," said he to me, in a low voice; "in high hope one day, in despair the next. We shall set out to-morrow."

These last words betrayed such poignant grief that I could not help cursing in my heart that pitiless coquetry which could wound the feelings of so ardent a lover.

"Ah!" he resumed, "she has not yet forgiven me for that confounded bow of red ribbons which I was unable to procure for her."

At this moment his rival advanced to the estrade, and uncovering, presented his hat to Sacramenta with a very gallant air. She received it with a smile, without interrupting for a moment the evolutions in which she was engaged. Calros's face appeared quite impassible, and he contented himself with making an almost imperceptible gesture to one of his partisans. This person then advanced in his turn and did the same. Custom demanded that, in a case like this, the maiden should show preference to neither; she therefore continued to dance with the two hats in her hand. The advantage of seeing his hat placed upon the head of the dancer would by right belong to the third gallant; and, as I expected, Calros was the one who profited by this usage. The two rivals then exchanged looks of mutual defiance, while the first, untying his sash of China crape, formed it into a rosette, and stepped forward to suspend it to the bare shoulder of Sacramenta.

The guitars, now struck with the greatest vigor, made almost as much noise as a band of trumpeters, and the voices of the singers increased in proportion. The men were exchanging looks of evident satisfaction, but the women were chattering among themselves, evidently envying the homage paid to Sacramenta. This young girl kept her feet in motion; her complexion was heightened by a reddish glow, which lent an additional charm to her radiant black eyes. A vague apprehension, however, seemed to agitate her bosom. At once happy and miserable, she dared not turn her eyes upon him whose heart yearned for her with such true affection. In spite, also, of Calros's apparent calm, the involuntary working of the muscles of his face disclosed the torture he was suffering.

"Courage!" said I to him, in a whisper; "have you not on your heart the suchil flower?"

Calros raised his head, as if the remembrance of that had restored all his confidence. He seized his machete, and went to suspend it at Sacramenta's shoulder. I then understood the meaning of the prediction that I had heard some time before. Sacramenta danced with the machete and *chamarra* of two of her suitors. It was a singular sight to see a long, sharp, glittering blade dangling from the nude shoulder of the young girl, in such close proximity to her heaving bosom.

A sudden silence now fell upon the crowd, similar to what sometimes takes place at a bull-fight when the arena has received its first stains of blood. All at once a loud and imposing male voice near the orchestra exclaimed "Bomba!" The instruments ceased to sound, and the song died away. The voice was that of Calros's rival, who now chanted a couplet expressive of his confidence in his mistress's tenderness, while the friends of the Jarocho repeated the last line in chorus. Calros then answered in a high key by saying that he would not have a divided heart, and that his rival was a traitor.

The Jarocho replied in another recitative, by inquiring if he had spirit sufficient to meet him in fair combat. Calros then, with a smile upon his face, expressed his willingness to meet this traitor, this vagabond, this false friend.

Whether Sacramenta was weary of the dance, or overcome by the general emotion which was manifested when this last couplet was chanted, I know not, but she stepped hastily from the estrade, and her companions followed her. Instructed by past experience not to wait for the commencement of the melee, as their instruments generally suffer in the fray, the musicians hurriedly retired. Some customary pieces of ceremony were still, however, to be gone through; the suitors must redeem the pledges given to the dancer. The customary fee for these is half a real each. The two rivals advanced, one after the other, and filled both hands of Sacramenta with silver coin. While she was receiving the forfeits, in the midst of murmurs of applause excited by the prodigality of the two Jarochos, and which she could not refuse without being guilty of rudeness, her two little outstretched hands trembled involuntarily, and her pale lips tried, but in vain, to smile. Calros fruitlessly sought a look of encouragement from her. Pale and mute, and evidently laboring under an emotion too powerful for concealment, she kept her eyes fixed upon the ground. The machete would decide the question; and the pleasures of the fête were going to be wound up by my host in spite of his sage resolutions, when an old woman, elbowing her way through the crowd, reminded him of the oath he was about to violate. She was the mother of his dead relative.

"It is a shame, *ñor* Don Calros," cried the beldame, "to take a new quarrel upon you when your cousin's death has not yet been avenged."

The Jarocho was evidently taken aback at this unseasonable interruption, and he made all the efforts he could to induce the old woman to retract what she had said, but to all his reasons she had one unvarying reply.

"Well, ña Josefita," said Calros at last, good-humoredly, "you are making a great work about nothing, and are mistrusting my good intention; for, if I fight this man, am I not keeping my hand in exercise?"

"And should you happen to be run through the body, who will then avenge my son?"

"You are right there," replied Calros, thrown off his guard by this argument; "but that's just the way: the women are always mixing themselves up in business that does not concern them. Any one may now take my place," he continued, with an ill-natured air, "if my adversary consent."

His rival bowed, and, poising his hat jauntily over his right ear, placed at the same time his hand upon the hilt of his machete, and with his right leg thrown slightly in advance, exclaimed, with an air of haughty condescension, "What do I mean by all this? Will the good folks of Manantial allow it to be said that they suffered their fandango to be terminated without bestowing the customary honors upon their visitors? Now," he continued, his eyes winking with increased rapidity, "if I can not knock a man down for the sweet eyes of ña Sacramenta, I shall forfeit to any one who draws the first blood a bottle of Catalonian brandy."

Loud shouts of applause interrupted the orator, who, raising his head with an air of assurance, thus went on: "I must say, however, that, having expended my last real not an hour ago, I can not pay and must conquer. Will any one here fight me on these conditions?"

This ridiculous fanfaronade, quite in the spirit of a Jarocho, was welcomed enthusiastically by the by-standers. As for the speaker, looking upon Calros, who was biting his thumbs, he cried impudently, "Come, now, Don Calros, you have no lack of friends to take your place."

But the enthusiasm of the crowd had died away. The prospect of paying the forfeit in one's own person, and out of one's own purse, did not appear to be welcomed by any of the on-lookers, and I was not without some apprehension that Calros would revert to his former idea by asking me to become his substitute. Happily, an unexpected incident occurred which saved the honor of the villagers of Manantial.

By the same road that I had reached the village the evening before, a horseman was descried galloping along at his utmost speed. All eyes were turned upon the new-comer, who appeared to be a stranger, and whom I recognized as one of the horsemen who had interrupted my game with Cecilio. The unknown alighted, and, without saying a word, tied his horse to one of the wooden pillars of a house; then, still silent, he stepped to the estrade, drew his machete, at whose hilt fluttered a bow of red ribbons, with its point traced a circle in the sand, and then stuck his sword in the centre.

A dead silence welcomed this strange visitant. The sword stuck in the ground seemed to me to convey a defiance to all the village. The antagonist desired by the rival of Calros appeared to have stepped in at the proper time. The general gaze was now directed to the former boaster, but he evidently did not feel inclined to take up this unlooked-for challenge. The stranger, who looked like one of those Paladins on whom a vow of silence has been imposed, advanced as haughtily as he had come to one of the *ventorillos*, called for a glass of brandy, and raised it to his mouth; but, with the air of a man who disdains to assist his courage by artificial stimulants, instead of drinking it, he tossed the liquor over his shoulder. He then cast upon all the by-standers a proud glance of defiance.

All the villagers viewed the unknown with admiration, but none seemed so impatient to measure their strength with this brilliant champion as Calros. If the reader remember, he was not in favor with Sacramenta, owing to the affair of the bow of red ribbons. Now at the hilt of the stranger's sword hung a bow of ribbons of the very color she wanted.

"Viva!" he whispered to me; "the old woman may go to the devil; Sacramenta shall have her ribbons."

He then went and planted his sword beside that of the unknown. The challenge was accepted. The stranger courteously carried his hand to his hat, and, having considered his adversary for a moment, cast a rapid look among the group of females, as if singling out some one on whom to bestow the homage of his valor. He was not long in discovering the beautiful Sacramenta, and, stepping toward her, exclaimed, with admirable self-possession, "The fandangoes of Medellin have lost all their attraction since *ña* Sacramenta is no longer there to enliven them with her presence. May I flatter myself that she has not forgotten them, and one of her most fervent *apasionados*?"

The young woman was going to reply, when Calros, whose jealousy was ever awake, approached the unknown, and said, "Pardon me, Señor Cavalier, but I have a particular liking for red ribbons. Will you surrender those that adorn your machete as forfeit for the first blood drawn?"

"With pleasure," answered the stranger. "I should hardly have ventured to offer them in homage to Doña Sacramenta; henceforth they shall have a certain value in my eyes, as being the price of blood shed for her."

After saying these words with a gracious smile, he uncovered himself, and plucked his sword out of the ground. Calros did so too. A polite altercation then took place between them as to who should be the first to place his hat on his head; but this was soon decided by bonneting at the same time. The most experienced of the spectators undertook the task of selecting a spot free from the sun's rays. This done, the combatants stood face to face, the villagers surrounded them, and they waited for the signal to begin. If the stranger was as skillful as he was brave, Calros would find in him a tough opponent, and the issue might probably be unsuccessful to this ardent lover of Sacramenta. The word was given, and the combat commenced. Their blows were so furiously put that it looked more like an encounter for life and death than a contest for the first blood.[63] Sometimes the swords cut the air with a mournful sough; sometimes they struck one another with a shrill clang. It was evident, however, that the stranger looked more to the honor of his antagonist than to his life. Now, in combats of this sort, the great point is to guard the hand. A wounded hand is the greatest stain upon the reputation of the most renowned swordsman. The loss of life even is not such a disgrace. Unluckily, the red ribbons, fluttering at the hilt of the unknown's sword, protected his hand more securely than even the best steel guard could have done. It was to deck the beautiful hair of Sacramenta that Calros was exposing his life; it was to guard these ribbons from stain that the Jarocho stood so grimly on his defense. In the course of the combat the swordsmen had now gone over a considerable space of ground. The tumultuous crowd wavered to and fro, and followed the two combatants as they were successively displaced. Neither had yet received a scratch, when the sword of the stranger, striking that of Calros, glided along the whole length of the blade. A moment after, my host's fingers being cut, he was just about to drop his machete, but a rude parry he made to save his arm failed, and the blood poured out from a wound above his wrist. At the same instant a bloody stain appeared upon the shoulder of the stranger. The two swords were lowered at once, and the combat was decided without it being possible for me to say which of the two had been first wounded; but the skilled and experienced eyes of the witnesses had decided that question. The unknown did not even appeal to their judgment; but, detaching the silk bow which adorned his machete, fixed the much-coveted ornament upon its point, and held it out to his adversary, thus confessing himself conquered. This last act of courtesy won him all hearts; and, in spite of his defeat, he partook with his rival in all the honors of victory. One thing only remained, which my host perhaps desired more. During the whole time the combat had lasted, a deadly paleness had overspread the countenance of Sacramenta, but that soon gave place to a more lively color when Calros advanced toward her. While she was receiving the precious ribbons which he had so valiantly fought for, the tumultuous heavings of her bosom, a sweet and radiant smile, and looks no more cast down to the ground, all proclaimed in the most eloquent manner to the happy Jarocho that his beloved attached as much value to the bow of scarlet ribbons as he had done to the withered suchil flower which had fallen from her hair the night before.

This last episode had passed unnoticed by almost every body. The men surrounded the stranger, who this time invited them to a *ventorillo*. Calros soon joined the company, and the two rivals began a contest of prodigality, to the great delight of all the villagers, who, as they swallowed the brandy in long draughts, congratulated themselves on having had such a brilliant fandango as would furnish matter for conversation for a week to come. For my part, after some words had passed between the former rivals, I was on the point of addressing the stranger, when the general attention was directed to a horseman who was seen advancing at full gallop. This cavalier was no other than the person with whom the unknown had agreed the evening before to meet at Manantial. When he saw the blood which stained his shirt, the new-comer cried, "Have you passed a pleasant time here, friend Julian?"

"Better than I could have expected, friend Ventura," answered the stranger.

"Well, did I not tell you what would happen?" said the horseman, pointing to the sky, which, having been covered with clouds for some time, now betokened a coming storm. "We shall have some hard work presently upon the beach. Will you accompany me?"

"Willingly," answered the unknown, sadly, "for I am afraid I have nothing to hope for here."

And, remounting his horse, after shaking every one by the hand, the two friends went off at a gallop. A general break-up then followed. The passage at arms between Calros and Julian had closed the fête in a worthy manner.

Who were Julian and Ventura? None of the Jarochos around me seemed to know them; but I intended to interrogate Calros about the strangers on the first opportunity. When night had come, and we were lying together under the veranda of my host's cabin, I was on the point of questioning him about the two mysterious individuals, when the light tread of a person walking over the dry grass interrupted me. It was the old woman Josefa. Carefully draped, in spite of the heat, in her *rebozo*, which allowed only her two sparkling dark eyes to be seen, the old woman presented a complete specimen of those sorceresses that are still to be found in Mexico among so many other remnants of the Middle Ages.

"I have been charged with a message for you," said she to Calros, "and from the lips of one dear to you, who will welcome you on your return, if you ever return alive. You will be told when to set out as soon as you are ready."

The Jarocho rose briskly, and followed the old woman. An hour afterward he returned. He knew that *her* most fervent wishes accompanied him in his perilous enterprise, and his brow was radiant with delight.

"It is, however, very hard to leave Sacramenta," he remarked, "but I have no longer a pretext for deferring my departure, and we shall set out to-morrow morning."

"So be it; but what road do you intend to take? Do you know to what place the murderer has fled?"

"We shall keep by the coast. Old Josefa assures me that the pilot Ventura will put me on his traces. He is at Bocca del Rio. Down there we shall certainly meet him."

When Calros named Ventura, I was desirous to satisfy my curiosity by asking who he was. I inquired if he knew this Ventura, and, above all, Julian, whose chivalrous conduct had singularly interested me; but, as I obtained nothing but vague replies, I was confirmed in my design of accompanying my entertainer to Bocca del Rio, where I hoped to meet the two friends.

Next morning we saddled our horses before dawn, and, as soon as it was daylight, quitted the village, which was still enveloped in its usual morning fog.

FOOTNOTES:

[58] Local name for a sword.

[59] A kind of shed erected for the sale of brandy, tepache (a fermented liquor made from ananas), and other intoxicating liquors.

[60] This dance is called bomba.

[61] A little village about three leagues from Vera Cruz.

[62] Uncle, an expression of endearment, applied to men advanced in years.

[63] The Jarochos know nothing of scientific fencing, and trust altogether to strength and agility of body.

THE PILOT VENTURA.

CHAPTER I.

Vera Cruz.—Bocca del Rio.

The place where Vera Cruz now stands is not that on which Cortez first disembarked. It was not till the end of the sixteenth century that Count de Monterey, the viceroy, laid the foundations of the present city. Destined to become the key to New Spain, Vera Cruz was built by the conquerors with all the splendor which they usually lavished on their undertakings. The houses were made large and spacious, and the streets crossed each other at right angles, to allow the fresh sea-breezes to circulate freely, and to temper the intense heat of the atmosphere. Still faithful to that antipathy to trees, which seems a distinctive trait in their hygienic principles, the Spaniards chose, as a site for the first maritime city in Mexico, a vast sandy plain, enlivened by scarcely a spot of verdure, and not even containing a single spring of water. Even before it was first visited by the yellow fever, a situation so unfavorable gave to Vera Cruz a melancholy appearance, which it has preserved to this day. The town, though scarcely all built upon, nevertheless quickly attained a very high degree of prosperity. It was from its ill-sheltered roadstead that those rich galleons sailed which conveyed to Europe a mass of wealth far surpassing the much-vaunted treasures of Potosi.

Few remains of its former grandeur are now to be seen. Built on too large a scale for its decreasing population, this city, once so flourishing, never tried to struggle against that decline which is soon made known to the traveler by its empty houses and deserted streets. The wind from the sea exercises in full force its destructive agency; and the terrible periodical gales are sometimes so violent as to tear down the crumbling walls of the palaces, and lift from their beds the rusty cannon which serve for posts upon the quays. In Vera Cruz you are reminded of the cities of the East, as well from the rich and picturesque costumes of the people of the neighboring coast and of the interior, who flock to the town, as by the dull appearance of the houses and public buildings. Every where you observe domes of various colors, steeples shooting high into the air, balconies ornamented with massive gratings; and, as if to increase the resemblance still more, the women of the upper classes are never seen in the streets. If you wish to get a glimpse of them, you must penetrate into the interior of the houses, or, rather, go out after sunset. Then, the murmur of mysterious voices, the rustling of a fan, and some pale figures, blanched by the rays of the moon, sitting behind a Venetian blind half opened, reveal the presence of the fair Vera Cruzans to the stranger, whom the freshness of the night, and the delicious coolness of the sea-breeze, have brought out upon the streets.

Washed on one side by the ocean, which is gradually wearing away its admirable mole, surrounded by heaps of sand, which the wind is continually shifting, Vera Cruz, at the present moment, submits with indifference to the progressive encroachment of the sand-hills and the daily ravages of the waves. The north-east wind carries before it, in dense whirling masses, large bodies of sand. For many centuries a line of movable hills has been thus gradually formed behind the city. These hillocks, improperly called *medanos*, are continually augmented by fresh additions, and are ever changing, according to the caprice of the wind, their place and figure. Some rise in the air like pyramids, from the top of which small portions of sand are constantly flying off like a never-failing bank of fog. The great number of these medanos, many of which attain a height of from fourteen to more than thirty feet, threatens to bury the town; but, as the danger is still distant, and in hot countries one's existence hangs merely by a thread, the inhabitants leave to their posterity the task of providing against that emergency. Another disadvantage still more serious is, that the medanos hinder the rain-water from flowing away. Small lakes are thus formed at the bottom of these sand-hills; and the parched-up ground is gradually converted into a fenny marsh, from which arise the most pernicious exhalations. A thick layer of mud fertilizes the sand, and all the noxious plants which abound in low, moist grounds are here produced in countless profusion. During the rainy season this rank vegetation spreads and grows round all the margin of the ponds. The mangroves shoot their branches down to the ground. They take root there, produce new trunks, and soon form impenetrable thickets—haunts of numberless reptiles of every kind. A thick crust of greenish scum carpets the surface of the water. The fermentation which sets in on the return of hot weather in these frightful marshes disperses deleterious miasmas abroad, and removes to a distance the swarms of musquitoes. For three months of the year, however, the impetuous squalls which usually prevail sweep away all pestilential vapors, and momentarily purify these sinks of putrefaction.

The reader may perhaps remember that, the day after the fandango at Manantial, I had set out with Calros to seek the murderer whom he had sworn to punish. On leaving the village, there were signs abroad which showed the near approach of one of those tempests caused by the north wind, termed by seamen northers. A strange, dreamy sort of languor seemed to brood over all nature; the suffocating heat caused our horses to foam and pant, although our pace was designedly slow, and our lungs sought in vain for the freshness of the morning air.

We had traveled only a few hours on a road overshadowed by trees, when a dull, hollow, rumbling noise was heard. It was the sound of waves; we were approaching the sea without being able to discover its whereabouts. A few minutes afterward we debouched upon the beach, and I could not help contemplating with delight that ocean which bathed the shores of Europe. In the distance we descried Vera Cruz, with its spires and domes, and the fort San Juan de Ulloa, that stood like a rock among the billows, above which shot the tall, slender masts of the shipping in the roads.

The state of the sea gave every indication of a tempest, of which we had recognized the first symptoms in the wood. The waves gently licked the sand; a more than usually keen smell was distinguishable; the fish were evidently uneasy, leaping high out of the water; and the sea-birds wheeled round and round in the air, uttering mournful cries. Thick clouds were already sweeping up over the town. All at once a large cleft was observable in them. The Sierra of San Martin, which extends from Tuxtla to the mouth of the Goazacoalco, was suddenly stripped of the veil which had, till now, hid the range from our eyes, and its sharp peaks were brought out in bold relief against the deep blue sky.

"Woe betide the ships that are in the gulf just now!" said Calros, "for the north wind will advance upon them sword in hand;[64] this will be a tempestuous night. We shall know something more about it this evening at Bocca del Rio."

I made no reply at first. I was gazing on the ocean. To-morrow I intended to bid adieu to Mexico, and to embark for France. Contending emotions were striving for mastery within me. The joy at my return, long desired as it had been, was tinged with a momentary feeling of dejection. The country that I was about to leave had satisfied my thirst for adventure, and I wished ever afterward to lead a more calm and equable life. Calros's remark reminded me that I had not yet left this life of peril, from which I fancied I had been freed too easily. When, after saying nothing for a few moments, I told him—a little confused, I own—that I intended to embark in the first American ship that was leaving the roads, Calros objected with an air of chagrin, reminding me of my promise to accompany him to Bocca del Rio; and he then pointed out the threatening appearance of the sea. Not a single ship will lift her anchor here for four days, he added; and this last argument was decisive. I then agreed to his terms. I arranged to spend one of the four days of detention with him at Bocca del Rio, to assist in the search for the murderer. That port is only twelve miles from Vera Cruz. Calros intended to go through the city on the way to his village. For my part, I resolved to stay in town to make arrangements for my departure, after which I meant to rejoin Calros in the evening.

A short time after this we entered Vera Cruz. Upon the arid, sandy plain which surrounds the town, some muleteers had pitched their tents, waiting impatiently for the time when they could fly this pestiferous coast, which carries off some of their number at almost every trip. Farther off, a few negro porters, accustomed to this burning climate, were wrestling and struggling on the sand, paying no regard to the fine clothes they wore. I could not help smiling involuntarily when I compared in my own mind their condition with those of our porters at home. After renewing my promise to Calros of meeting him soon, I repaired to the countinghouse of my correspondent. I shall pass over in silence the worthless incidents which occurred during this day, till the time when I had to quit the town and set out for Bocca del Rio.

The wind now began to blow strongly from the north. When I reached the shore, after passing the outskirts of the town, great black clouds, preceded by drifting scud, veiled the face of the sky, and an icy blast, charged with cold from Hudson's Bay, struck me at intervals upon the face. The waves broke on the beach with a mighty roar, and the water came up as far as my horse's feet in large sheets of white foam. The farther I advanced, the wind seemed to increase in fury, and the night was growing darker and darker. Forced sometimes to turn my back to avoid the clouds of drifting sand, I now and then had a glimpse of the town that I repented of having left. At regular intervals, the light-house of San Juan de Ulloa blazed up in all the beauty of its revolving light, sometimes gleaming on Vera Cruz shrouded in darkness, and then on the roadstead white with foam. For a moment I discerned the ships at their anchors pitching up and down on the broken swell, and almost driving on each other. The light soon turned, and all was dark. It was scarcely the season for a nocturnal excursion. I advanced, however, with a resolution that deserved some credit, and had already approached the wood at the extremity of which lies the village of Bocca del Rio, when I fancied I distinguished a cavalier somewhat in advance of me. I hastened toward him. Enveloped in a large blue cloak, he seemed at a distance like a Franciscan. The noise of the tempest was so loud and overpowering that I was by his side before he perceived me. I then saw he was not a monk, but a peasant of the coast, whose *bayeta*[65] I had taken for a frock. With his hand upon his eyes to guard them from the dazzling glare of the lightning, the horseman rode on, casting keen glances toward one side, as if seeking to pierce the dark veil which hung over the ocean; but nothing could be seen but the white crest of the waves lashed into fury by the violence of the storm. I shouted to the stranger with all the force of my lungs, but the violence of the wind hindered my words from reaching him. All at once a loud report was heard in the distance. At the sound, as if it had been a signal he had been ardently expecting, the cavalier put spurs to his horse, and galloped off in the direction of the woods of Bocca del Rio. He was soon lost to view among the trees, and my only care was, in the midst of the lianas and underwood, to keep the straight path which led to the houses. I had reason to hope that, once among the trees and sheltered from the fury of the wind, I could follow the road with ease. As soon as I entered the wood, the noise of the waves gradually died away. I rode almost an hour beneath this leafy vault in complete darkness, and it was not without regret that I again perceived, by a flash of lightning, a long line of foaming breakers. I soon arrived at Bocca del Rio, so called from its situation at the mouth of the river; but, on issuing from the wood, an interesting spectacle met my view, which decided me to make a short halt.

FOOTNOTES:

[64] *Con espada en mano*, a local term to denote the fury of the north-east wind. It commonly blows for fifty hours when it is strong. If weak, it lasts sometimes five or six days.

[65] A kind of cloak of woolen cloth worn almost exclusively by the Jarochos.

CHAPTER II.

The Wreckers.—Narrow Escape of Ventura.

In spite of the violence of the tempest, the whole population of Bocca del Rio were assembled on the beach, and all eyes were fixed on the boiling sheet of foam, whose phosphorescent light contrasted strongly with the deep black of the heavens above. Not a sail was in sight. The distant boom of a gun, however, signaled that a ship was in distress, and that a pilot was required. In such a night as this, it was evident that nothing short of a miracle could save the luckless vessel from being dashed to pieces. Still, as another gun had not been heard, it was hoped that the ship exposed to the tempest had weathered the danger. Besides, a pilot who had left that morning before the *norther* began to blow had very likely got on board, and his consummate seamanship and skill eased some minds. A few, however, persisted in looking upon the ship as doomed.

I soon recognized Calros, whom curiosity had brought to the spot. Just when he was concluding his account about the general gathering of the people of the village, we heard another heavy boom, and this time more distinctly than the last. A flash was soon followed by a third report, and at the end of a few seconds the dark mass of a vessel was distinctly seen, driving on shore with as much rapidity as if she had been impelled by sails. Apparently no power could now save her. A by-stander, however, remarked that there was still a chance of safety, if she succeeded in reaching a part of the bay, opposite to which ran a kind of natural canal, where she might glide softly on to a sandy beach; but if, on the contrary, the luckless ship were driven on the rocks, she would infallibly go to pieces as soon as she grounded. Unfortunately, no one could exactly make out the place in question in the dark, since we could not light any fires for fear of guiding her in a wrong direction.

All the manœuvres of the ship appeared to be now directed to impelling her in the direction of the canal that was covered by the waves. Sometimes she drifted broadside on, sometimes she ran right before the gale, in the direction of the shore. A cry of joy suddenly arose that was heard above the roaring of the tempest. About a gunshot from the place where we were standing, a beacon-fire flashed up with a brilliant flame. Had some courageous fellow hazarded his life to point out the passage into the place of safety? We fancied that the people on board put the same construction upon the light as we did, for the ship was seen advancing toward the light with great rapidity, looming larger and larger as she approached the shore. The light was waved backward and forward, but was kept always in a straight line. A single jib was the only sail that could be set to assist her in answering her helm. Sometimes, when the wind lulled for an instant, her motion appeared to be checked, but a fresh gust soon gave her a new impulse. At last, carried on the top of a high wave, the vessel hung for an instant upon her larboard quarter, then upon her starboard; she then started forward and canted on her broadside, her timbers grinding heavily against the ground. A cry of distress reached our ears, heard distinctly above the roar of the winds and waves; at the same instant the light went out, like one of those glow-worms which flit through the air at night in fenny places, and lead the incautious traveler into quagmires. The schooner was a complete wreck. All we could now do was to save the crew and passengers. While some were deliberating on the means that should be adopted for that purpose, a man was seen making his way along the bows of the wrecked ship, and, by the light of a lamp which shone full upon his face, I distinguished a person who was no longer unknown to me since his visit to Manantial—I mean the pilot Ventura. Some words that he directed to us through a speaking-trumpet were heard very indistinctly, but a line that he held in his hand left us in no doubt as to his meaning. Ventura was begging us to launch a boat to take the end of a rope on shore. But it was impossible that any thing could swim amid these breakers. A boat was then lowered from the bows of the schooner, several seamen got in, and pulled hard to reach the shore; but, in a few minutes, struck by a sea, it filled with water and disappeared.

One man only succeeded in reaching the shore, almost exhausted with cold and fatigue. He was the pilot Ventura. Paying no attention to the questions the people put to him, he unwound a line that was fastened round his body, and ordered them to hold on by the end so as to assist in saving the remaining sailors on board the schooner. A hundred hands immediately seized the rope, and held it with the strength of a capstan. That done, the pilot gave me the details of the dark and mysterious proceeding which I had just witnessed. The ship had been lost through a false light. The beacon-fire that had drawn her upon a reef of rocks had been lit by the perfidious hands of one of those wreckers to whom every shipwreck is a godsend. While telling a story which reflected so much credit upon himself for his courage, Ventura's eyes wandered about among the crowd, seeking to discover the malicious individual who had caused the loss of the schooner. I could hardly help thinking on the person whom I had seen in advance of me before my arrival at Bocca del Rio, and who, on the first signal of distress given by the ship, had galloped off so furiously in the direction of the sea.

"Curse them!" cried Ventura, on finishing his account; "to the devil with those wreckers whom the north wind brings to the coast to rob the shipwrecked and pillage the cargo! Above all, confound the rascal who led us ashore to gratify his own infernal cupidity!"

While he was speaking, the vibratory motion given to the cordage announced that the sailors of the ship were striving to reach the land by its assistance. In fact, partly by swimming, partly by wading, the shipwrecked seamen were not long in reaching the shore, though not without great difficulty and danger, as the sea was running higher, and the wind had increased in fury. The vessel, which was an American schooner, had been bound to Alvarado with a rich cargo of contraband goods, which was destined to become, to all appearance, a prey to the waves and the inhabitants of the coast; but, with American prudence, the lading had been insured for a sum at least equal to its value, and the captain, knowing it was an affair between the underwriters and the proprietors of the ship, interested himself only to procure shelter for himself and crew. The peasants received both him and his men with every demonstration of hospitality, incited, no doubt, by the consideration of profiting without scruple, during the night, by the waifs which the sea would not be long in throwing up. For my part, I intrusted my horse to one of the villagers, after taking the precaution of placing in my belt the pistols which were in the holsters. My intention was to remain upon the beach, that I might not lose a single portion of the strange scene which the organized pillage of a wreck promised me.

The women and children having been sent away, a small number of men only remained upon the shore, waiting impatiently for the moment when the sea would give back a part of the cargo that had been ingulfed in it. Ventura caused all the lights to be extinguished, and the beach became dark, if not still. The hoarse noise of the waves was as loud as the thunder overhead. Sometimes the pale light of the moon illumined the foaming breakers with which the sea was covered, and you got a glimpse of the ill-fated vessel pounding to pieces upon the rocks.

"Wherever there is a corpse," said the pilot, pointing to the schooner, "there you will find *zopilotes*[66] or sharks. We shall soon see the wretch that caused the loss of the vessel, and it will be a shame if we allow others to share in any thing that the sea may throw upon our coasts."

No sound, however, save the wild war of the elements was heard, and, while waiting for the wreckers, I had leisure to examine the situation of the different places. A few paces from us was the mouth of a river, whose banks were covered on both sides with thick brushwood. On our side of the stream stood the houses of Bocca del Rio, and between it and us ran a thick range of mangroves, which would, owing to the darkness, hide us completely from view. Upon the suggestion of the pilot, we agreed to lie in ambush at this spot.

We were not long kept in suspense. A body of men on horseback soon appeared, riding along the bank of the stream. They stopped upon the beach.

The troop halted a short distance from the mangroves as if in doubt, and a horseman advanced alone to reconnoitre.

"The rascal has gone away to get assistance," said the pilot to me, in a low voice.

"And some mules, doubtless, to carry away the spoil," remarked one of the river-men.

In the horseman who had left the main body I was not long in distinguishing the man whose odd behavior had raised my suspicions while on my way from Vera Cruz to Bocca del Rio. Astonished, no doubt, to find the place which he had left so full of life some time before, quite deserted, the man, still enveloped in the same blue bayeta, continued silently to examine every place, and at last advanced near the mangroves. He soon, however, returned to his comrades.

The remains of the schooner's cargo, which the tide was washing on shore, could now be plainly seen. This was a sure indication that the most valuable parts of the lading would not be long in being thrown up. The wreckers could no longer restrain their impatience. They stationed themselves in a long line along the strand, so that nothing could escape them. The man in the blue cloak, who seemed to be the chief of these wretches, rode his horse into the waves, to have a better view of the boxes and bales floating about.

"Will any of you lend me a gun?" asked the pilot.

One of our party handed him his musket. Ventura seized it. At this moment the dark profile of the chief wrecker and his horse, relieved by the white foam of the sea, presented an admirable mark. He fired, and we saw the cavalier fall from his steed, and disappear beneath the waves. The other wretches took to flight. Immediately after, a man came out of the water, and walked up the beach, the ball which Ventura had intended for him having only struck his horse. The pilot ran toward the villain to prevent his escape. A struggle took place in the darkness. Just when we had come up to assist the pilot, he was thrown to the ground by the marauder, whose poniard happily had glided over his clothes without injuring him. It was impossible to overtake the fugitive, as he fled as fast as his legs could carry him, fancying, probably, his opponent had been killed. Ventura rose with difficulty.

"I was not able to hold him," said he, passing his hand over his body; "but that's nothing. I recognized the fellow; it is Campos! I am not hurt a bit; but it is a wonder that the rascal did not pin me to the ground with his dagger. I am curious to know, however, where the deuce the scoundrel got that horse."

"Did you say that the miscreant's name was Campos?" cried Calros; "Tereso Campos?"

"Yes, Tereso Campos."

"That's the man I am seeking," returned the Jarocho, grasping my hand.

"Are you in search of him?" asked the pilot; "and why?"

"To kill him," answered Calros, quite naïvely.

"Well, I warrant you we shall find him to-morrow; and if the proprietor of the horse he stole join us, as he ought to do, the scoundrel will be very fortunate if he escape."

"You hear, Señor Cavalier," said Calros to me; "you have a like interest with us in avenging yourself upon Campos."

"Why?"

"Because, if I am not mistaken, it is your horse he has carried off."

I replied with perfect disinterestedness that, with the exception of the saddle, which was a costly one, I did not attach the slightest value to the sorry hack of which he had deprived me. But my objection was overruled, and I was obliged to yield. The reader may perhaps remember that I had sent my horse to the village in the charge of one of the inhabitants, but the man had tied up the beast to a tree near the beach, intending to return for it in a short time; and Campos, meanwhile, had stepped in and appropriated the animal.

Before advancing up the country in pursuit of the fugitives, a very delicate business still remained to be accomplished. This was the equitable division of the spoils from the wreck, vast quantities of which had been thrown up by the waves. I was not long in perceiving that the wrath of Ventura was chiefly directed against the marauders, because they were poaching on his preserves. At first, a few isolated portions of the rigging had been collected, then casks of wine and brandy, which were soon followed by large quantities of boxes filled with various articles. As they were thrown upon the shore, they were seized and piled up in a dry, sandy hollow till the distribution was made. I must say that Ventura conducted himself on this occasion with the strictest impartiality; he reserved nothing to himself beyond his share but a number of small boxes containing a goodly number of yards of fine Irish linen, as a sort of recompense for the dangers he had run. All was arranged to the full satisfaction of the river-men, who carried their booty away with such expedition that, in a short time, not a single article was to be seen on the sands.

We at last settled what was to be done during the remaining hours of the night, which was already approaching its meridian. In an hour hence we agreed to meet on the bank of the river at a place that the pilot pointed out to us. He, meanwhile, went home to secure his share of the plunder. The Jarocho had contemplated with a disdainful indifference the pillage of the shipwrecked cargo. Before quitting the shore, he threw a last look upon the sea, which was still beating with remorseless fury against the timbers of the ill-fated schooner, and then upon the broken barrels and boxes which the tide was still floating to land.

"All that," said he, with a melancholy smile, "is not to be compared to a fandango under the palm-trees, nor a look from Sacramenta."

I could not help thinking that the Jarocho was right; but it was scarcely the moment to lose one's self in amorous reveries. A short walk took us to the village; and, after a frugal repast, a necessary precaution before setting out to encounter new fatigues, we directed our steps in silence to the place where Ventura was waiting for us.

FOOTNOTE:

[66] Black vultures that abound in the streets of Vera Cruz, which perform the part of public scavengers by clearing the streets of carrion, &c.

CHAPTER III.

Excursion up a River.—Vengeance overtakes Campos, the Murderer.

In a little creek, overshadowed by some gigantic willows, we found the pilot engaged in putting the oars on board a small boat that was moored to the bank. I was rather averse to a march through the woods, and it was with a feeling of pleasure that, instead of a pedestrian excursion, I saw we were to be conveyed to our place of destination in a boat. I communicated my satisfaction to the pilot.

"Here," said he, "we only travel in two ways, on horseback or in a 'dingy.' We leave to the newly-landed Galicians the resource of *striding a path*.[67] You can row, of course?" addressing himself to Calros.

He answered in the affirmative, and we took our places in the skiff. As I was only a passenger, I stretched myself on my cloak at the bottom of the boat to shelter myself from the wind. Though we were at a considerable distance from the mouth of the stream, the river was swollen with the tide, and the water lapped the sides of the boat with great fury. We set out, and, impelled by two pairs of strong arms, soon began to glide rapidly along the surface of the dark water. The usual imposing stillness of American forests was on the banks. At a distance you heard the dull, heavy roar of the wind raging among the trees. The banks of the river were very undulating. Sometimes its bed widened considerably, and we then kept in the centre of the stream. At other times the water flowed between high, precipitous rocks, under a thick canopy of mahogany and cedar trees, from whose branches long-trailing parasitical plants hung over our heads. Charmed with the beauty of the river, I forgot completely the object of our journey. I was soon reminded of it, however, by the pilot.

"Every one," said he, "in this world has his enemies. For my part, I know more than one individual, and Campos among others, who would be very glad to know that at this late hour of the night, in the midst of these solitudes, which alcalde has never visited, they could meet Sinforoso Ventura unarmed and defenseless."

"Have we no arms?" Calros inquired. "Are the pistols of my friend here, my machete, and your musket, to be reckoned as nothing?"

"In an open country such arms would be of the greatest service; here they are of no use. A person hidden in any of the trees which overhang the stream could pick out any of the three he chose, and send a ball through his head; or, by throwing the trunk of a tree across the river, might capsize our boat, if he did not smash it to pieces. What do you think of that?"

"I dare say you're right," answered Calros. "Luckily, nobody is to know that you are to be pulling up the river to-night."

"I am not so sure of that," said the pilot; "there are spies and traitors every where. If any of the marauders we put to flight this evening has the slightest inkling of our plans, be sure that his comrades will be apprised of it time enough to meet us at a part of the river I know. We have already rowed two hours," he added, shaking his head, "and the place is not far off. You now know what we have to fear. Consider, therefore, whether we shall push on, or land, and wait till daylight."

"I can not lose a minute," returned the Jarocho, coldly. "If we pull well, we shall reach the village where Campos lives in an hour."

"It is quite the same to me," Ventura replied. "Let us proceed."

A dead silence succeeded these words. Knowing now the dangers we had to run, I went and seated myself in the bow, to try to make out, if it were possible, the ambuscades that threatened us; but the darkness was so great that I could discover nothing. The leafy vault under which we moved threw a thick shadow over the bed of the river; at times, however, a gust of wind shook into the water, like a shower of golden rain, large cucuyos, which fell from the trees above us. Not a single star was to be seen through the interstices of the foliage. A quarter of an hour had now elapsed without in the least justifying the suspicions of the pilot. The Jarocho lay on his oars to take breath, and the boat, moved by the current, turned broadside on to the stream.

"Keep her head to the stream," cried the pilot, sharply. "Even supposing that we have no ambuscades to fear, the wind may, perhaps, have uprooted some dead tree, and should it happen to hit the side of our boat, it would cant over to a dead certainty; but if we are struck on the bow, it may do us no harm. The tide runs up as far as this, and sharks not uncommonly come up with it."

This last observation disclosed another danger which I had not suspected; and, in the presence of the increasing perils of this nocturnal expedition, I thought, with some bitterness, on the comfortable *farniente* and refreshing sleep I should have enjoyed had I been in my hotel at Vera Cruz.

Calros did not require a second warning, but resumed his oar with new vigor. We soon arrived at a place where a high rock on each side of the stream approached each other, narrowing very considerably the bed of the river. About a dozen paces farther up, the passage became so contracted that both oars could not be worked, and it was only by the assistance of a boat-hook that the pilot, by fixing it among the lianas, could pull us up against the force of the current. The river widened considerably at the head of this narrow pass, and allowed us again to ply our oars; but as the stream grew broader, the banks rose in proportion. On the right and left, high rocks curved gently inward, and then ran sheer down into the water, like the arch of a bridge broken at the key-stone. Under this vault every stroke produced an echo. We advanced by chance, and the darkness was so intense that we did not know but what every pull would send us up against the wall of rock on either side.

"One would need to have the eyes of a tiger-cat to see in this place," cried the pilot.

"Have we far to go now?" asked Calros.

"A few vigorous strokes will send us there," answered Ventura; "but the most embarrassing thing is to discover the entrance to the narrow reach that runs up from this basin. This reach is as narrow as the one we have just left."

"Put out the boat-hook to feel if we are not running against the rocks."

I did what he ordered me. The boat was still in the middle of the stream. The boat-hook, though stretched out as far as I could reach, struck against nothing.

"All right," I cried. "I can touch the rocks on neither side."

The rowers again plied their oars, and the light skiff flew up the river. All at once the boat-hook, which I was holding at right angles to the boat, hit against a rock, and bounced out of my hands. The shock over-set me completely. A cracking of broken branches was heard. The skiff suddenly stopped.

"What's this?" cried the pilot, who had run to the bow, and was fumbling with his hands among a tangled mass of lianas and branches. "Demonio! the rascals have pitched a dead tree into the river higher up, and the current has carried it down here. We can advance no farther. How shall we get out of this mess? One or two large stones, hurled from the top of these rocks, might crush us to pieces before we could clear the passage."

This took us completely aback, and not another word was said. The only plan seemed to be to return to the reach we had just left; but the boat was so strongly fixed among the branches of the fallen tree that it could not be disengaged. Some moments passed in a fruitless endeavor to overcome this obstacle. Suddenly a voice called out right above us, "Who is there?"

"*Gente de paz,*" I replied, prompted by the pilot.

"That's not enough. There are three of you, and I must hear three voices."

"Caramba! well," cried the Jarocho. "Tell Campos that I am here—I, Calros Romero, of Manantial."

"And ask him also," added the pilot, haughtily, "if he remembers the name of Sinforoso Ventura, of Bocca del Rio."

A shrill whistle was heard in the woods. It was repeated behind us, showing that both banks were guarded. Two or three seconds elapsed, that seemed as long as so many years. Shadowy forms appeared on the rocks above our heads, threatening cries were heard, and quivering lights danced upon the water. The pilot was not long in firing upon the scoundrels; but they had the advantage in point of position, and wielded arms more terrible than ours. The flash of the gun lighted up all surrounding objects. Meanwhile an enormous stone, which they had succeeded in moving to the edge of the rocks, fell close to the boat, and splashed us with water from head to foot. The pilot cried out as if he had been hurt. We felt the boat lurch under us heavily, and then, torn from the rude embrace of the branches, drift rapidly down the stream. When I opened my eyes, for we had been both blinded by the spray, Ventura had disappeared. I called aloud several times. There was no reply.

"'Tis all over with him!" cried Calros. "He is at the bottom of the river. We must see to ourselves now."

A speedy retreat was the only chance of safety left us. The Jarocho seized the oars and began rowing vigorously. Not a sound was heard but the dip of the oar in the water. Had our enemies retreated, or were they waiting for us at the narrow reach we must unavoidably pass? We could not escape the fate that seemed to be awaiting us. We were soon in the dangerous pass. The trunk of a guaiacum or cedar hanging over the water—the noise of the wind in their branches—an iguana leaving its bed of dry leaves—a squirrel frightened by the working of the oars—the slightest sound, or the least object that we saw, all kept our minds on the rack, and our hands on our arms. We stopped at short intervals, after which Calros resumed his oars with new ardor.

We reached at last a spot where the vegetation was not so abundant, and one of the banks was destitute of wood. We landed there. A rapid survey convinced us that this was not the place for an ambuscade. We decided to remain a short time to rest ourselves, and we should afterward consider whether to continue our journey by land or water. The sun was just beginning to make his appearance. What was our surprise, when, as we were about to throw ourselves upon the ground, we heard a voice calling to us! The voice was that of our late companion Ventura. We thought at first that we were laboring under a hallucination; but in a short time we could no longer doubt about the resurrection of our brave friend, who appeared on the opposite bank, waving his hand to invite us to carry him across. To cross the stream was with Calros the work of an instant.

"And by what miracle are you still in this world?" I asked of Ventura. "The cry of agony you uttered still rings in my ears."

"That cry saved my life. As soon as I felt that we ran the risk of getting crushed to pieces without being able to defend ourselves, I jumped among the branches that stopped our passage, and, on seeing the immense stone which they had pushed into the river, I raised a great shriek. The rascals, fancying from the cry that I was mortally wounded, decamped as quickly as they could. Once out of the water, I followed the course of the river, knowing that you could not be far off. I was right, as you see. We shall now resume our journey. As for you, Señor Calros, who are so impatient to revenge yourself upon Campos, I have hit on a more expeditious plan than the one we are now following. I have some friends in the village in which Campos lives. We shall go and visit them; and in two hours all your wishes shall be fully satisfied."

The arrival of the pilot had brought back to Calros's mind all that boiling impatience which his exhaustion of body had alone kept under. He would not listen to a halt. A short discussion then arose as to whether we should continue our journey by land or water. Ventura was of opinion that we ought still to make use of the boat and reascend the river, as we should probably fall in with no more enemies, and the force of the current had very likely removed all obstacles to our passage. We therefore took our places in the skiff without loss of time, Calros and Ventura pulling, and I between the two rowers, glad at finding that, from my inexperience in rowing, I should not be expected to give any assistance, and would be at full liberty to admire the glorious landscape that unfolded itself before our eyes, bathed in the first light of dawn.

The river, so dark and sombre the night before, seemed now to smile in the sunlight. Light vapors arose from the surface of the water, drawn up by the heat, which had taken the place of the coolness of the evening before. Numerous aquatic plants covered its surface, and the furrow which our boat cut in passing through them soon closed up again, leaving not a trace of our presence. No sound was heard save the working of the oars in the row-locks, and a green woodpecker tapping with long, regular strokes the trunk of a dead tree.

My companions were quite indifferent to the glorious beauty of this solitude. I must confess, however, that I allowed myself to be distracted from the contemplation of these charms to listen to the conversation of the two men, which was becoming more and more animated. Besides relating the grievances which he had endured from Campos, the pilot, in the course of his narrative, caused a chord to vibrate in the heart of the chivalrous lover of Doña Sacramenta. Calros was painfully surprised on learning that Julian, his antagonist in the fandango at Manantial, was his rival. Julian, being the pilot's friend, had no secrets from him. His passion for Sacramenta dated from the time when the parents of the young girl lived in another village called Medellin, before they had come to reside at Manantial. After the departure of Sacramenta for Manantial, Julian had not lost all hope of seeing her again, and of winning her affections. Old Josefa, the woman whose son Campos had killed, and who was seeking every where an avenger for her son's murder, had been often invited from Manantial to Medellin for the purpose of exercising the black art, in which she was considered an adept. It was through her that Julian received news of Sacramenta, and the old crone had even promised to exert her influence with the girl in his favor, if he succeeded in putting her on the traces of her son's murderer. This condition Julian had been able to fulfill through the friendship of the pilot, as the latter, by his ancient relations with Campos, was well aware of all this wretch's crimes. Julian had thus informed her that Campos was her son's murderer, and that the pilot Ventura would lend her a hand in securing him. Josefa had, on her side, kept her word. She had used all her influence with Sacramenta in Julian's favor, "and was successful," said the pilot, with an arch smile, "since the amorous Jarocho had been invited to attend the fête of Manantial by the young girl herself, to challenge, in her honor, the bravest champion in the village." The pilot did not know that the old crone Josefa, in her eagerness to have her son avenged, had likewise excited the passion of Calros, in order that she might make him more eager in the search after Campos. Calros and I could alone complete the revelations of Ventura. I did not say a single word, however, because I feared to excite the Jarocho's jealousy still more by untimely consolation, and because I knew that his soul was torn by violent and contending emotions. The pilot, seeing us both sunk in thought, turned to Calros and said,

"Now, when I think of it, it was you that challenged my friend Julian. It was you that was victor in the combat held in honor of the fair Sacramenta. Well, shall I tell you? Julian confessed to me that, even after his defeat, he had not entirely lost hope; so much so that he is talking about quitting Medellin, and you will perhaps see him some of these days quietly settled in Manantial."

"Are you sure of what you say?" asked Calros, in an altered tone.

"Has my good friend Julian ever deceived me?" answered the pilot. "Trust me, he is not a man that is under the influence of illusions. If he never come to Manantial, it is because he will have the best of reasons for staying away."

This was rather much, and Calros asked him no more questions. With eyes fixed mechanically on the water around him, the poor fellow plied his oar with a kind of feverish energy. His body was with us, but his mind had fled away to the woods of Manantial.

We had now gone as far as we could on the river, which had now dribbled down to a mere streamlet, flowing between low banks. Upon one side fields of green sugar-cane, waving in the wind, stretched to the foot of a chain of hills which rose at a short distance from the stream.

"We must land here," cried the pilot; "the village is behind these hills."

FOOTNOTE:

[67] Ensillar la vereda.

CHAPTER IV.

The Duel.—Awful Death of the Murderer.

We leaped ashore. The pilot tied the "dingy" to the bank, and led the advance. We soon reached the village. All was quiet there. The greater part of the inhabitants were still in their hammocks under the verandas of their cabins, but they saluted the pilot as he approached with the greeting of an old acquaintance. After replying briefly to the questions that were put to him, Ventura asked where Campos was. He pointed to Calros, and explained why he had come thither. This news was welcomed with enthusiasm by the idle and pugnacious peasants; but in a *diversion* in which there was so much interest, the greatest secrecy must be employed, and every one rivaled his neighbor in discretion. The hut of Campos was noiselessly approached, and he was found inside stretched in his hammock. I could not help admiring the rare command of countenance which this man showed when he saw the pilot, whom he believed to be lying at that moment at the bottom of the neighboring river. He rose quietly, looked at us with a disdainful curiosity, and did not appear to be moved at seeing Calros.

"Who put you on my traces?" he asked of the Jarocho.

"*Tia* Josefa," was the reply. "It was by her order I came here from Manantial."

"A word is enough to the wise," answered Campos. "It is well; I am ready for you."

The conditions of the duel were immediately discussed, with a calmness and dignity which I did not expect in two such adversaries. Neither Calros nor the pilot deigned to make the slightest allusion to the events of last night. It was a duel to the death which was to be fought, and at such a solemn moment all recrimination was reckoned silly and trifling. The place of meeting was mutually agreed on; and Campos left to procure his seconds, while we directed our steps thither. I walked behind Calros, silent and sorrowful.

"Whatever happen," said he to me, in a low voice, "whether I fall or remain alive, in any case, you will have no message to deliver to *her* from me."

After walking about half an hour on a footpath that ran at right angles with the river, we arrived at the edge of one of those marshy ponds so common in certain parts of Mexico. On one side was a clump of trees, and on the other rose lofty hillocks of fine moving sand, which was gradually filling up the lagoon by its ceaseless shifting. We there waited the arrival of Campos and his seconds. Calros strode over the ground, a prey to feverish anxiety, for the Jarocho was not one of those lackadaisical lovers who rush out of life the first check they receive. The ground measured, and the situation chosen, the antagonists stood face to face. The signal was given; and I heard, with a beating heart, the clash of the two swords. I had turned my head away; but, hearing a cry of rage, I was drawn irresistibly to cast a look upon the combatants. A man had run to the top of one of the sand-hills; he brandished the stump of a machete, and blood was trickling down his side: this was Campos. His flight had been so sudden and rapid that his adversary was still immovable in his place. One of his seconds approached to hand him a sword in the place of the one that had been broken, but he came too late. Exhausted by the effort he had made in clambering up the hill, Campos staggered and fell upon the sand. For a moment we thought he would have kept himself on the mound, but the movable substance rolled away from beneath him, and the unhappy wretch, after struggling fearfully for a few moments, rolled down into the marsh, and was ingulfed alive in an avalanche of sand.

Nothing now remained but to secure the flight of Calros. We left in all haste the scene of action, and arrived at the boat before the alcalde of the village had detached a single alguazil in pursuit. Aided by the current, the light skiff glided like an arrow down the stream, the trees and rocks seeming to fly behind us. After a two hours' row, we reached the mouth of the river, and landed under the willows which overshadowed the pilot's abode. We required his services no farther, and therefore bade him adieu. Before parting, he tried to induce Calros to stay with him.

"I was looking out for a brave and resolute fellow to make a man of him like myself. I have found one in you. The sea-shore is preferable to the woods. It is to enrich the dweller on the coast that the norther blows three months every year. Remain with me; you will be rich in that time."

But a complete dejection now possessed the mind of the Jarocho; he shook his head moodily in token of refusal.

"Well, I am sorry for it," said the pilot. "I shall always miss a comrade who can handle an oar as well as a machete. We two could have done a good stroke of business together. Good-by, then; every one must follow his destiny."

We parted, and I accompanied Calros to the hut where he had left his horse. Some wood-cutters, during my absence, had found my hack a short way off in the woods.

"I must bid you farewell here," said Calros. "You will soon see your native land, and I—"

He left the sentence unfinished; I finished it in thought, and pressed him to return to Manantial. I attempted also, but in vain, to prove to Calros that his despair was at least premature.

"The words of the pilot," he replied, "agree but too well with a voice that has been incessantly calling to me, 'Sacramenta never loved you.'"

"But," I answered, "if you intend to bid an eternal farewell to your mother and the village in which Sacramenta lives, why did you refuse the offer of the pilot? Your life would then have some definite aim."

"That's of no consequence. The Jarocho is born to live free and independent. A bamboo hut, the woods and the river, a gun and nets, are all that is necessary for him, and these I shall find every where. Farewell, señor; don't tell any body that you saw me weep like a woman."

Pulling his hat over his eyes, Calros gave the spur to his horse. It was not without a lively sympathy that I followed with my eye the retiring figure of one whose exalted passion and adventurous humor had shown the character of the Jarocho in the most pleasing light. I had to gain Vera Cruz on foot this time, as my horse had lost both saddle and bridle. I dragged him along, however, with a halter behind me. Oppressed by heat and thirst, I stopped at a hut by the way-side, and the host accepted of the poor brute in compensation for the refreshment with which he had supplied me.

Two days afterward I embarked on board the good ship *Congress* for the United States. I could not leave Mexico without regret, for the society to be found in that country had for me all the attraction of a romance, with every particular of which I had a strong desire to become acquainted.

THE END.

Milton Keynes UK
Ingram Content Group UK Ltd.
UKHW040831071024
449371UK00007B/730

9 789362 096494